When Language Breaks Down

Doctors, nurses, and other caregivers often know what people with Alzheimer's disease or Asperger's 'sound like' – that is, they recognize patterns in people's discourse from sounds and silences, to words, sentences, and story structures. Such discourse patterns may inform their clinical judgements and affect the decisions they make. However, this knowledge is often tacit, like recognizing a regional accent without knowing how to describe its features. The absence of explicit knowledge of discourse patterns may be partly because research and practice associating neurocognitive function with language has tended to focus on (often isolated) linguistic 'deficits' as signs or symptoms of brain injury or disorder rather than beginning with comprehensive descriptions of discourse. In contrast, this is the first book to present models for comprehensively describing discourse specifically in clinical contexts and to illustrate models with detailed analyses of discourse patterns associated with degenerative (Alzheimer's) and developmental (autism spectrum) disorders. The authors also suggest how clinical discourse analysis, combined with neuropsychological and imaging data, can add to our understanding of neurocognition. The book is aimed not only at advanced students and researchers in linguistics, discourse analysis, speech pathology, and clinical psychology but also at researchers, clinicians, and caregivers for whom explicit knowledge of discourse patterns might be helpful.

ELISSA D. ASP is Associate Professor of English Linguistics in the English Department and Linguistics Coordinator of the Linguistics Programme at Saint Mary's University. She is also Adjunct Professor in the Faculty of Medicine at Dalhousie University.

JESSICA DE VILLIERS is Associate Professor in the Department of English at the University of British Columbia.

When Language Breaks Down

Analysing Discourse in Clinical Contexts

Elissa D. Asp and Jessica de Villiers

CAMBRIDGE UNIVERSITY PRESS
Cambridge, New York, Melbourne, Madrid, Cape Town, Singapore,
São Paulo, Delhi, Dubai, Tokyo

Cambridge University Press
The Edinburgh Building, Cambridge CB2 8RU, UK

Published in the United States of America by Cambridge University Press, New York

www.cambridge.org
Information on this title: www.cambridge.org/9780521718240

First published 2010

Printed in the United Kingdom at the University Press, Cambridge

A catalogue record for this publication is available from the British Library

Library of Congress Cataloguing in Publication data
Asp, Elissa D.
When language breaks down : analysing discourse in clinical contexts /
    Elissa D. Asp, Jessica de Villiers.
        p.   cm.
    ISBN 978-0-521-88978-0 (hardback)
    1. Language disorders.   2. Discourse analysis.   3. Alzheimer's disease –
    Patients–Language.   4. Autism spectrum disorders–Patients–Language.
    I. Villiers, Jessica de.   II. Title.
    RC423.A82   2010
    616.85′5–dc22
    2009044694

ISBN 978-0-521-88978-0 Hardback
ISBN 978-0-521-71824-0 Paperback

Contents

Figures

Tables

Acknowledgements

We would like to thank our friends and families for their encouragement and support while we worked on this book. To John Foster and Arnaud Goupilliere we are especially indebted – for making us tea and dinner and cleaning up afterwards, for making us go out in the sunshine sometimes and for cheerfully putting up with us while we worked. We would also like to thank our mentors. Elissa is especially indebted to Dr Kenneth Rockwood, Professor of Medicine (Geriatric Medicine and Neurology) at Dalhousie University, Halifax, Nova Scotia. As well as mentoring her in developing research on discourse in Alzheimer's disease and providing access to data and patients, Dr Rockwood, together with his team, have consistently modelled what interdisciplinary research and clinical care can be. Elissa was also privileged to be invited to participate in the Halifax Symposia on the Treatment of Alzheimer's disease from 2003 to 2008 which brought outstanding international scholars in many disciplines to address particular themes associated with Alzheimer's and dementia. Elissa also wants to thank Jennifer Klages, for generously giving her access to data on vascular cognitive impairment, the Nova Scotia Health Research Foundation for their support and Saint Mary's University which has twice given her sabbatical leave to work on the book and projects related to it, and her colleagues in the English department who may flinch but vote in favour of leave to research discourse effects of cholinesterase inhibitors and other similarly unliterary topics.

Jessica would like to thank Peter Szatmari, whose mentorship and encouragement made much of this work possible. He has been a great advisor, collaborator and supporter. She would also like to thank the Department of English at UBC, her research team and language group, the Faculty of Arts at UBC and the Offord Centre for Child Studies at McMaster University for supporting her work in many ways. She is very grateful to the Offord Centre for Child Studies for giving her access to data and other research supports. She gratefully acknowledges financial support from the Social Sciences and Humanities Research Council and the Canadian Institute of Health Research.

We also both want to acknowledge the mentoring of Michael Gregory. He taught us much of what we know about language and discourse analysis, and although he didn't believe linguists had any business talking about brains or neurology, we think he would have liked this book. Other linguists who influenced our work because of their own are Noam Chomsky, William Downes, Jonathan Fine, Ruqaiya Hasan, Michael Halliday, Rodney Huddleston, Richard Hudson, Ray Jackendoff and Sydney Lamb. We also would like to thank reviewers and readers of our manuscript in its various stages for helpful and encouraging comments, and Andrew Winnard for believing in the project and supporting us in it. Finally, we thank the individuals and families who participated in our studies. Our work is for them.

Transcription conventions

SP1 speaker 1
SP2 speaker 2
IV interviewer
CG caregiver
P patient (in caregiver and patient interviews)
CHI child
RES researcher (in semi-structured conversations with researcher)
(1) line 1
(5) line 5
( ) material in parentheses is inaudible or there is doubt of accuracy
(( )) double parentheses indicate clarifying information, e.g. ((laughter))
(.) a pause which is noticeable but too short to measure
(.5) a pause timed in tenths of a second
noticeable pause, unmeasured
long pause, unmeasured
: colon indicates an extension of the preceding vowel sound
\<text>[>] overlaps following text
\<text> [<] overlaps preceding text
… some text intervening
Bold bold is for prominent information (presented as new or emphasized)
Under underscore is for information that is the focus (unmarked starting point) of a construction
//text// tone group
//2 text// tone 2
xxx unintelligible
[if] uncertain
^ silent beat

Many of the transcription conventions used are borrowed or adapted from Gail Jefferson's system. (See for example Jefferson 1985; 2004.)

Introduction

This book is predicated on the relatively uncontentious notions that discourse patterns – what people do when they talk or write – can provide trained observers with information about cognitive functions and affective states in speakers and, further, that cognitive functions and affective states may be signs of integrity of neurological function and structure. Neurolinguists, psycholinguists, aphasiologists, psychiatrists, psychotherapists and speech pathologists all take some variation on assumptions like this as their point of departure in studying brain–behaviour relationships and treating some neurological and affective disorders. However, discourse – people's talk and text – is inherently complex and apparently unstable and, worse, the neurological substrate and processes that support even superficially simple things like 'how words are represented in the brain', let alone 'what happens in brains when people talk' are matters of active debate and investigation rather than scientific givens. In the face of so much uncertainty and complexity, most of the work done on language–brain relationships has, very sensibly, centred on theoretically discrete and/or methodologically isolatable phenomena associated with particular semantic, morphosyntactic or phonological structures or processes. Work on discourse in clinical environments as another means of investigating neurocognitive (dys-) function, although often called for, has been less common.

This situation is changing now because of technological developments and, we think, a sea-change-like shift that is taking place in attitudes to brain–behaviour relationships. On the technological side, recent developments in neuroimaging techniques are providing new tools to investigate neural structure, chemistry and function, and developments in machine-mediated text analysis tools, storage and search capacities have made corpus-based discourse studies much more doable. The change in attitudes to brain–behaviour relationships is also at least partly technologically mediated insofar as imaging and other techniques enabling *in vivo* investigation of the effects of cognitive activity suggest that behaviours can have measurable effects not just on activation patterns but also on neurochemical and neuroplastic (structural) responses. What is novel in this is not that behaviour can alter neurochemistry and structure – therapy for people with brain injury or dysfunction presupposes and evidences this. Rather, it is that the new technologies can make changes observable and measurable, and so present new possibilities both for understanding brain–behaviour relationships and, consequently, for developing new therapies to help people with neurological disorders or injuries. There are other factors that contribute to this drift – salient among them are recognition of the limits and risks of pharmacological interventions and an increased, computationally mediated, capacity to conceptualize complex interactions. The first three factors suggest that people interested in neurological disorders and diseases should have access to very detailed accounts of the discourse patterns (and other behaviours) of the populations that they study and treat; the computational capacity to store and process the data produced by such studies means projects that used simply to be unworkable can now be fruitfully undertaken.

It is in this environment that we offer this book as a first pass at 'clinical discourse analysis' or CLDA. It is intended as an introduction to the use of structurally, pragmatically and linguistically based discourse analysis techniques to investigate relationships between discourse behaviours and patterns and neurocognitive (dys)function in clinically defined groups. Because we work with teams specializing in the care of people with autism spectrum disorders and degenerative dementias, most of the examples we use refer to discourse samples from these groups. However, the techniques that we discuss and model for discourse analysis were originally developed for description of normal speech and writing and are applicable to any sort of speech sample, including corpora representative of the speech associated with other neurological disorders.

Our primary audience is discourse analysts (including linguists and cognitive scientists) – senior undergraduate or graduate students, faculty and researchers interested in investigating relations between discourse and neurocognitive functions. For instance, we see the book as a useful adjunct to courses in discourse analysis and clinical linguistics. However, it should also be of value to nurses, speech pathologists, clinical psychologists, neurologists and psychiatrists interested in the potential of discourse analysis (or working with discourse analysts) for informing clinical judgements of diagnosis and change and for addressing their own research questions. Finally, we wanted our book to be interesting and readable for non-professionals, especially caregivers, interested in Alzheimer's disease, autism spectrum disorders or just generally in discourse and neurocognitive function. So, although some parts of the book are unavoidably technical, we have worked to make the descriptions of discourse patterns in Alzheimer's and autism speakers accessible for a general audience. Readers will no doubt let us know whether or not we succeeded.

In the chapters that follow, we first orient readers to clinical discourse analysis (chapter 1) and the theoretical and clinical contexts and disorders our work engages (chapter 2). Chapters 3–5 present descriptive resources which allow coding of spoken discourse in terms of conversation analysis and intonation (chapter 3), grammatical resources for meaning (chapter 4), and means for extracting patterns from these and relating the patterns to contexts of culture and situation presented as articulated aspects of memory (chapter 5). Chapters 6 and 7 address questions in study design associated with various discourse tasks and model applications for diagnosis (in autism spectrum disorders) and treatment monitoring (in Alzheimer's disease). Chapter 8, on cognitive models, inferencing and affect, and chapter 9 on modelling information across domains, situate the analytic constructs presented in neurocognitive and clinical perspectives through review of relevant neuropsychological, imaging and lesion studies and through detailed illustrations of the analyses and inferential processes involved in clinical discourse analysis. We close with remarks about the future and potential for clinical discourse analysis.

1   Introduction to clinical discourse analysis

> Discourse represents that aspect of mental activity that most clearly reflects the intimate and over-lapping connections among cognition, language, and communication.
>
> (Ulatowska *et al.* 1985)

1.1   What is clinical discourse analysis?

Clinical discourse analysis is the term we use to describe the analysis of language behaviour observed in clinical contexts. Language behaviour includes well-defined areas of clinical research addressing syntax, vocabulary, phonology, conversation skills and cohesion. It also includes areas less commonly described in clinical research such as argument roles, situational features and functional variation. The focus of clinical discourse analysis is natural language behaviour which requires examination of all these aspects of language use. Even the smallest of texts require analysis that can explore multivariate features.

Consider the following sentence:

(1) I can remember my Mom.

It is extracted from a brief sample of spoken discourse elaborated below. The sentence has an interactional function: it makes a statement which is modalized for capacity (*can*). It has a predicate that references a cognitive process (*remember*) and two argument roles, an experiencer (*I*) and a percept (*my mom*). It has an unmarked clause order: subject occurs first in English statements unless there is a reason to emphasize some other element of structure. One might also assume that the speaker interprets the situation as an informal one in that she chooses to refer to her mother as *Mom* rather than *mother*.

The larger text from which this example is taken appears in Text 1.1 below.

Text 1.1 My Mom

Ah the same thing with the – what was it we just discussed? – the stove. I can remember my Mom, she was as smart as a ticket. She was ninety-six years old when she died and she would, you know, she had everything under control. But I knew I knew that I couldn't do that I couldn't go and I don't know. Now I'm lost again.

The speaker is a 76-year-old woman, Cleo, with moderate Alzheimer's disease (AD). She is responding to a question about her ability to use the stove, and commenting on her mother's competence in old age as compared with her own difficulties. Grammatically, her speech is well formed. Most sentences are complete. They have appropriate subject–verb agreement, and subordinate and co-ordinate clause structures that are typical for her age group (Mackenzie 2000; Kemper *et al.* 2001b). She uses idioms *she was smart as a ticket, she had everything under control,* and a metaphor *I'm lost again.* She also uses cohesive features such as pronouns and other referring expressions appropriately, with reference supplied either in prior or subsequent text. However, there are conversation and fluency features which reflect planning difficulties and repairs: she hesitates (*the same thing with the*) and checks reference (*what was it we just discussed?*) but then supplies it herself (*the stove*). She has false starts (*she would*) which she repairs (*you know, she had …*); repetition (*I knew I knew*)*;* and one predication (*I couldn't go*) appears incomplete or tangential in that it does not refer to anything in either prior or subsequent discourse.

Cleo's abilities and difficulties, including her ability to monitor and repair her discourse, and her explicit recognition of difficulty (*I don't know, I'm lost again*) are characteristic for her age and stage of Alzheimer's (Asp *et al.* 2006a). Recognizing that this pattern is typical requires not only that all its elements be described, but also that samples described address both intra- and inter-individual variations relative to diagnosis, dementia phase, potential treatment effects and contexts of use. Thus clinical discourse analysis inherently requires both frameworks that enable comprehensive descriptions of language in use and the development of specialized text collections, or 'corpora', representative of the language used by speakers.

As the above brief description suggests, clinical discourse analysis not only involves description of formal linguistic features such as syntactic structures, but also characterizes patterns of meaning which may be relevant in understanding neural function in speakers. Consider Text 1.2: it is a transcript of a conversation between a research technician and a six-year-old boy with autism.

Text 1.2 Lions

(1) CHI: what would scratch you.
(2) CHI: wouldn't that be terrible?
(3) RES: umhum.
(4) CHI: awful!
(5) CHI: stink.

(6) CHI: and then you hate lions.
(7) CHI: stink hairy.
(8) ...
(9) RES: do you like lions?
(10) CHI: na I hate lions.
(11) RES: you hate <lions> [>]?
(12) CHI: <bushy> [>] and hairy stinky.
(13) ...
(14) RES: what's your favourite animal?
(15) CHI: an I hate lions.
(16) RES: yeah.
(17) RES: you hate lions.
(18) RES: but what what animal do you like?
(19) CHI: stinky and then I li ugly:
(20) RES: how about bunny rabbits?
(21) RES: do you like bunny rabbits?
(22) CHI: yes:
(23) RES: do you?
(24) CHI: why yes!

The text reflects some normal features of conversational interaction. Ted initiates a topic (*lions*). He knows when it is his turn to speak and when to let others have a turn. He develops his topic, giving characteristics of lions (*bushy, hairy* and *stinky*). And he expresses his attitude to lions (he hates them). However, when asked to shift topic and say what his favourite animals are, he doesn't collaborate in topic development but rather repeats the points that are of interest to him, that lions are *stinky* and *ugly* and he hates them. He also repeats *hairy, stinky* and *I hate lions*. Together, inability to shift focus and repetition, particularly of single words and phrases, create an identifiable pattern in this text. For instance, it suggests that Ted has difficulties managing topic and may have trouble staying with the drift of the conversation. Of course, such features may occur in the discourse of children who do not have autism. However, if such patterns appear as normative rather than exceptional in the discourse of an individual or group with diagnoses of autism spectrum disorders (ASDs), they may in fact reflect discourse patterns characteristic of ASDs. Identifiable recurrent patterns are the business of clinical discourse analysts.

Clinical discourse analysis is not as such a theory or discipline. Rather it is a goal-directed set of practices aimed at describing and explaining language behaviours as a means of investigating neurocognitive function. This implies a need for theoretical and descriptive flexibility. At present, there are few studies which investigate and attempt to fully characterize natural language behaviour of speakers with particular neurological disorders or diseases, although there is widespread recognition of the need for such work. We attempt to address this need by combining conversational analysis with comprehensive linguistic description of functions and structures as they relate to contextual variables.

As we use it, the term 'discourse analysis' refers to the types of description mentioned and not its more widely used sense associated with, for instance, the 'discourse of capitalism' or the 'discourse of libertarianism'.

1.2   What use is clinical discourse analysis?

Clinical discourse analysis can characterize language behaviour (i.e. discourse) from which inferences can be drawn about neurocognitive function. Discourse is a sensitive sign of global and specific function. In clinical contexts, its analysis can enable the development of tools for diagnosis and evaluation of treatment response. These may supplement existing measures and provide information for developing new therapies. Comprehensive descriptions of discourse patterns produced by speakers with neurological disorders may also lead to new understanding of brain–behaviour relationships.

Moreover, clinicians internalize the characteristic behaviours of the treatment groups they meet, and may use this information in making clinical judgements. Discourse analyses can make the basis for such clinical judgements explicit, replicable and generalizable. Such explicit characterizations can lead to the development of useful models for researchers, healthcare workers and families and thus help people to understand the behaviours they recurrently notice.

1.3   What use is this book?

Over the last thirty-five years, there has been increasing recognition that language behaviour is supported by a wide range of neural capacities, including attentional and memory systems, and that it is context dependent. While there is significant interest, a growing literature, and some established descriptive techniques and norms, there is as yet no agreed upon and validated set of practices which allow comprehensive analyses of language behaviour in clinical contexts. In the chapters that follow, we articulate a range of descriptive and theoretical tools and examples that may be useful for these purposes.

1.4   Sample analysis

Below we present and discuss in non-technical language, an example of discourse analysis. We illustrate how discourse techniques can highlight distinct, observable patterns of language behaviour which may be signs of neurocognitive function.

Text 1.3 The magic of the universe

(1) CHI: what's my favourite what?
(2) RES: your favourite game on the computer.

(3) CHI: well there's ex # well there's uh # eh # there's the there's this strange unusual game.
(4) CHI: uh well # there's a la a computer called an IBM Aptiva comes with games.
(5) CHI: uh # like my favourite is the # is from I is from a: place where there's a k.
(6) CHI: it's the game's about # it's a it's about a light bodied cube # k running getting the opposite colour on another light force called endorfun which is spelled e n d o r f u n.
(7) RES: umhum?
(8) CHI: and uh uh: light bodied cubes flying everywhere.
(9) CHI: and I have the power.
(10) CHI: I feel the magic of the universe.
(11) CHI: And et cetera et cetera et cetera.
(12) RES: is this a game you play by yourself James?
(13) RES: or with a partner?
(14) CHI: just myself.
(15) RES: hm.
(16) CHI: I am really completely good at it.

The speaker, James, is fifteen years old and has been diagnosed with autism. In this text he has a conversation with a researcher about his interests. James takes turns appropriately. In the first paragraph, he uses an echo question for clarification of a request for information. Subsequently in lines (3–6) and (8–10) he responds to and develops the request for information, identifying his favourite game as *strange, unusual*, the computer that it comes on (4), describing the game itself (5–6) and the player's role (9–10). In (14) he responds, again appropriately, to a question about the number of participants and evaluates his own ability as a player (16). This is very much a two-way conversation. James stays on topic throughout and pauses long enough at regular intervals to allow the interviewer to give feedback (*umhum*? (7), and *hm* (15)) and to ask for details (12, 13). He doesn't need to be prompted for topic development. His syntactic structures are varied with some simple and some co-ordinate and complex structures.

James' discourse is also characterized by pedantic features and dysfluencies. Specifically, he repeats information and phrases, supplies technical details, and has some initial difficulties organizing his talk. He uses redundant attributes (*strange, unusual* (3)) and degree modifiers (*really, completely* (16)). He fully repeats the phrase *light bodied cubes* when he refers to it a second time and repeats *et cetera* twice. He introduces technical details using one kind of grammatical structure, a reduced relative clause using *call*. He gives the brand name of the computer (*an IBM Aptiva*) on which the game is found and provides the spelling for *endorfun*. His description of the player's role (*I have the power; I feel the magic of the universe*) comes from the game and has a rehearsed quality.

In topic initiation there is also repetition: *well there's*, repeated three times, suggests the topic is in fact being reinitiated from the beginning (*well* is normally discourse or topic initial (Schiffrin 1987)). In fact, there are marked difficulties in setting the topic. There are eight pauses, five hesitations, eleven false starts and three repaired clauses (3, 4, 6) in the first half of the discourse where James is describing his favourite computer game without actually naming it. His dysfluency occurs perhaps because he does not know or remember the name of the computer game. The dysfluency features disappear when James is talking about his role in the game and his speech becomes more formulaic.

Cumulatively, the amount of repetition, the technical specificity and formulaic elements are features typical of pedantic speech in autism. This is thought to occur across autism spectrum disorders (de Villiers *et al.* 2007). Even an informal analysis of a short sample such as James' *The magic of the universe* isolates specific features which contribute to the characterization of 'pedantic speech'. While the neural substrates of autism spectrum disorders are not currently known, articulating how dysfluency and pedantic speaking pattern together may shape research questions about neurocognitive function in autism spectrum disorders.

The steps by which one moves from observation and description of a discourse pattern in an individual or a group with a diagnosed neurological disorder to hypothesizing possible neurophysiological cause(s) for the pattern are only a beginning in understanding brain–behaviour relationships. Hypotheses, once generated, need to be checked if they are to be of any use. Checking requires designing research projects. For these, a clinic setting really is essential. Even if discourse data for clinical populations were readily available outside clinic settings, there are other issues of access. Access to accurate diagnostic information for participants, to neuropsychological and neurological expert opinion and evaluation, to neuroimaging as a potential source of information about neural structure and/or function are all essential if hypotheses are to be investigated in ways that have the potential to be useful. And for obvious ethical reasons, utility is a goal of research in clinical discourse analysis.

That said, knowing how to analyse the data, and being willing to work with and in interdisciplinary teams is enough to begin with. We hope this book will be useful to people who might be so inclined and, paraphrasing Orange and Kertesz (2000: 173), that clinical discourse analyses will become a window into the cognitive, linguistic and social performances of people with neurological disorders.

2 Theoretical and clinical contexts

2.1 Introduction

This chapter is intended to situate clinical discourse analysis in terms of relevant linguistic and non-linguistic fields and to orient readers to the developmental and degenerative disorders discussed. Sections 2.2 and 2.3 briefly sketch diagnostic criteria, epidemiological information, current treatment options and potential associations with neurophysiology in each area. Section 2.4 focuses on the theoretical background and sources for clinical discourse analysis. These include conversation analysis, ethnographic and interactional sociolinguistics, functional linguistic discourse analysis, cognitive and philosophical pragmatics, and formal (generative) linguistic models. Section 2.5 addresses the roles of neurology, neuropsychology, psychiatry and neuroimaging as essential in developing understanding of relationships between discourse behaviours and neurological disorders. Finally, section 2.6 addresses the role of normative discourse patterns in evaluating descriptions of the discourse of clinical groups.

2.2 Autism spectrum disorders

Autism spectrum disorder (ASD) is an umbrella term for a continuum of neurodevelopmental disorders, the causes of which are unknown. ASD manifests during infancy and is estimated to affect one in every 165 children (Fombonne *et al.* 2006). The first account of autism was published by Leo Kanner (1943). Since that time, an expansion in diagnostic criteria has led to the inclusion of more diagnostic categories in the autism spectrum. ASD now includes autism, Asperger syndrome and pervasive developmental disorders not otherwise specified.

   ASDs affect more than one domain of functioning and are generally characterized by three core deficits:

1) impairments in socialization and interaction (e.g. lack of shared attention, lack of peer relationships),
2) impaired language and communication (delay or lack of functional speech, difficulties with conversation and pragmatics),

3) stereotyped behaviours and restricted interests (e.g. a desire for sameness or routine). These behaviours vary depending on an individual's age and level of functioning (American Psychiatric Association 1994).

In trying to understand the underlying causes of the three core deficits of autism, research has focused on cognition, neurology and genetics. Cognitive explanations have postulated as underlying causes: difficulty in theory of mind processing (Baron-Cohen *et al.* 1985; Baron-Cohen 1995); executive dysfunction (Russell 1998; Hill 2004) and a unique, locally oriented processing style (Frith and Happé 1994; Happé and Frith 2006). Some investigations of the neural circuitry associated with these explanations have found evidence of disturbances in functional connectivity. Specifically, a number of functional neuroimaging studies have found underconnectivity in autism and a processing style involving reduced reliance on prefrontal regions (Just *et al.* 2004; Koshino *et al.* 2005; 2008). Genetic studies looking at inherited risk for autism have found evidence that genetic factors play a role in autism. Current genetic research focuses on risk factors as well as genes that have an effect on variation in clinical expression (Nicholson and Szatmari 2003; Szatmari 2003).

Autism is a lifelong disorder. Given the high prevalence of ASDs, the need for services to diagnose and treat autism is overwhelming. With varying needs, and high costs of early intervention, treatment options are limited and much research is directed toward improving detection and intervention. Perhaps the most studied treatment option for ASDs, Applied Behavioural Analysis (Cooper *et al.* 2006), engages children in socialization, communication and behavioural learning with one-on-one teaching for up to forty hours per week. Other interventions may involve parent education, support programmes, advocacy, self-advocacy and combinations of physical and speech therapies, medication and social skills training. Often interventions focus on changes in the environment that can expand opportunities for engagement and social participation, including the communicative patterns of people who enter into social networks with people with ASDs. For example, peers and caregivers may be taught ways to start a conversation with someone with an ASD. They may also learn ways to use discourse that help facilitate conversational participation. While some people with less severe forms of ASD can function well and even excel without treatment, many people with autism are unable to function in everyday life into adulthood.

Communication difficulties in ASDs are widely varied. Early on, parents may observe an absence of communicative behaviours such as poor eye contact, lack of shared attention and lack of playing peekaboo. Many children with autism never develop functional verbal communication, while others have speech that stands out as being unusual. Frequently observed speech characteristics of autism include flat or unusual intonation (Fine 1991; Fine *et al.* 1991; de Villiers *et al.* 2007), the use of repetitive or stereotyped language (Tager-Flusberg 1996) and echolalia (Prizant and Duchan 1981). In Asperger syndrome, language development may be typical or even advanced, with complex syntax and wide vocabulary. Stereotyped phrases are often used and speech may have a scripted or pedantic quality, resembling a written register (Ghaziuddin and Gerstein 1996; de Villiers *et al.* 2007). Casual conversation often poses a distinct challenge for people with Asperger syndrome, especially in topic management, sustained conversation and contextual relevance. Overall the communication difficulties found in ASDs may be characterized as making insufficient use of contextual information in social language use (de Villiers 2005).

While there is no single speaking style that uniquely reflects speech difficulties in ASDs, the following text, from a 12-year-old speaker with autism illustrates one kind of difficulty in conversation:

Text 2.1 Free Willy

(1) RES: do you have some movies that you like?
(2) RES: what's the last movie that you saw?
(3) RES: what was it about?
(4) RES: did you see a movie at Christmas time?
(5) CHI: <yeah: ## yeah> ((faint)).
(6) RES: pardon?
(7) CHI: yeah.
(8) CHI: I did.
(9) RES: what movie did you see?
(10) CHI: Free Willy ((faint)).
(11) RES: pardon?
(12) CHI: Free Willy.
(13) RES: Free Willy.
(14) RES: was it good?
(15) CHI: good.
(16) RES: I've never seen that movie.
(17) RES: can you tell me what it's about Patrick?
(18) CHI: it's Free Willy.
(19) RES: it's Free Willy.
(20) CHI: I watched that show.
(21) CHI: Free Willy.
(22) RES: did you watch it at home?
(23) RES: hm?
(24) CHI: ## yeah.
(25) RES: did you watch it at your house?
(26) CHI: yeah.
(27) RES: tell me about Christmas Patrick.
(28) RES: did you have a good Christmas?

(29) CHI: yeah.
(30) CHI: I have a good Christmas.
(31) RES: what did you get for Christmas?
(32) RES: did you get presents?
(33) CHI: presents.
(34) RES: what did you get?
(35) CHI: I get: toys.
(36) CHI: I should get toys.
(37) RES: get toys?
(38) RES: what kind of toys?
(39) CHI: I: um I # didn't bring it.
(40) RES: pardon?
(41) CHI: I bring it.
(42) RES: you'll bring it?
(43) RES: did you bring it to school?
(44) CHI: ## yeah.
(45) RES: yeah?
(46) RES: what was it?
(47) CHI: Free Willy.
(48) RES: Free Willy hm.

The speaker, Patrick, is a cooperative participant in the conversation, who nevertheless speaks very quietly and at times appears to require prompting in response to questions or requests for information (2–4, 23, 28, 32). While he follows the rules of turn-taking, he rarely offers elaboration. Patrick also presents difficulties with tense forms (*I have a good Christmas* (30); *I get toys* (35); *I bring it* (41)). In addition, there is some confusion about whether or not he has brought a toy (or video), Free Willy, to school (39–44). Patrick's talk thus reflects difficulties in morphosyntactic, referential and experiential aspects of discourse development. He offers too little information and has difficulty organizing what he does say so that it has obvious relevance to the immediate context of the researcher's questions. As we shall show in the following chapters, there are other patterns of ability and challenge within the ASD spectrum. What they have in common are varying degrees of difficulty in producing the kinds of contribution that meet the information needs of addressees and/or the demands of the immediate context.

2.3   Neurodegenerative disorders associated with aging

There are a number of neurodegenerative diseases associated with aging such as Alzheimer's disease, vascular cognitive impairment, Lewy Body disease, Parkinson's disease, Creutzfeldt-Jakob disease, and the spectrum of fronto-temporal dementias. With the exception of Parkinson's disease, they are all associated with 'dementia'. Dementia refers to changes in cognitive function and/or behaviour associated with neurodegeneration rather than identifying a single disease. While there is some debate as to the combination of features necessary and sufficient to constitute dementia, there is consensus that such a diagnosis is to be given when people exhibit chronic changes in cognition and function which impair their ability to carry out activities of daily living independently, and these changes are not caused by psychiatric disorders such as depression or anxiety, by traumatic brain injury, or other physical causes such as nutritional deficiency, exposure to toxins, infections or brain tumours.[1]

Some of these diseases, such as Creutzfeldt-Jakob disease and the frontotemporal dementias, are relatively rare. The sporadic type of Creutzfeldt-Jakob disease associated with aging has an estimated incidence of one in one million worldwide (Public Health Agency of Canada 1999). The infectious and familial forms of this disease are rarer still. Estimates of the prevalence of frontotemporal dementias vary from 2% to 12% of all dementias (Bird *et al.* 2003; Kertesz 2006; Knapp *et al.* 2007).[2] They constitute a group of neurodegenerative disorders which initially affect frontal cortical regions – judgement, behaviour and language may be separately or simultaneously impaired. As they progress, memory and other cognitive functions are also affected. The frontotemporal dementias tend to have earlier onset, so that frontotemporal dementia may account for up to 50% of dementia cases in people less than 60 years old (Graff-Radford and Woodruff 2007). In rare cases, they are inherited through an autosomal dominant gene and onset may be earlier. Lewy Body dementia is a neurodegenerative disease which can occur by itself or together with Parkinson's and/or Alzheimer's disease and is estimated to account for between 3 and 26% of all dementias (Zaccai *et al.* 2005 for review). It is characterized by the presence of 'Lewy Bodies', abnormal proteins called alpha-synuclein distributed in cortical and subcortical brain regions, as well as by diffuse neuritic plaques (Baba *et al.* 1998). Dementia with Lewy Bodies most typically causes fluctuations in cognition, attention and alertness, vivid visual hallucinations and impaired motor control (Parkinsonism). As it develops, memory and other cognitive functions also become impaired. Parkinson's disease also involves deposits of the alpha-synuclein protein, initially in subcortical brain regions (the basal-ganglia). The initial effects of Parkinson's are usually limited to impaired motor control and typically develop after age 60, but between 25–40% of people with Parkinson's later develop dementia (McKeith *et al.* 1996; Galvin *et al.* 2001; Nussbaum and Ellis 2003).

The most familiar of the neurodegenerative causes of dementia, because of their prevalence, are Alzheimer's disease (AD) and vascular cognitive impairment (VCI). Global statistics for dementia (used inclusively for the neurodegenerative diseases associated with aging) suggest that approximately 24 million people worldwide have dementia, and that 4.6 million people develop dementia every year (Ferri *et al.* 2005; Alzheimer's Association 2007). Projections suggest that the number of people living with dementia will double every twenty years (Ferri *et al.* 2005). AD accounts for approximately 60% of dementia cases. Estimates of VCI suggest that it accounts for about 20% (Hill *et al.* 1996) of dementia cases though prevalence may vary by region and gender (Knopman *et al.* 2003; Rocca and Knopman 2003; Knapp *et al.* 2007). Community-based neuropathological studies suggest that AD and VCI frequently co-occur in individuals (Massoud *et al.* 1999; Neuropathological Group 2001; Jellinger and Attems 2007), suggesting that diagnosis and treatment of 'mixed dementia' should be more common (Langa *et al.* 2004; Jellinger 2007).

AD is normally sporadic (not inherited) and typically affects people after the age of 65, with about 10% of people over this age being affected. Among people over 85, estimates of prevalence range from 30 to 50%. In about 5% of cases, AD is familial, occurring as a consequence of genetic mutation. People with the autosomal dominant forms of AD may develop symptoms in their 30s and 40s (Knapp *et al.* 2007).

Currently, criteria for identifying AD based on the DSM-IV-TR (American Psychiatric Association 2000) and the recommendations of the National Institute of Neurological Disorders and Stroke–Alzheimer's Disease and Related Disorders (NINCDS-ADRDA) working group include clinical evidence of gradual, progressive development of memory impairment and one or more impairments in language, motor abilities, ability to recognize and identify objects, and executive function (McKhann *et al.* 1984). For a diagnosis of AD, the DSM-IV further specifies that these deficits significantly impair social and/or occupational function and are not due to other physical or psychiatric conditions or to toxin exposure. A definite diagnosis of AD can only be achieved at autopsy. Otherwise diagnoses are 'probable' or 'possible' and are clinical judgements which may be supported by neuroimaging or evaluation of cerebrospinal fluid.[3]

Some of the structural and functional features of AD neuropathology are well established. These include the formation of amyloid plaques and neurofibrillary tangles first reported by Alois Alzheimer in 1907. Biochemical markers of these pathological changes in AD may be assessed by cerebrospinal fluid *in vivo* (Blennow and Hampel 2003). There is also impaired neurotransmission associated with loss of cholinergic neurons in the nucleus basilis, reduction of nicotinic and muscarinic receptors in the cortex, and dysfunction of the major excitatory neurotransmitter – glutamate (Mesulam 2000; Bleich *et al.* 2003; Hynd *et al.* 2004; Jacob *et al.* 2007; Kashani *et al.* 2008). Neuroimaging may show early localized atrophy in the medial temporal lobe, particularly the hippocampus and entorhinal cortex; reduced temporal-parietal and frontal lobe function in blood flow and metabolic studies, and altered neurochemical concentrations in *in vivo* imaging of metabolites (Fox *et al.* 1999; Silverman *et al.* 2001; Kantarci *et al.* 2007; Matsuda 2007). Global brain atrophy is evident in late stage AD (Mesulam 2000).

Although there are a number of biomarkers and established neuropathological correlates, the actual cause of AD is not known. Studies investigating cause focus on the role of genetics and molecular mechanisms involved in the deposition of amyloid plaques, the formation of neurofibrillary tangles, cholinergic dysfunction and neuronal death. Studies of risk factors for the development of AD point to age, genetics and lifestyle factors such as diet, exercise, social and intellectual engagement as well as potentially precipitating physical conditions such as head injury, hypertension, obesity, low oestrogen, elevated cholesterol and diabetes (Jellinger 2002; Gustafson *et al.* 2003; Mayeux 2003; Luchsinger and Mayeux 2004; Blennow *et al.* 2006). The overall picture with respect to lifestyle and health conditions is that anything that promotes oxidative stress and/or increases demands for neuroplastic responses in the brain may increase the likelihood of developing AD (Mesulam 2000; Mamelak 2007).

2.3.1   Vascular cognitive impairment

Criteria for vascular cognitive impairment (VCI) require that there be evidence of cerebrovascular disease established by focal neurological signs and symptoms and/or by brain imaging; that cerebrovascular disease is judged to be causally connected to dementia (if present), that the onset is typically abrupt, and that the disease course is stepwise and fluctuating (Roman *et al.* 1993). Prevalence estimates for VCI suggest that it is the second most common cause for dementia, accounting for approximately 20% of all dementias in Europe and North America (Hebert *et al.* 2000; Rocca and Knopman 2003; Knapp *et al.* 2007). As with AD, there is an inherited form of VCI, cerebral autosomal dominant arteriopathy with subcortical infarcts and leukoencephalopathy, or CADASIL (Ruchoux and Maurage 1997). It occurs as a result of a genetic mutation on a gene (NOTCH 3) which affects blood vessels in the brain and heart. Prevalence is uncertain, but Razvi *et al.* (2005) estimated genetically proven CADASIL to occur in 1.98/100,000 of people in the west of Scotland and suggested that the mutation prevalence is likely to be higher (4/100,000).

With the exception of CADASIL, VCI is not a disease with a single etiology, but rather a range of cognitive states brought about by impaired function or total obstruction of vasculature supplying blood to the brain (O'Brien *et al.* 2003). Reduced blood flow reduces oxygen and nutrient supplies, which in turn cause dysfunction and tissue death. Damage may be localized, or consist of multiple large or small lesions distributed in cortical and/or subcortical regions. There is also a variant, small vessel disease, in which arterosclerotic conditions of the small vessels in the brain reduce the blood supply (hypoperfusion) which may result in a dementia syndrome (Pantoni and Simoni 2003). The location and extent of the damage will be reflected in the dementia symptoms of affected people (McPherson and Cummings 1996). However, a common pattern is for prefrontal systems to be impaired, which may be reflected variously in behavioural changes, executive dysfunction, attention limitations and general cognitive slowing (Almkvist *et al.* 1994). Memory may be relatively spared at least early in the course of the disease (Desmond 2003; Sachdev and Looi 2003; Moorhouse and Rockwood 2008). Risk factors for the development of VCI include untreated high blood pressure, heart disease, a history of stroke, atherosclerosis, diabetes, high cholesterol, obesity and lifestyle factors contributing to these conditions such as diet, exercise, a history of smoking or substance abuse (Roman 2005; Alagiakrishnan *et al.* 2006; O'Brien 2006). As noted above, AD and VCI often occur together (Langa *et al.* 2004). The relationship between them is still a matter of research and debated (Skoog and Gustafson 2003).

At present, there are no cures for either AD or VCI. Treatments address prevention and symptoms. Reducing risk factors through drug therapy (for instance, for high blood pressure, diabetes, high cholesterol) and lifestyle modifications of diet, exercise and toxin exposure may help prevent dementia or slow the processes of neurodegeneration (Roman 2005; Black 2007). Drug therapies developed to address cholinergic and glutamatergic system deficits in AD improve neurotransmission and have consequent benefits in improved cognition and function for some patients (Birks 2006; Burns *et al.* 2006; McShane *et al.* 2006). There is also some evidence that these drugs may have some neuroprotective effects. For instance, the cholinesterase inhibitors have been associated with reduced atrophy *in vivo* (Krishnan *et al.* 2003; Tune *et al.* 2003) and work in animal models suggests that memantine may limit neuronal damage associated with hyper-phosphorylated *tau* (Li *et al.* 2004). The cholinesterase inhibitors are also used to treat VCI patients and appear to have similar effects (Burns *et al.* 2006). Research into new drug therapies is aimed at preventing or reducing the development of plaques and tangles thought to be the principal causes of neuronal damage in AD (Blennow *et al.* 2006; Klafki *et al.* 2006) and treating vascular disease in both VCI and AD (Gorelick 2003; Inzitari *et al.* 2004).

There are some widely recognized patterns of language deficits associated with AD including early word-finding difficulties, and what has been described as 'lexically empty' and paraphasic speech (Nicholas *et al.* 1985; Bayles *et al.* 1987; Dijkstra *et al.* 2004). There is also evidence of reduced capacity for processing complex syntactic structures although prototypical syntactic patterns are preserved until AD becomes severe (Kontiola *et al.* 1990; Lyons *et al.* 1994; Bickel *et al.* 2000; Kemper *et al.* 2001). People with AD often modalize their discourse quite heavily and may have difficulty producing or understanding complex narratives or instructions (Patry and Nespoulous 1990; Erlich *et al.* 1997; Nespoulous *et al.* 1998; Asp *et al.* 2006a). They also very characteristically have repetitive speech (Ready *et al.* 2003; Cullen *et al.* 2005;

Asp *et al.* 2006b; Rockwood *et al.* 2007). As the disease progresses, communication may be severely impaired and ultimately people with AD become mute, though the desire to communicate may remain intact (Bayles *et al.* 1992; Ellis and Astell 2004).

Because of the variability in VCI, there is no single profile of language or discourse abilities or deficits. Rather language impairments will vary depending on the cause, location and type of neural damage. For example, dementia following a stroke may include any of the aphasic syndromes depending on the location of the stroke (McPherson and Cummings 1996). A number of studies investigating VCI caused by diffuse subcortical ischemic damage have found that patients have reduced letter fluency as compared with category fluency on word-list generation tasks (e.g. Lafosse *et al.* 1997; Mendez *et al.* 1997; Tierney *et al.* 2001; Duff *et al.* 2004; Poore *et al.* 2006). These tests ask participants to name all the words they can think of beginning with a particular letter (letter fluency) or all the animals they can think of (category fluency). All these studies compared performance of VCI patients with AD patients in the interests of finding clinically relevant ways of distinguishing the two dementia syndromes. The general pattern, not always confirmed statistically, is that AD patients perform better on letter fluency and VCI patients perform better on category fluency though both groups may perform worse than control subjects on both measures. The assumption is that subcortical damage affects prefrontal function on which letter fluency tasks depend more than temporal lobe functions which are engaged in category fluency. Jones *et al.* (2006) extended the analysis to preclinical phases of AD and VCI and found that category fluency does distinguish the groups, but that compromised prefrontal function in preclinical AD participants matches that of VCI participants so that letter fluency is similar between groups. Other studies, also comparative of AD and VCI patients' language, have reported conflicting results not only for fluency tasks (e.g. Looi and Sachdev 1999) but also for syntax. Kontiola *et al.* (1990) suggest that in AD syntax is more compromised than in VCI, whereas Hier *et al.* (1985) and Powell *et al.* (1988) report the converse. Recent studies directly evaluating syntax in VCI are lacking as are studies of discourse, though Shindler *et al.* (1984) noted increased perseveration and intrusions for VCI patients.

In short the linguistic picture for VCI is very limited. Studies have been mostly comparative (with AD) and there has been little work on areas such as syntax and almost none on discourse in VCI. This paucity is perhaps a result of both the somewhat disappointing findings of early studies that sought to use linguistic features to distinguish VCI and AD and the heterogeneity of VCI itself. Those findings that there are mostly point to the effects of impaired prefrontal function in VCI caused by diffuse subcortical damage – the characterization of discourse for the various groups within this spectrum has yet to be undertaken. Diagnostic techniques which allow better discrimination between the subtypes of VCI make the prospect of developing research strategies which address the linguistic and discourse signs associated with particular vascular pathologies more possible.

2.4   Theoretical sources

Our approach to discourse analysis is eclectic, drawing from such theoretical sources as conversation analysis, generative linguistics, functional linguistics and pragmatics. Here we outline the kinds of phenomena and assumptions of these different linguistic approaches.

2.4.1   Conversation analysis

Conversation analysis is the analysis of talk. It examines all kinds of spoken interactions and it focuses on turn-taking, topic and fluency. **Turn-taking** has to do with who gets to talk when and how turns at talk are ordered in relation to each other. For example, questions require responses and the type of question asked shapes in some respects the type of response given. Yes/no questions (e.g. *Do you like chai?*) require answers ranging between positive (*yes*) and negative (*no*). There are thus both sequence (question before response) and semantic relations between the pair of utterances. Highly regularized relations in turn-taking of this type have been described as adjacency pairs (Sacks *et al.* 1974; Levinson 1983). Studies of turn-taking address not only sequencing and semantic relations between turns at talk, but also means of facilitating or inhibiting speakers' access to 'the floor' through use of features such as supportive questioning, interruption and speaker selection. **Topic** refers to what is discussed and interacts with turn-taking, for instance insofar as speakers' relative access to the floor affects the extent to which topics of interest to them are discussed (Danes 1974). **Fluency** refers to features associated with information processing and monitoring discourse. Features such as hesitation, pause frequency and duration, speakers' repairs to their own or others' discourse and so on, are studied by conversation analysts. Within conversation analysis, the goal of these analyses is typically to explicate the meaning contributions of such behaviours to talk. There is also a concern in conversation analysis with identifying turn-taking, topic and fluency conventions, and associated speaker expectations for performance. Moreover, conversation analysts describe the variation in such conventions and expectations associated with different types of conversational interaction and in different institutional environments (e.g. Atkinson and Heritage 1984; Sacks 1992a; 1992b; Heritage and Maynard 2006).

In clinical contexts, conversational norms associated with turn-taking, topic and fluency may inform assumptions in terms of which individual speakers' performance may be assessed. The clinical setting also introduces concerns for features which conversation analysts do not typically consider. For instance, in the clinic, concern with fluency may be associated with motor control (e.g. stuttering), with rate of speech, with integrity of semantic systems, or with executive function processes such as attention, working memory, or information maintenance and monitoring. Similarly, topic management and turn-taking might be means of investigating ability to (interactively) construct relevance, in terms of perseveration, tangentiality, attention, confabulation, or social skills development. These may in turn be linked to neural functions or structures implicated in different disorders. Thus while the primary business of conversation analysts has been to identify and describe the semiotic function of elements of conversational interaction, in the clinic these elements may become the means of investigating relationships between behaviour and cognitive and neurological functions.

2.4.2   Generative linguistics

Generative linguists have directly presented the fact of language competence as cognitive and psychological capacities of speakers (Chomsky 1957; 1995; Jackendoff 2002). The motivation is to provide explanations for the universal ease with which children acquire languages and the apparently infinite potential for speakers to say new (never spoken before) things. Formal generativists typically ask not *what do speakers know?* but *what is it that speakers would need to know in order to acquire a language? what kinds of mechanisms and information might support language acquisition?* and *what formal properties do languages need to have in order at least rationally to allow for linguistic creativity?* The attention to acquisition and creativity has meant that generativists have emphasized the role of syntactic (and other) structures in cognitive architectures and so have contributed perspicuous and relatively simple ways to represent relations in and between syntactic structures and structural potentials.

2.4.3   Functional linguistics

Functional linguistics is concerned with semiotic potential and language use. Functional linguists are thus more or less directly concerned with questions such as *what do speakers know* that let them communicate relevantly and successfully in context. Systemic–functional grammars address the text–context relationship in part by positing linguistic systems as shaped by their cultural and situational contexts of use. Within these frameworks, it is possible to describe particular languages and varieties in terms of experiential, interactional and organizational functions. These functional potentials constitute the semiotic resources from which speakers can select meanings to produce texts which are contextually relevant (e.g. Halliday 1976; 1985; Halliday and Hasan 1989). Concern with functional differentiation within the systemic–functional framework has also meant that there has been explicit attention to areas such as affect and evaluation in grammars and discourse (e.g. Martin and White 2005). Because of the concern with texts and discourses, functional linguists have borrowed and developed models of generic structures, scripts and schemas from European functional and structuralist traditions, cognitive sciences and conversation analysis. These cognitive models incorporate semiotically rich articulations of textual and contextual information into the linguistic model so that accounts of discourse schemas and genres can be represented as part of the semiotic resources of a language or variety (e.g. van Dijk 1977; 1981).

2.4.4   *Pragmatics*

Pragmatics broadly addresses speakers' ability to infer logical and presup-positional relationships between sentences based on the content of what is said, its relevance in context and speaker intentions. Pragmatics took as its point of departure, questions raised by Austin (1962) about how individual sentences could function as speech acts and how literal content might differ from intended or interpreted meaning. For example, Austin drew attention to the fact that we do not simply make statements, ask questions and give com-mands, but that a sentence such as *I hereby name this ship Floatsome* spoken in the appropriate context by a person with socially designated authority to name the ship, actually performs the action of naming. Similarly, *Let's call the kitty Oblong* does not merely make a suggestion but actually (assuming the naming is accepted) may perform the action of naming a new kitten. Austin made the further point that all our utterances constitute speech acts insofar as they perform actions, though they need not overtly state the act they perform. For instance, a statement such as *there is a bug on your shirt* may be offered as information. However, it is also possible that it might be spoken with the intention to warn, as an expression of alarm, or even as a joke. Addressees' ability to interpret the statement appropriately depends in part on inferring the speaker's intention relative to available contextual information. For example, one can imagine a variety of situations which might motivate a speaker such as knowledge that bugs in this area are poisonous, an affective state (the speaker is afraid of bugs), or in the context of humour that the addressee has an image of a bug on her shirt.

Pragmatics broadly conceived is thus concerned with the problems of explaining textually and contextually based inferential processes involved in communication. Aspects of these problems have been addressed with different emphases and methods in relevance theory, cognitive pragmatics, ethnography and interactional sociolinguistics as well as directly in some models of language and discourse processing (e.g. van Dijk 1977; 1981; Lakoff 1987; Gregory 1988; 2009a; 2009b; 1998; Jackendoff 2002; Hudson 2007). Relevance theory pays particular attention to inferencing from text to context (e.g. Grice 1975; Sperber and Wilson 1986; 1995). Interactional sociolinguistics studies are interested in figuring out how the micro-bits of talk, performance both in terms of linguistic behaviour and conversational behaviour, instantiate and construct meaning in context through interaction (e.g. Gumperz and Hymes 1972; Atkinson and Heritage 1984; Clark 1996; Schegloff 2007). Where relevance theorists may be more concerned with abstract relations that characterize inferential processes and may therefore work with hypothetical examples, interactional sociolinguists are concerned with performance and thus work on instances of talk. For example, interactional sociolinguists are prepared to investigate the communicative value of superficially meaningless fragments such as hesitation phenomena and false starts (e.g. Clark and Fox Tree 2002). Ethnographic studies have also focused on 'communicative competence' (Hymes 1971) with particular attention to intercultural differences in conventions associated with many different discourse features (Hymes 1962; 1974). Studies compare differences not only in linguistic systems but also in conversational norms and generic expectations for narrative, expository and other types of discourse. Ethnographic work thus informs analyses about potential and real variation in discourse associated with cultural contexts.

The discourse analysis that we do is eclectic in the sense that it is informed by all of the above. The grammar that we use is functionally organized (by experiential, interactional and organizational meaning potential) and generative (we use a formal syntax). It explicitly incorporates insights from pragmatic, cognitive and interactional perspectives not only in the grammar but also in the overall architecture and it assumes that ethnographic locations supply the content (and may influence the form) of that architecture. That is, we assume that context, insofar as it is relevant to inferential processes in discourse, is cognitive – matters of speakers' access to information available in the interaction and the semantic and episodic memories it activates.[4] Moreover, the information available in the semantic and episodic memory of speakers depends upon the cultural contexts in which they live and the generic situations in which they participate in instances of everyday life. We also assume within this framework that cognitive processes such as inferencing are, in fact, executive function processes. Some of these relationships are schematically suggested in Figure 2.1.

Figure 2.1 is not intended as a 'model' or paradigm of anything. Rather, its purpose is just to suggest, reading across rows, some of the areas of correlation between contextual parameters, linguistic and discourse phenomena, their hypothesized neurocognitive reference domains, and the kinds of study that characterize the type of information represented. (Neuropsychological and physiological

Contextual parameters	Discourse and linguistic correlates	Neurocognitive reference domains	Description domains
Context of culture	Language and dialect variation	• Language(s) and dialect(s) knowledge • Semantic memory representations of culturally specific 'knowledge of the world'	• Models/grammars of languages and varieties • Ethnographies • Encyclopaedias
Context of situation	Functional variation by register and genre	• Semantic/episodic memory • Representations of typical ways of doing and saying things, organizing and affectively responding to information (knowledge of genres, registers, scripts, frames, schemas etc.)	• Ethnographies of speaking • Conversation analysis • Genre and register descriptions
Instantial situation	Discourse	• Linguistic processes: selection, retrieval, sequence/order, articulation • Executive function processes: information selection/inhibition, retrieval, maintenance, monitoring • Executive control function: judgement, planning, reasoning • Affect: emotional states and evaluative responses	• Interactional sociolinguistics • Analysis of instances of discourse • Information and discourse processing models • Pragmatics

Figure 2.1 Context, language and discourse relations to neurocognitive domains and inquiry types

models for 'semantic memory' and 'executive functions' are not included here simply because the focus of Figure 2.1 is 'what information' needs to be represented, rather than how or where that information is neurally instantiated.)

Figure 2.1 also says nothing about vertical relations within columns. Some of the relationships between the elements in context of culture, context of situation and instantial situation may be thought of abstractly as inheritance relations of model(s) to instance(s) (Hudson 2007). That is, any particular instance of discourse will inherit properties from speakers' knowledge of linguistic and contextual models which the instance of discourse both references and instantiates. Selection of particular linguistic and discourse features are mediated by ongoing executive functions associated with information processing and with executive control functions of planning, reasoning and judgement (Royall et al. 2002). We assume that executive functions and executive control functions relate instantially available information to speakers' semantic and episodic models and that affective states in the speaker in the instance modulate these processes.

2.5   Other sources

In this section we discuss the roles of neurology, neuropsychology, psychiatry and neuroimaging in developing understanding of relationships between discourse behaviours and neurological disorders. Our primary goal here is to emphasize the need to work with a multi-disciplinary team in clinical discourse analysis. We do not aim at anything that could be considered a full characterization of these specializations, but rather just to indicate the types of expertise necessary for developing and testing hypotheses, and interpreting results.

Neurologists, psychiatrists and (neuro)psychologists are all involved in diagnosis, assessment, and treatment of people with neurological and/or neuropsychiatric dysfunction. There are significant areas of overlap in their expertise, research and practice. However, each specialization differs to a certain extent in focus and in the types of care and intervention they typically provide. Neurologists specialize in understanding the nervous system; that is, the brain, spinal cord and nerves. This means that they may be consulted not only about dysfunction but also about insult or trauma to these systems. In relation to neurophysiology and behaviour, neurology is one of the disciplines which have the authority and potential to provide explanatory models and attribute cause relative to neural substrata.

The focus in psychiatry is understanding mental health. This means that psychiatrists' focus may include emotive, psychological and behavioural disorders with uncertain neurological etiology such as depression, anxiety, anorexia and schizophrenia. They are also often involved with many of the disorders (such as Alzheimer's) that engage neurologists. Many psychiatrists and neurologists specialize in periods of the life span (e.g. paediatric or geriatric psychiatry) or in particular disorders (e.g. vascular disease). They may also be engaged in epidemiological and preventative research.

Neuropsychologists focus on identifying neural structures and functions associated with neurological and psychiatric disorders. They develop and use assessment tools for differential diagnosis, evaluation and rating and are expert in measurement techniques. They may specialize in particular human processes such as perception or cognition.

Neurologists, psychiatrists and neuropsychologists may all employ neuroimaging as means of investigating neural function and structure *in vivo*. Neuroimaging offers additional evidences that may support diagnoses or neurological hypotheses. They do this by imaging structure using computed tomography (CT), magnetic resonance imaging (MRI), diffusion tensor imaging (DTI) and by imaging distributions of metabolites using magnetic resonance spectroscopy (MRS). Function can be assessed through blood flow, oxygen and glucose uptake using positron emission tomography (PET), single photon emission computed tomography (SPECT) or functional MRI (fMRI), or by evaluating electrical activity using electroencephalography (EEG) or magnetic fields produced by electrical activity using magnetoencephalography (MEG) (e.g. Toga and Mazziotta 2002). There are also novel technologies for imaging microstructure and functional processes in neurons, cells and vasculature.

Current studies investigating language and discourse abilities that involve an imaging component most commonly use one of the functional imaging techniques. However, there is potential (given the right team, circumstances and questions) to bring the other technologies to bear in relating discourse features to neural structure and function.

An example of a functional investigation is Mason *et al.*'s (2008) investigation of the relationship of inferencing in discourse to theory of mind abilities using fMRI. Building on considerable evidence that people with autism have a deficit with reading other people's mental states, they compared two groups of speakers, 18 with a diagnosis of high functioning autism and 18 matched controls, in their abilities to draw inferences about situations, intentions and emotional states in a reading task. They compared left and right hemisphere regional activations and functional connectivity between groups on task performance and found that the group with autism activated a similar network, but had less left activation, lower functional connectivity and activations were not differentiated across tasks. That is, the group with autism employed the same kinds of cognitive strategies regardless of the specific inferential process. Mason *et al.* conclude that the activation patterns during complex information processing are similar to controls but less efficient in autism.

This study illustrates ways in which various specializations may interact in coming to understand (or even address) a particular set of brain behaviour relations in the context of a particular disorder. Minimally, the areas of expertise the study brings together are neurology, pragmatic aspects of discourse analysis, fMRI imaging expertise (design, execution and analysis), statistics and diagnostic assessment expertise. These relationships are schematically indicated in Figure 2.2.

The point of Figure 2.2. is to suggest the collaborative and inherently interdisciplinary nature of research which explores discourse in clinical settings. While particular tasks such as diagnosis or discourse analysis will be carried out by researchers independently, shaping the questions, establishing the methodology for addressing them, doing the investigation that leads to results and interpreting the results require consultation and collaboration if the work is to have potential value for health care.

2.6   Discourse norms

The goal of this section is to clarify the role of normative patterns in grammar and discourse (behaviour and processing) in interpreting patterns in clinical settings. Most grammars characterize the linguistic structures and relations that may (or may not) occur in a language. What constitutes 'a language' may be assumed (based on a speaker's intuitive investigation of their own knowledge of the particular language) or it may be established through examination

Assumptions

Theory of Mind is supported by a localized and functionally dedicated neural network
(neurology, psychiatry, neuropsychology, neuroimaging)

In autism there are deficits in Theory of Mind
(neurology, psychiatry, neuropsychology)

This may be reflected in differences in inferencing in discourse
(neurology, psychiatry, neuropsychology, discourse analysis)

Questions

Is the neural network supporting Theory of Mind differentially activated between controls
and people with autism on discourse comprehension tasks designed to engage this network?
(neurology, psychiatry, neuropsychology, discourse analysis, neuroimaging)

Ethics

Does the question merit the resources and participation demands?
What if any potential harms may be involved in participation?
(Principal Investigator and supporting institutions)

Method

Participant selection (diagnosis by psychiatrist)
Recruitment, data collection
Task design (neurologist/psychologist/discourse analyst)
fMRI design (technician/physicist; radiologist/neurologist)
Statistical design (psychometrist, biostatistician)
Study coordinator

Investigation

Analysis and interpretation of linguistic data (discourse analyst)
fMRI analysis and interpretation (technician/physicist; radiologist/neurologist)
Statistical analysis (psychometrist, biostatistician)

Results

Disseminate

Figure 2.2 Interdisciplinary relations in clinical discourse analysis

of demographically representative and functionally salient samples of speech or writing. Increasingly, the speech samples used in developing grammatical descriptions are based on large electronic corpora such as the British National Corpus, the parallel American National Corpus, and the COBUILD corpus of English. Corpora may be specialized for region (e.g. Canadian or Indian English), mode (e.g. spoken or written), function (e.g. science language, first or second language acquisition), or some combination of mode and function (e.g. spoken academic English). Some smaller corpora are already analysed phonologically, morphologically and/or syntactically.

Even where grammars and corpora are demographically or functionally specialized, the goal is still to investigate and provide normative representation of typically occurring speech and/or writing. Grammars and corpora can thus be used to explicitly establish 'normal' speech and discourse patterns. They also can provide models for conceptualizing problems, recognizing differences, and may provide data for hypothesis testing. Because grammars and corpora are normatively based they provide essential reference material for clinical (and other) types of discourse analysis.

What normatively based grammars and corpora do not do (for obvious reasons) is represent (or indeed systematically exclude) the speech or discourse of groups with identified, diagnosed, motor, cognitive or affective disorders. It is also the case that sampling techniques for corpora vary and grammatical descriptions and postulates may or may not be validated either in corpora or by other means. Clinical discourse analysis can thus use grammars and representative corpora as reference material but must develop specialized techniques and corpora to address the requirements of the medical setting and the specific patterns relevant for treatment groups. For example, descriptive techniques may require validation by inter-rater reliability assessment, and theoretical assumptions about neural representation of grammatical constructs require validation or support from neuropsychological, pathological or imaging sources. Specialized reference corpora which characterize disorders, including their stages and level of severity, are necessary for research purposes. Further, it is necessary to control such reference material by comparison with, for instance, demographically similar groups without the disorder, and/or with different disorders depending on research goals.

It may also be necessary to develop functionally varied corpora where investigation is directed to understanding the competence of speakers across a range of different situation types. For example, in developmental disorders such as ASDs, verbal communication may be relatively successful in one context (e.g. school or work) but challenging in others (e.g. phatic communion in casual social settings). In studies where participants are involved in drug or other therapeutic interventions or where disorders change with time, it is also valuable to sample periodically (longitudinally) to assess change from a 'baseline' state.

Combining cross-sectional and longitudinal sampling with matched controls is another very rich way to investigate discourse within a study group. Thus, the choices made with respect to reference corpora for establishing norms or 'baseline' patterns will depend on the research goals in the particular study, but the need for such reference corpora is a given in health research and so also in clinical discourse analysis with potential translational value.

The clinical discourse analyst thus not only needs to be able to do discourse analyses and all that that entails, but also needs to know enough about the disorder(s) she is investigating and to be able to explain the relevance of linguistic and discourse findings to clinicians. This kind of work can happen in the context of single case studies, and indeed, despite our remarks above about corpora, the case-study approach can be extremely informative as a point of departure for research, and for illustrative purposes. But if the goal is ultimately to contribute to the possibilities for helping people in clinical contexts, then an appropriate corpus and research team is called for.

3 Talk and speech – conversation analysis and intonation in English

3.1 Introduction

In this and the following two chapters we present descriptive resources which allow coding of spoken discourse in terms of conversational, grammatical, pragmatic and contextual features. Features that are coded can be counted. This allows both 'pattern finding', a replicable way of proceeding inductively to characterizations of discourse (a specialized kind of data mining), and 'hypothesis checking' where analyses in terms of the presence, absence, frequency and/or co-occurrence of discourse features are hypothesized to be associated with particular disorders, neurocognitive states, or changes in neurocognitive states.

Our goal is pragmatic: we do not enter into debates or account for the historical development of particular concepts or constructs, but present criteria for description that allow understanding and reliable coding of discourse features. Often this means that we are presenting 'hybrid' models, synthesized from works in functional, ethnographic, interactional and formal linguistic traditions. We refer readers to these works but discuss them only when such discussion seems essential for understanding.

The order of presentation, from conversational to contextual analysis, is intended to proceed from the familiar to, perhaps, less familiar ways of describing discourse. However, as is inevitably the case, some terms appear that presuppose knowledge of others presented later. For the most part, we address this by providing examples and/or glosses of terms and references. We use normative examples rather than examples from clinical contexts in presenting the grammar. Normative examples are practical insofar as they do serve to illustrate without the addition of marked features or other distractions. (See appendix A for some basic grammatical terminology.) Two terms presupposed in all of the following discussions are **clause** and **utterance** so we offer definitions of these first.

For English, **clauses** can be defined syntactically as consisting of a verb, its arguments and adjuncts as in *Cosmo saw Tess yesterday,* where the verb *saw* takes two arguments, an Experiencer *Cosmo* and a Percept *Tess* occurring as subject and complement respectively. *Yesterday* is an optional element (syntactically an adjunct) realizing a time circumstance. Clauses which function independently can also be assigned a speech function. That is, they can be used alone to ask a question, make a statement or exclamation, or give a command. This means that the following Examples (1)–(4) are all clauses by either or both criteria:

(1) Tess listened to the mouse very intently.
This has a speech function (statement), a verb (*listened*), two arguments (*Tess, to the mouse*) and a manner adjunct (*very intently*).

(2) Where did Cosmo leave his monkey?
This has a speech function (question), verb (*leave*), and three arguments (*Cosmo, his monkey, where*).

(3) What a fabulous day!
This has no verb but has a speech function (exclamation).

(4) Cosmo loves (chasing the monkey).
The bracketed dependent clause has a verb *chasing* and arguments (*the monkey,* tacitly *Cosmo*), but no speech function.

This description of clauses refers to ideational and interactional features which are distributed across morphosyntactic and semantic systems. Clauses are also 'organized' as units of information, some of which is 'given' and some of which is presented as 'news'. Organized information units in discourse are most commonly identified in terms of their prosodic features as 'intonation units' (Chafe 1980; 1994; 2001) or 'tone groups' (Halliday 1970; 1994; Halliday and Greaves 2008). Intonation is discussed in more detail in Section 3.3. For now, a tone group can be thought of as a sound segment that includes a major pitch movement over information presented as news. Typically, but by no means always, a simple clause will be spoken as a single tone group.

For many practical purposes, researchers may be content to work with minimum discourse units synonymous with one, two or all aspects of the clause as just described. If one is interested in, say, measures of information density or speech function distribution, a clause may be the only unit one needs to refer to. However, there are phenomena which researchers may want to analyse which do not meet criteria for a clause: incomplete utterances, minimal responses, idiosyncratic vocalizations and isolated hesitation fillers are examples. We use the term **utterance** as a label to include such heterogeneous bits of speech.

Utterances may be independent clauses which, as just described, are roughly equivalent to instantiated speech acts (e.g. Searle 1969; 1979). Practically, this can be operationalized simply as any unit which has a speech function (i.e. is used to state, exclaim, ask or order). Utterance must also include any spoken (or written) element that signals ideational, interactional or organizational information about a speaker's message. Thus, a minimal response *umhm* inserted in another's discourse will be included as an utterance signalling at least that the speaker of *umhm* is attending to the discourse. Typically, such utterances have distinct prosodic organization and one might be tempted to use Chafe's (1980; 1994; 2001) intonation unit as the defining 'minimum discourse unit'. But incomplete utterances often don't meet this criterion – they are not only partial clauses but partial tone groups – and hesitation fillers such as *uhm* and *ah* may be articulated with a level tone (monotone). If the analyst is interested in a speaker's processing abilities, these data matter as utterances. While they do not meet criteria for speech function or for intonation unit, they do contribute ideational, interactional or organizational information about a speaker's message. So we offer the somewhat inelegant but comprehensive hybrid definition of an utterance as any unit which

- can be assigned a speech function, and/or
- has a distinct tone group and/or
- is a linguistic signal of ideational, interactional or organizational information about a speaker's message.

The result is that, with the exception of the laughter (8) which is not linguistic, each line in the Text 3.1 will be treated in our analyses as an utterance by one or more criteria.

Text 3.1 Scalding
The discussion is about activities of daily living for a patient (speaker 1) who has moderate AD. It has been suggested that she might make a mistake with the hot water taps in the bath. Speakers 2 and 3 are caregivers.

(1) SP1: I still say that that's not something that's that a normal person wouldn't do.
(2) SP2: Well you could get scalded.
(3) SP2: No no
(4) SP2: hell no
(5) SP2: I'm normal
(6) SP2: I would never do that.
(7) SP1: No no
(8) SP1: ((laughter))
(9) SP2: I'm normal /?/
(10) SP3: fingers

The utterances *I still say that that's not something that's that a normal person wouldn't do* (1); *Well you could get scalded* (2), *I'm normal* (5), *I would never do that* (6) and *I'm normal* (9) all have speech functions (they are statements) and meet all other criteria. The other utterances cannot readily be assigned speech functions. But (3), (4) and (7) are spoken as single tone groups and realize information. The emphatic *No no* (3) and *hell no* (4) of the second speaker are spoken as two tone groups so they are treated as two utterances rather than one. They contradict the suggestion that 'a normal person' could make a mistake (with the hot water tap in the bath) and thus have ideational and interactional information value. However, given this speaker's intervening *well you could get scalded,* (3) and (4) are not clearly elliptical statement forms of '*no that's not something that a normal person wouldn't do*'. (That is, their 'speech function' must be inferred; it is not formally instantiated.) Similarly, the first speaker's *no no* (7) appears to affirm the second speaker's negative assertion through reiteration of the negation, though these ideational and interactional values are inferred rather than explicitly stated. (Consider that the speaker could have said *no, no, of course, you are normal.*) The third speaker's *fingers* (10) is a fragmentary index of ideational value but overlaps with the second speaker's *I'm normal* and no attempt is made to complete or repair the utterance. This may signal something about this speaker's interactional (lack of) commitment to the utterance. She could restate it.

In effect, we treat as an 'utterance' any verbalization that engages linguistic systems. A majority of utterances will also meet classic definitions for speech act or intonation unit, but others do not. In clinical studies where the goal is to link behaviour to neurophysiology, with or without pathology, such behaviours should be included in descriptions where they may have relevance. Our hybrid coding for utterance allows this.

3.2   Conversation analysis

Conversation analysis examines all kinds of spoken interactions: conversations, interviews, telephone exchanges, lectures, speeches and oral narratives are a few examples of the many types of spoken interaction. One focus of conversation analysis is on the regularities of information exchange. Sacks, *et al.*'s (1974) ground-breaking work on turn-taking showed that, among peers, speakers take fairly regular turns at talk and that they follow a usually tacit set of rules about 'what can follow what'. Conversation analysts have also contributed an inventory of elements of talk such as speaker turn, topic, control of the floor, speaker selection, adjacency pairs and so on; they have identified different genres of talk in terms of these elements, and they have accounted for meaningful patterns in our everyday speech which we sometimes think of as meaningless. For instance, our use of words such as *um* and *uh* have been shown to have a non-random pattern relative to following pause length: *uh* precedes a short pause; *um* occurs before a longer pause (Clark and Fox Tree 2002). In effect, this means that these apparently 'meaningless' hesitation fillers function as signifiers for information structure. In Table 3.1, we define and exemplify terms in conversation analyses and give examples of coding options.

Table 3.1. *Terms from conversation analysis*

Topic
Ideationally consistent stretches of discourse may be developed over several turns through cohesive chains. Lexical selections, arguments, predicates and adjuncts are related to each other such that speakers can make a judgement that what is talked about is 'the same or a different topic'. A discourse may be about a single topic or more than one (see Coates and Cameron 1988; Coates 1996).

Topic initiation occurs normally at the beginning of an interaction. Initiation of new topics typically occurs at clause boundaries (sometimes called transition relevance places, TRPs).

Topic development occurs when an initiated topic is expanded in subsequent turns which are cohesive with (i.e. refer back to) the initiated topic. The topic being developed will typically become background information (rather than new information), occurring for instance in subject position with pronominal rather than full lexical reference.

Topic shift occurs when the ideational focus of talk changes. New participants, processes or circumstances will be referred to. The discourse may still have some cohesive ties with previous talk but will not be 'about' the previous topic. The turn introducing a topic shift will typically have previously mentioned information represented either as news or as an element of another constituent presented as news so that it can then become topic for the discourse. Entirely new topics that do not refer back to prior discourse may be introduced at almost any point. These are regarded as TOPIC INITIATION rather than topic shift.

Text	Coding	Count
SP1: I saw John last night.	TI: JOHN	TOPI 1
SP2: Oh yeah. And is he well?	TD: WELL [JOHN]	TOPD 1:1
SP1: Yeah. He's fabulous.	TD: FABULOUS [JOHN]	TOPD 1:2
SP1: He has a new job, new flat, new baby.	TD: NEW JOB, FLAT, BABY [JOHN]	TOPD 1:3
SP2: Cool.		
SP2: What's the baby's name?	TS: NAME [BABY]	TOPS, T 2
SP1: Kitty.	TD: KITTY [BABY]	TOPD 2:1

Notes on coding:
- Interactional elements such as the *cool* which is an evaluation of the preceding news are not included in the topic analysis. Evaluations like this one signal a speaker's reaction to the topic rather than developing or changing the ideational content.
- Counts for topics, developments, shifts and so on can reference speakers (if one is interested, for instance, in the level of speaker participation).

Turns – taking a turn at talk. Turns can be of any extent, from minimal (umhum) to extended monologue. For practical reasons, we treat **turn** here as **turn at talk**, rather than as a unit isomorphic with clause or utterance (Schegloff 1968; Sacks *et al.* 1974). Turns can be initiating (5), or responding (6). Elliptical responses to questions can be verbal or non-verbal (e.g. head nodding). Both may be counted and coded.

(5) SP1: Well I saw John	**Coding:** Initiating TI
(6) SP2: And was he well?	**Coding:** Responding TR
	Count: # of turns and/or # of turns per speaker

Table 3.1. (*cont.*)

Hesitations

Sounds (*uh, um, er, like*) inserted to fill pauses in discourse (see Example (7)).

Alternatively, a sound may be lengthened (Clark and Fox Tree 2002; Jefferson 2004) (see Example (8)).

(7) Well I *uh uh uh* saw John   **Coding:** H; **Count:** 3
(8) A::nd I saw John   **Coding:** HL; **Count:** 1

Pauses – hesitations in discourse with no vocal filler. Length of pause can be timed using a stop watch or computer programme. Counts may be specified for total number of pauses, or pauses judged as short, medium or long by a normative standard. In general, pauses of less than a quarter of a second are short, those of about half a second are medium and pauses of more than one second are long (Campione and Veronis 2002). (Campione and Veronis suggest a categorization of brief (<200 ms), medium (200–1000 ms) and long (>1000 ms) pauses.) (See also Goldman-Eisler 1968 and Jefferson 2004.)

(9) Well I uh (2) saw John   **Coding:** (2) *2 second pause*; **Count:** 1

Repairs – non-initial correction of utterance (Jefferson 1974; Schegloff *et al.* 1977). Repairs may be **self-initiated** (10) or **other initiated** (11). In **signalled repairs** the repair is overtly signalled as such (12).

(10) I saw Jack, John last night   **Coding:** RSI: repair self initiated; **Count:** 1
(11) SP1: I saw Jack
    SP2: *John?*   **Coding:** ROI: repair other initiated; **Count:** 1
    SP1: yah *John* last night   **Coding:** SRSI: signalled repair, self initiated;
(12) I saw Jack, *I mean* John last night   **Count:** 1

False start: Speaker begins an utterance, stops and restarts (13). The repair can repeat the same start (14) or start differently (15) (see for example MacWhinney 2000; MacWhinney and Osler 1977).

(13) I'll tell, I'll tell you about that later;   **Coding:** false start: FS; **Count:** 1
(14) I'll tell, I'll tell you about that later;   **Coding:** false start repeated: FSR; **Count:** 1
(15) I'll tell, we can talk about that later   **Coding:** false start different: FSD; **Count:** 1

Incomplete utterances lack an obligatory predicate, argument or full argument not supplied by the context as in Example (16).

(16) We certainly…; We were about…   **Coding:** IU; **Count:** 1

Overlap: Speech overlaps that of a previous speaker (17). Overlaps can be distinguished as *interruption* where the first speaker does not have an opportunity to continue (18) versus *co-construction* – overlapping speech where first speaker continues speaking (19). Brackets can be used in transcripts to indicate overlapping segments of speech (see Sacks *et al.* 1974; Coates 1996; MacWhinney 2000).

(17) SP1: I saw John <outside> [<] on the street.   **Coding:** overlap OL; **Count:** 1
    SP2: <Me too> [<]
(18) SP1: I <saw> [>]   **Coding:** interruptive overlap IOL; **Count:** 1
    SP2: <When are> [<] you leaving?
(19) SP1: I saw John <outside> [>] on the   **Coding:** supportive overlap SOL; **Count:** 1
    street
    SP2: <cool> [>]

Extended exemplification is taken up in subsequent chapters where we analyse particular discourses.

3.2.1   Additional features

Other features in conversation researchers may want to code for include:

Latching   A person starts speaking immediately after the previous speaker finishes with no intervening pause (Jefferson 1985; 2004). Frequent latching can show high levels of engagement and close monitoring of information in the discourse on the part of the latching speaker.

Relevant audible non-linguistic behaviour   (E.g. laughter, crying, blowing, sighing, clicks.) Such behaviour may indicate affective, attitudinal or attentional features of an interaction, a participant or a patient group and so may be important in transcripts. We code these in brackets. It is useful to set the representation, for instance ((laughter)), as part of the transcription protocol as it can then be readily quantified (or removed) from transcripts as needed.

3.3   Intonation patterns in English

3.3.1   Phonological hierarchy

Phonology has to do with speech sounds. The area of phonological study most relevant for discourse analysis is **prosodic phonology**. Prosodic phonology, sometimes referred to as 'supra-segmental phonology' is the study of speech sounds associated with the pitch, length and loudness of sounds. It is contrasted with segmental phonology which refers to minimum contrastive sound segments, or **phonemes** such as the English pairs /p/ and /b/ in *pat* and *bat* or the vowel sounds /æ/ and /ɛ/ in *pat* and *pet*. M. A. K. Halliday (1970; 1994) posited a hierarchy of phonological units above the phoneme as a constituent hierarchy as follows:

- a syllable will consist of one vowel phoneme and optional consonants before it (in the 'onset') and after it (in the 'coda');
- a foot will consist of one initial stressed syllable and optional unstressed syllables;
- a tone group will consist of at least one foot. The one required foot will be the site of a major pitch movement.

Halliday uses the analogy of music such that the syllable is the equivalent of a beat, the foot a bar, and by extension, the tone group is a phrase. Prosodic organization structures information in two multifaceted ways:

Tonicity and given/new information   In each tone group there will be a foot containing a syllable which will be more prominent: it will be a little louder, longer and will have a bigger pitch movement than others. This more salient syllable is called the **tonic syllable** and it signals that the speaker is presenting the phrase that it occurs in as important information, or **news**. Typically, it occurs on the last lexical item in a phrase or clause. Compare

(20) She's a good student.
(21) She's good.

If you say these normally and then hum the tune that you've used you'll find that the biggest pitch movement in (20) occurs on the first syllable of *student* while in (21) it occurs on *good,* the last lexical item in each clause. The location of tonic prominence within the tone group is key in interpreting new information in spoken discourse. For instance, if the tonic syllable is shifted to *she* in either example then there is contrastive emphasis on *she* and the interpretation would be that there is some other person who is not a good student. It is possible to simply move tonicity within the tone group to (almost) any element and create patterns of contrastive emphasis in this way. There are also a number of syntactic resources (outlined in Chapter 4, Section 4.4.2 on message organization) which enable changes in the site of tonic prominence, and therefore changes in what speakers present as new information.

Intonation and speaker stance   The **direction** (falling/rising), **height** (high/low) and **width** (wide/narrow) of the major pitch movement reflect the speaker's orientation to what they are saying in terms of

- **certainty about polarity** (yes/no-ness) where falling tones are broadly certain and rising tones are uncertain;
- **commitment** where lower tones express greater commitment on the part of the speaker to what they are saying;
- the **width of pitch range** used. This does not correspond to any single generalization except perhaps that the use of a wider pitch range is broadly, stereotypically, associated with excited/uncontrolled speech.

(There are cultural differences in the pitch ranges associated with excited or uncontrolled speech (Lakoff 1975).)
Notation conventions for prosodic phonology include that:

- the tone group is enclosed in double slashes //tone group//
- feet are separated from each other by single slashes /foot/

- tones (numbered 1, 2 etc.) are inserted at the beginning of the tone group, after the double slashes and before any indication of a silent beat (^)
- the tonic syllable is either underlined or in bold face (**tonic**)

Thus, //1 *where are you / **going** //* is a single tone group spoken on tone 1, consisting of two feet, the second of which is the site of the tonic ***go*** and //2 ***where*** *are you / going //* is the same except that the tonic is on ***where*** and the tone is tone 2.

Beyond these broad patterns, Halliday (1970) posited a system of five primary tones with more or less specific values as follows. (Also see El-Manoufy 1988; Brazil 1995; Gussenhoven 2004; Halliday and Greaves 2008.)

Tone 1 falling is the neutral tone for statements (as in Figure 3.1a) and WH questions (Figure 3.1b). The basic form has a level pretonic, with falling tonic from mid/mid-high pitch.

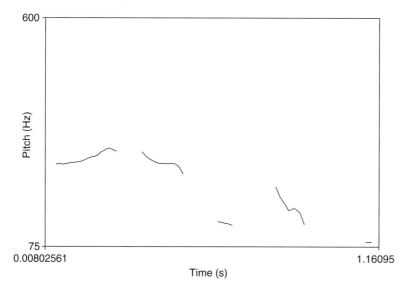

Figure 3.1a Tone 1: falling
Statement: John's lost his flashlight

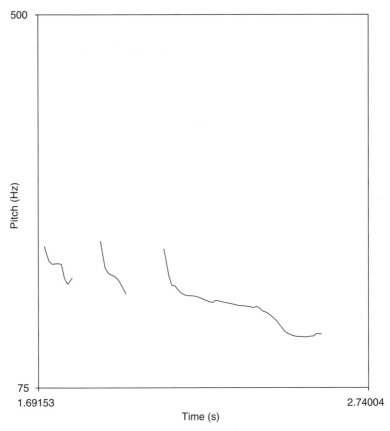

Figure 3.1b Tone 1: falling
WH question: What did John lose?

Tone 2 high rising (Figure 3.2a), **or falling-rising (pointed)** (Figure 3.2b) with a level pretonic is the neutral tone for yes/no questions:

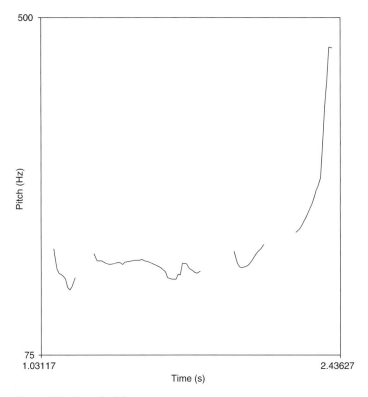

Figure 3.2a Tone 2: rising
Question: Did John lose his flashlight?

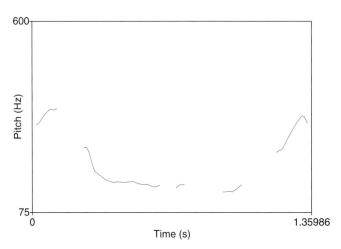

Figure 3.2b Tone 2: falling-rising (pointed)
Polar question: Did John lose his flashlight?

Tone 3 low rising with a mid level pretonic expresses incompleteness or dependence, as in Figure 3.3.

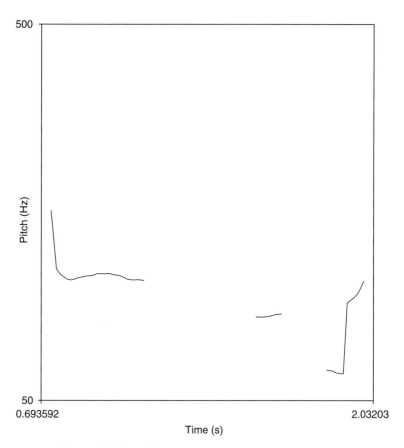

Figure 3.3 Tone 3: low rising
Statement: John lost his flashlight.

In **tone 4 falling-rising (rounded)**, the pretonic steps down from high to mid and is used to make statements about which there is some reservation and to express conditions (as in Figure 3.4).

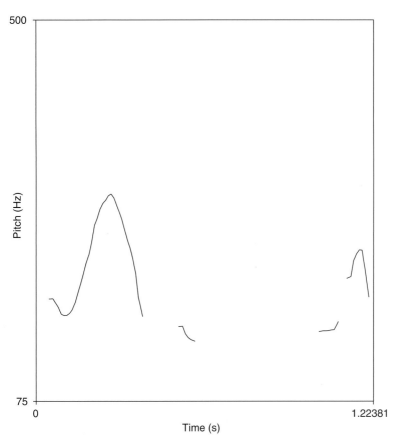

Figure 3.4 Tone 4: falling-rising
Statement: John lost his flashlight.

In **tone 5 rising-falling (rounded)**, the pretonic steps up from mid to mid-high and is used to positively assert that what is said is so (see Figure 3.5).

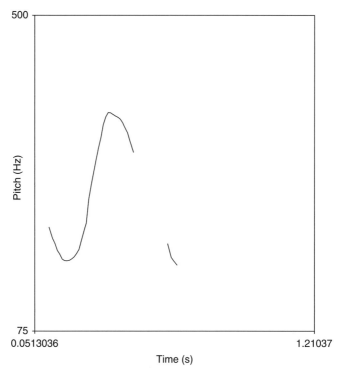

Figure 3.5 Tone 5: rising-falling
Statement: John lost his flashlight.

Halliday also posited two 'compound tones', tone 13 (a falling tone and then low rising tone) and tone 53 (a rising-falling tone followed by a low rising tone). These compound tones were hypothesized to occur when a speaker wants to highlight two points of prominence. The first tone would carry the main point. Other authors simply regard these as sequences (Halliday 1994). Sequences such as a series of tone 2, then tone 1 are normal for lists as in Figure 3.6.

Speech function and tone interact in predictable ways in English such that there is an unmarked or neutral tone selection for each primary speech function and the selection of other tones are marked for various kinds of interactional

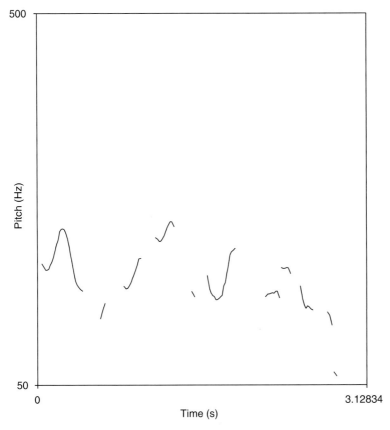

Figure 3.6 Tone 2, 2, 1: listing sequence
Statement: John lost his flashlight, his hat and his mittens.

and/or affective meaning. For example tone 1, the falling tone, is the unmarked tone for statements, WH questions and commands, while the rising tone 2 is the unmarked tone for yes/no questions. Use of a rising tone with a statement produces something which is often interpreted as a question. However, the combination of tone 1 and a yes/no question results in something that, at best, sounds cold and detached, while tone 2 and a command produces something which may be difficult to interpret as a speech act at all.

4   Grammar

4.1   Introduction

In this chapter, we outline in sequence a grammar for specifying **interactional**, **ideational** and **organizational** features of discourse in English. We use a functional organization for the grammar because we find this perspicuous for discourse analysis. The grammar owes much to Michael Gregory (2009a; 2009b). However, in many cases our approach is once again hybrid; we present a model that draws on social and cognitive perspectives on language, based on our experience of what works. Section 4.1 presents a grammar of interaction. In Section 4.2 we outline the grammar of ideation and Section 4.3 presents the grammar of organization. We presuppose that readers have a basic syntax for English. As much as possible, technical and model-specific terms are limited. Appendix A presents basic grammatical terminology and Appendix B lists the coding options suggested in this chapter.

4.2   A grammar of interaction

The interaction relationship has to do, initially, with two types of activity speakers can engage in. The first involves the **negotiation of role relationships** relative to an addressee and the second involves **speakers' expressions of attitude and evaluations**. **Role relationships** are most easily understood in institutional settings with highly generic situation types such as the classroom, court room or clinic, where boundaries may seem relatively fixed: teacher/ student, judge/defendant, doctor/patient, nurse/patient are examples of such role relationships (Goffman 1959; 1961). Less obviously hierarchic and institutionally dependent are peer relationships among colleagues, friends, siblings and partners. We refer to the **negotiation** of role relationships because, while there may be expectations about behaviours for speakers filling particular roles, in fact in every instance of interaction there is the possibility that those expectations may be met, or directly or indirectly challenged or ignored by participants (Goffman 1974). The defendant who challenges the moral authority of the judge, or the judge who asks a guilty defendant to specify the duration of their sentence, the patient who demands a particular treatment or the doctor or nurse who asks the patient for treatment recommendations are examples of speakers acting outside their expected roles. More commonly, speakers make linguistic choices in interactions which, more or less subtly, signify their orientation to the expected roles for the situation; so the colleague or friend who is a little more knowledgeable on a given subject may act or be cast in the role of mentor with respect to that subject. Roles are negotiated through behaviours (Goffman 1974). The use of speech functions and address terms are perhaps the most obvious ways in which speakers assume and assign roles in relation to each other. Checks (such as tags) and intonation may also be involved in negotiating role relationships as well as reflecting speakers' attitudes and evaluations. We present criteria, values and possible coding for each of these in turn in Section 4.2.1 and then discuss attitudes and evaluations in Section 4.2.2.

4.2.1   Negotiation of roles

Speech functions   Particularly significant for the negotiation of role relationships are the possibilities for selection of SPEECH FUNCTION, summarized in Table 4.1. In broadly functional terms (e.g. Halliday 1994), **statements** and **exclamations** offer information to an addressee. **Questions** seek information from an addressee and **commands** direct the behaviour of an addressee.

Table 4.1. *Basic speech function contrasts*

Statements, Exclamations	offer information
Questions	seek information
Commands	direct behaviour

There are subtypes of each category with different functions. There are also 'normal' syntactic structures that express these meaning differences. To keep life simple (and descriptions replicable), we work with the grammatical features (morphosyntax and intonation) of each category. These are spelled out below and in Section 3.3 on intonation above.

Statements   The basic form for a statement is that a subject noun phrase (NP) or clause precedes a finite (tensed or modal) verb. The verb will agree with the subject in person and number though, given the amount of syncretism in modern English, this is only observable in the present tense contrasts between third person singular and other subjects (Huddleston and Pullam 2002) as in A and B.

A. Present tense verb agreement with third person singular subjects.
(*Verbs* are in italics. **Subjects** are in bold face.)

(1) **Sam** *watches* TV in bed.
(2) **He** *thinks* this is reasonable behaviour.
(3) **His mother** *believes* it is bad for him.
(4) **What worries her** *is* whether he actually gets enough sleep.

Examples (1)–(4) illustrate 'normal' unmarked statement patterns with third person singular subjects agreeing with third person singular present tense verb forms.

> Coding: Sam watches TV in bed. S

B. Present tense verbs with other subjects.

(5) **The children** *watch* TV in bed.
(6) **Sam and his dog** *watch* TV in bed.
(7) **I** *watch* TV in bed too.
(8) **We** *watch* TV in bed.
(9) **You** *watch* TV in bed.
(10) Also troubling *are* **the movies that he sees**.
(11) **I/we/you/Sam** *might* watch TV in bed.

In Examples (5)–(6) subjects are third person plural; in Examples (7)–(8), subjects are first person singular and plural respectively. In Example (9) the subject is second person for which there is no number contrast except in dialect varieties that include either *you/yous* or *you/y'all*. The verb form doesn't change: we follow Huddleston and Pullum (2002: 74–5) in calling this the plain present tense form. Example (10) illustrates a marked order in which one can see the importance of agreement in that it is the NP *the movies that he sees* following the verb that functions as subject and agrees with the verb. Example (11) illustrates the fact that modal verbs (*will, would, can, could, may, might, shall, should, must, ought*) operate like tensed verbs, but do not change form regardless of number and person of subjects.

Past tense verbs do not change form in relation to person and number of the subject. The verb *be* is an exception to these patterns: it has first person singular tense (*I am ...*), third person singular tense (*he is ...*), 'other' present tense (*we/you/they are ...*) and singular (*I/she was ...*) and plural (*we/you/they were ...*) past tense forms. Notice further that negating statements requires the introduction of a modal or tensed operator verb as in *I **don't** watch TV in bed* and that negative does presuppose positive. The unmarked tone selection for statements is falling (tone 1), but see Section 3.3 for other options.

Statements can be tagged as in *Sam watches TV in bed,* ***doesn't he?*** A tag is a clause consisting of a finite operator verb (tensed forms of *do/have/be* and modal verbs *will, would; can, could; may, might; shall, should; must; ought* and in some dialects *dare* and *need*) and a pronominal subject co-referential with the subject of the clause to which the tag is attached as in Examples (12)–(18) where the tags are in bold face.

(12) Sam saw an elephant, **did he**.
(13) The answer is obvious, **isn't it**.
(14) We've haven't finished, **have we**.
(15) Drive carefully, **won't you**.
(16) Call me when you get home, **will you**.
(17) ?Don't rush me, **will you**.
(18) Sam saw an elephant, **he did**.

Coding: Sam saw an elephant, did he. S-TAG

Tags are adjoined to clauses functioning as statements (12)–(14) or commands (15)–(17). Tags can have positive or negative polarity which can be the reverse of that in the main clause as in (13), (14), (15) and (17) or unreversed positive as in (12) and (16). (Negative main clause + negative tag as in **Sam didn't see an elephant, didn't he* doesn't occur.) There is also the option illustrated in (18), an emphatic tag in which the order of the elements of the tag are the same as those for the main clause. These options are summarized in Figure 4.1. (Example (18) is included here for comprehensiveness, as are (15)–(17).)

Tags work in conjunction with intonation patterns to signify positive or negative presuppositions and seek confirmation from addressees (e.g. Quirk *et al.*

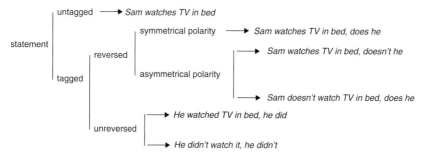

Figure 4.1 Options for statements[1]

1985: 810–13; Sinclair 1990: 433–4). The allowable intonation patterns are as follows:

> +falling ↓ + rising ↑
> +rising ↑ +falling ↓
> +falling ↓ +falling ↓

The broad patterns are that rising tone expresses uncertainty and falling tone, certainty, and that positive tags check the polarity of the main clause with neutral presupposition, whereas negative tags presuppose positive polarity. For example, a positive statement with falling tone asserts positive and expresses certainty. If it is negatively tagged with falling tone, the positive is presupposed and certainty is expressed by the tone. The result is that it emphatically asserts the positive statement as in *You saw him / didn't you /* and merely checks on the presupposed certainty of the proposition *you saw him*. The expected response is 'yes'. The same sentence spoken with rising tone on the tag *You saw him / didn't you /* ↑ differs insofar as the rising tone expresses doubt and so although the sentence still strongly presupposes positive *you saw him*, there is less certainty about the response.

Exclamations   Exclamations, summarized in Figure 4.2, may be either finite (with a tensed verb), or minor (with no verb at all). They often have an initial WH NP or WH AP construction as in the following. (Again, *verbs* are in italics. **Subjects** are in bold face):

(19) What a brilliant student **she** *is*!
(20) (What) a brilliant student!
(21) How wretched that you have to leave!

Coding: What a brilliant student she is! E

Questions   Questions have to be subclassified initially into **Yes/No** (polar) questions and **WH** questions (as in Figure 4.3). Polar questions seek yes/no responses, with graded options (*possibly, maybe, probably, certainly, of course* and so on) between the *yes/no* 'poles'. The unmarked tone for

Figure 4.2 Options for exclamations

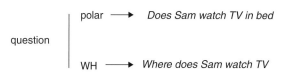

Figure 4.3 Options for questions

yes/no questions is rising (tone 2). WH questions seek information about a participant or circumstance indicated by an initial WH word (*what, where, when, who, why, which, how*). The unmarked tone for WH questions is falling (tone 1).

The central grammatical difference between questions and statements is that in a question a finite operator (tensed forms of *do, have, be*) or modal verb occurs before the subject element as in (22)–(27) where **subjects** are in bold face and *operators* (or modals) are in italics.

(22) *Can* **you** be ready by six?
(23) *Is* **anyone** hungry?
(24) *Has* **there** been much snow this year?
(25) *Would* **you** like some more?
(26) *Did* **the dogs** get fed?
(27) *Were* **the children** frightened by the film?

Coding: Can you be ready by six? QP

Notice that positive polarity in yes/no questions generally entails no presupposition about the polarity of the response, whereas negative polarity always presupposes, not necessarily a positive response, but that the speaker believes that the positive predication is more likely or ought to be true. The contrast will seem obvious if one considers likely contexts for examples such as (28)–(30):

(28) Weren't the children frightened by the film?
(29) Didn't the dogs get fed?
(30) Wouldn't you like some more?

Syntactically, **WH questions** have the same form as polar questions except that the operator verb is preceded by a WH expression which will be co-referential with an 'empty' argument, or circumstance position elsewhere in the clause. Co-reference can be indicated by assigning an *index* (conventionally starting with *i*, but in large data samples, better handled with numbers) to the WH expression and the empty position it refers to (marked with a *t* for 'trace') as in Examples (31–35).

(31) <u>When</u>$_1$ *can* **you** be ready t_1?
(32) <u>How much snow</u>$_2$ *has* **there** been t_2 this year?
(33) <u>What</u>$_3$ *would* **you** like t_3?
(34) <u>What</u>$_4$ *were* **the children** frightened by t_4?
(35) **Who** is hungry?

Coding: When can you be ready? QWH

Notice that (35) is an exception to the general pattern in that when the WH word refers to the subject position the order of elements is the same as for statements and there is no obviously 'empty' position corresponding to the WH expression. Notice too that patterns with negation are similar here: *What wouldn't you like?* presupposes that there are many things that you would like or, alternatively, that you are having difficulty stating a positive preference for something so the speaker seeks information about negative preferences in order to limit the set of total options. However, some WH questions actually entail that X positively is so, in which case it is not possible to negate them. **How much snow hasn't there been this year?* doesn't work for this reason.

Commands Commands must also be subclassified into **jussive**, **optative**, and **fiat**. Unmarked tone selection for all commands is falling (tone 1).

Jussive commands direct the behaviour of the addressee to do something. They have a base form lexical verb which may optionally be preceded by *you* or an indefinite pronoun subject as in (36)–(38).

(36) Call 911.
(37) (You) be quiet.
(38) Somebody call a doctor.
(39) Don't anybody move.
(40) Do be quiet.

Coding: Call 911. CJ

Examples (39)–(40) illustrate negated and emphatic jussives respectively. Both constructions require the insertion of base form *do.* Notice too that (37)–(39) illustrate the fact that the verb forms here are non-finite (not tensed) base forms. If the verbs were tensed, we would have *you are/were quiet; somebody calls/called a doctor; doesn't/didn't anybody move.* These are grammatically quite acceptable, but they are not commands: the first two are statements and the third is a question.

Optative commands propose a course of action to be (putatively) undertaken by both the speaker and the addressee (41). They are formed with *Let* followed by *us* (contracted to *'s* unless it is emphatic) as subject of the following verb. *Let* itself has no subject. The 'putative' descriptor refers to the fact that optative occurs quite frequently in contexts where the speaker is in fact proposing a course of action which engages the addressee as patient in a process carried out by the speaker (42) or where the speaker intends the addressee to carry out the action themselves (43).

(41) Let's go out for dinner tonight.
(42) Let's take your temperature. (imagine a nurse proposing this to a patient)
(43) Let's eat up all the veggies now. (imagine a parent supervising children's dinner)

Coding: Let's go out for dinner tonight. CO

Optative and jussive commands can usually be tagged, though the options are more restricted. Optative allows only positive *shall we* as a tag. Jussive allows positive or negative *will you, won't you* depending on the polarity of the main clauses.

Fiat commands are those rare utterances in which 'saying it makes it so': the *Let there be light* construction. Like the optative, they require *Let*, and do not allow a subject. The subject of the dependent clause is *there* or another third person NP as in royal fiat *Let this day be a holiday henceforth*. They are rare because few people have the authority or power to use them except when joking. Options for Command speech function are summarized in Figure 4.4.

Coding: Let there be light. CF

The ability to use commands may be correlated in some measure with the power and/or authority of the speaker relative to the addressee and in some circumstances certain forms may be 'required' by the situation (as in the pharmacist's necessary use of jussive in '*Take two tablets every six hours*'). The fiat and subjunctive almost never occur outside the context of religious texts. Certainly they cannot be used for anything other than comedic purposes (or by someone with a severely distorted view of the power of speaking) in ordinary discourse. But note that there are no isomorphic (one-to-one) correlations here. In some contexts, intimate and/or equal role relations may be signalled by use of, for instance, jussive imperatives. It is not possible to simply 'read off' role relations based on speech function selection. One has to look at what else is going on.

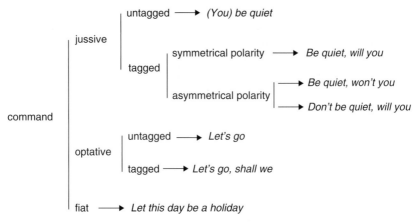

Figure 4.4 Options for commands

All the options for speech functions can be summarized as a system as in Figure 4.5.

Checks and intonation Also important in the negotiation of role are the use of checks. Tags as described above are one sort of check. Others include the use of words such as *eh, right, huh*, with rising intonation adjoined to statements (e.g. *you're finished, right? or huh? or eh?*).

Coding: You're finished, right? S-CHECK

Rising pitch on a statement can have a similar effect as a tag with rising tone. The statement positively or negatively asserts something; the rising tone signals that what is said is not certain and needs confirmation. This sort of intonation can be suggested in written texts by the use of a question mark (?) following a statement. (Notice that this is not the same as asking a polar question. The question *did you see them?* neither asserts nor presupposes that an addressee performed the action predicated of them. In contrast, *you saw them?* does assert this as an action of the addressee; and *you didn't see them?* presupposes the positive. The use of rising tone (2) adds a 'needs checking' feature.)

Coding: You're finished? S-RT

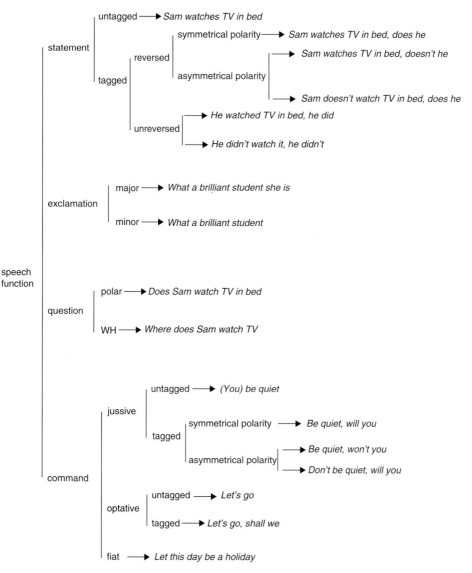

Figure 4.5 Options for speech functions

Address terms   Address terms are often, but not necessarily, realized as Vocative elements and can function as overt markers of the 'social distance' (on a graded scale with poles being NEAR/FAR) between speaker and addressee as in *Darling, Sammy, Samuel, Professor Samuel Johnson, Sir.*

Because address terms may overtly mark social distance, they can be used to index and negotiate role relationships not only in terms of the admissible level of intimacy, but also in terms of power. The parent–child relationship permits (indeed requires in many cultures) mutual use of familiar or intimate names. But young children lack power with respect to their parents and so may not be free to address them in any way they choose – whereas parents do have such freedom with respect to children. Similarly, North American professors may invite students to address them by their first names or by title and name. But the relationship is not reciprocal – students have little choice about the terms faculty use to address them, and students who address faculty by first name without invitation to do so may be regarded as attempting to shift the role relationship (Brown and Yule 1983; Gregory 1988; van Leeuwen 1996).

Coding: It's raining Sir. V+SD

All of the above features can be manipulated for 'politeness' (Brown and Levinson 1987), but there are also explicit 'POLITENESS MARKERS', These are the *please* and *thank you*s of everyday discourse. Their lexical category is somewhat obscure. They were originally verbs (*If it please you / I thank you*) but they have become idioms and behave a bit like adverbs. The degree of politeness required in any particular situation type varies from culture to culture.

Coding: Two beers, please. PM

4.2.2   Attitude and evaluation

The second major aspect of the interaction relationship has to do with speakers' ability to express their attitudes and judgements about what it is they are saying. Important elements here are the use of MODALITY which can express judgements about the relative probability of what is predicated (as in *It is raining / It might be raining, This should be the answer*), about the capacity or ability to perform some action (*You can understand this*), and about obligations (*You must/should eat your dinner*). Modals can also be used to seek or give permission (*May/can I go, you may/can go*). The value of particular modals varies with the contexts in which they are used. Modal *will* for instance is typically interpreted as expressing a prediction in *It will rain*, an intention in *I will go tomorrow*, and an obligation in *You will do your homework*. However, these different 'meanings' seem to be a function of their construction with other linguistic items rather than of the item *will* per se. For example, a prediction about self (*I will*) colligated with an action or process which self carries out will quite reasonably be interpreted as the expression of a speaker's intention to do something. But it seems unnecessary to say that *will* has more than one meaning. We would rather say that prediction has different values in different contexts. (For comprehensive discussions of the uses of modal verbs in contemporary English see Sinclair (1990) and Huddleston and Pullum (2002).) Probability and capacity values expressed by modal verbs can also be expressed through adjectives and adverbs with related meanings such as *possible/possibly, certain/certainly, is able, sure/surely, perhaps* and so on. Also relevant are indefinite degree expressions variously realized as NP + of + adjective (e.g. *sort of, kind of* as in *Sam is sort of fabulous*); NP AP as in *a little bit tired, somewhat clever.*

All of these resources constitute different ways to attenuate the forcefulness or degree of certainty with which something is expressed. Within the literature of pragmatics, they are broadly referred to as 'hedges' (Lakoff 1973). In clinical work, Nespoulous *et al.* (1998) and others have referred to discourse where these features are frequent as 'modalizing discourse'. Both the pragmatic and modalizing discourse approaches interpret these features as reflexes of speakers' psychological or epistemic states. In the heteroglossic approach presented within appraisal theory (White 1998; Martin and White 2005), these features are described as opening discourse to other views.

Coding: Sam is sort of MF fabulous.

Speakers can also evaluate the whole of a proposition by adding ATTITUDINAL elements to a clause. These can be ADVERBS such as *unfortunately, happily, sadly* and so on, or they can be relative clauses or noun phrases added to the end of a clause (*John broke his leg, which was unfortunate / John broke his leg, a pity*). This sort of marked expression of attitude is less common than the constant lexical choices of speakers which reflect positive, neutral or negative evaluations about referents as in *A gentleman called / A man called / Some birk called*. When coding attitude, it is useful to code positive attitude (ATT-P) or negative attitude (ATT-N).

Coding: Unfortunately ATT-N John broke his leg.

Every lexical choice we make indexes our attitudes to what we are talking about, and so all lexis is 'evaluative lexis', though we tend to notice (and may only want to code for) markedly negative or positive evaluations. Insofar as speakers orient themselves to others through shared values and

Table 4.2. *Modalization, attitude and evaluation*

Modalization
Expresses judgements about:
- probability
- permission (seek or give)
- capacity or ability
- obligation

Can be expressed by:
- modal verbs
- adjectives
- adverbs
- indefinite degree expressions (hedges)

Attitudinal elements and Evaluative lexis
Attitudinal elements – evaluate a proposition
- adverbs
- relative clauses or noun phrases added to the end of a clause

Evaluative lexis – reflects speaker's attitude to referents in a proposition
- positive
- neutral
- negative

judgements, expressions of attitude and evaluation are used in the 'presentation of self' and in the construction of social relationships (Goffman 1959; 1961; 1974; Berger and Luckmann 1966; van Dijk 1977; Martin and White 2005). Table 4.2 lists resources for modalization, evaluation and attitude.

4.3   Conceptual structure and the grammar of ideation

One thing a language does is relate semantic information to phonological structure. The semantic information may be conventionally signified by a range of linguistic phenomena including morphemes, words, argument roles, syntactic structures, discourse structures and patterns and occasionally whole discourses (Jackendoff 2002; Gregory 2009c). In some formulations, such as Jackendoff's (e.g. 1990; 2002), this set of relationships between semantic information and the linguistic and discourse structures and patterns that signify it is referred to as 'conceptual structure'. We use this terminology because the emphasis on the relational and functional character of the information matches our analytic experience and is neurally plausible. However, we do not imagine, as Jackendoff seems to (e.g. Jackendoff in preparation), that there is a dedicated amodal brain region that processes the relationships described in conceptual structure. Rather, we suspect that 'conceptual structure' will turn out to be a network of transmodal gateways (of the sort proposed by Mesulam e.g. 1998) linking information from modal and heteromodal association areas in widely distributed cortical and subcortical brain regions. This seems to be the sort of architecture implied by recent imaging and aphasia reviews (e.g. Bookheimer 2002; Stowe *et al.* 2005; Ferstl *et al.* 2008). We take up these matters in more detail in Chapters 8 and 9 – here we simply want to note that we do talk about conceptual structure but assume that the neural architecture is open to revision.

Semantic phenomena may be descriptively represented in taxonomic hierarchies at different levels of abstraction and we assume can be usefully thought of as decomposable into feature bundles, although these do not exhaust semantic meaning potential. Thus it is possible to think of words or morphemes as designating bundles of meaning features which may be more or less abstract such that the most abstract are superordinate concepts (animal), less abstract concepts (dog) are basic level, and most specific (Peekapoo) are subordinate level concepts (Berlin and Kay 1969; Rosch 1983; Lakoff 1987).

It seems reasonably clear that subordinate, basic level and superordinate concepts may be represented differently in neural systems. Evidence from Alzheimer's and aphasia studies (e.g. Chertkow and Bub 1990; Nespoulous *et al.* 1998; Marczinski and Kertesz 2006) suggest this insofar as subordinate and basic level semantic systems may be degraded, damaged, or be inaccessible independently of superordinate concepts. Thus a speaker with Alzheimer's may be able to say that a picture of a terrier is an *animal*, but not that it is a *dog* or a *terrier*. There is also evidence from Alzheimer's and aphasia studies to support the notion of semantic decomposition into features insofar as speakers may show differential impairment for semantic categories (Warrington and Shallice 1984; Warrington and McCarthy 1987). For instance, a speaker may have access to a lexicon for 'living things' but not to 'tools' (or the converse) (Marczinski and Kertesz 2006; Devlin *et al.* 2002; Ilmberger *et al.* 2002). Such a speaker might be able to recognize and identify dogs, cats and rabbits and assign them to the same category, but not be able to do the same thing with hammer, saw and chisel (Warrington and Shallice 1984; Warrington and McCarthy 1987). Thus, while the supporting neural systems are not entirely known or understood, there is significant evidence to assume both feature decomposition and taxonomic ordering of semantic features. This is as we might expect given our capacity to use referring expressions which rely on semantic decomposition. For example, English personal pronouns refer to superordinate contrasts such as human/non-human and gender (masculine/feminine/neuter) to establish the identity of a referent. To use them appropriately, one needs to be able not only to know the feature set of the pronoun, but to decompose the potential referents into comparable feature sets and match them. Explanations of fundamental processes such as reference are inexplicable unless we can decompose

Table 4.3. *Conceptual hierarchy with features*

	Superordinate Category	Basic Level Category	Subordinate Category
Example	Thing (animal)	Dog	Peekapoo
Features	• concrete • living • mammal	• four footed • domestic • has hair • barks	• (crossbred) • pet • very small • longer back than height • long woolly fur • tan/brown
Properties associated with features	• Concrete: entails shape, size, colour etc. • Living: moves, breaths, needs food • Mammal: warm-blooded animal which lactates and has one or more infants at a time	• Four footed: shape feature • Barks: defining activity for category • Domestic: used by people for food, work, pets	• Shape, colour, types of hair are specific • Pet: function
Evaluation features	In isolation, superordinate level categories rarely have evaluations attached to them. However, there is positive value attached to being *alive* rather than *dead* or *inert*.	Examples • Positive: 'useful, companions' • Negative: Fights, can be vicious, unclean, 'scavengers'	Examples • Positive: 'cute' • Negative: 'stubborn'

words and other signifiers into semantic features. Table 4.3 models differences in superordinate, basic level and subordinate categories.

In grammatical constructions, the semantic values of words do not account completely for the meaning of any particular clause. For example, in *Cosmo the cat ate the hazelnut chocolate and chewed the gardenia*, *cat* is a basic level concept for which we might specify features [DOMESTIC ANIMAL; PET; MEOWS]; *Cosmo*, a proper name, indicates some particular individual cat. However, these meanings do not account for the role of 'intentional doer of action' (Agent) that *Cosmo* has in both these clauses. The verb *eat* requires as one of its participants an Agent. That is, the intentional doer of an action, or Agent, is a bundle of semantic features associated both with the verb *eat* and with a syntactic position: Agent occurs as subject in unmarked cases. Agent clearly also occurs with many other verbs and other word classes. Similarly, *the hazelnut chocolate* and *the gardenia* also fulfil a role relative to their respective verbs *eat* and *chew*. Both may be described as Patient, an entity which pre-exists and undergoes a change of state in a process. And once again, a great many verbs require the argument role, Patient.

4.3.1   Argument roles

Argument roles are feature bundles expressing superordinate concepts related to events, relations and states. All clauses involve a predicate and (almost all involve) one or more arguments. Those arguments which must or can occur and their default positions with respect to each other are specified by the predicate(s). The arguments required and the positions in which they occur vary from language to language but there are probably a core set which recur in all languages (Fillmore 1968; van Valin and LaPolla 1997). In the description of particular languages one may want to elaborate argument roles to account for the variation and semiotics of the language. Argument roles express part of ideational meaning. An effect of this is that syntactic structures which most frequently are used to express particular argument roles may acquire their own meaning potential by association (cf. Jackendoff 2002). (This may be the source of the common conflation of syntactic positions such as Subject with semantic roles such as Agent.)

In the following we present a list of argument roles together with their features and distributions developed for the description of English (Gregory 2009b).

4.3.2   Agent – the 'doer' of an action

Agent must be +capacity for intention. This is testable through purpose adjuncts (*in order to, deliberately*). For example, JOHN is Agent in *John killed the ducks in order to feed his family*. But DISEASE is not Agent in *Disease killed the ducks*. (Notice that **Disease killed the ducks deliberately* does not work.) Agent need not be +intention. It only requires the capacity for intention so that JOHN is still Agent in *John killed the ducks accidentally*. With one exception (see below), Agent is realized by a noun phrase [NP] only and is subject in active clauses. In passive clauses, Agent occurs as an adjunct and is marked by $_{BY}$NP as in *The ducks were killed by John*. In NPs, Agent may appear as specifier to N', (*John's race* refers to the race that John ran), or it may appear marked either by BY (*the killing of the ducks by John*) or OF + posses-sive NP (*the book of Chomsky's*). The exception noted above is that Agent may be realized as a derived adjectival modifier of N' (as in *the American bombing of Iraq / parental abuse of children*). In the absence of a Theme, only the $_{BY}$NP constructions are unambiguously Agentive in NPs. (Thus, *John's murder* is ambiguous, referring either to *John* as Agent (he committed a murder) or as Patient (he was murdered by someone) (WH for Agent = WHO).

Coding: John AGENT killed the ducks.

4.3.3   Instrument – an entity used in the performance of an action

An instrument can be concrete or abstract. It is realized as a $_{WITH}$NP or $_{BY}$NP if Agent is also realized as in *John killed the ducks with a knife* (concrete), *John solved the problem with/by logic* (abstract). Instrument may be realized as Subject (in active clauses only) as in *The coat-hanger opened the door*. However, if Instrument and Agent are both realized, Agent must be Subject: *John opened the door with the coat-hanger*, but not **the coat-hanger opened the door by John*. In NPs, Instrument appears in $_{WITH}$NP constructions (*John's opening of the door with a coat-hanger*) although $_{BY}$NP constructions may be possible for some speakers, or as specifier to N' (*the key's opening of the door*). (WH = HOW, WITH WHAT)

Coding: The coat-hanger INSTRUMENT opened the door.

4.3.4   Cause – the inanimate cause in events

Cause must be without the capacity for intention and is realized by subject NP as in *The wind eroded the cliffs*, or $_{BY/WITH}$NP in passives (*The cliffs were eroded by/with the wind*), or by non-finite ING clauses as subject as in *The government constantly devaluing the dollar hurts everybody*. Cause frequently occurs in causal constructions, e.g. *The music prevented them from hearing each other* and alternates with $_{BECAUSE\ OF}$NP (*They were prevented from hearing each other because of the music*). Note that the alternative, to treat Cause as a metaphoric Agent, is not really plausible since potentially agentive NPs look metaphoric in Cause constructions. *The wind blew the roof off the house* is +Cause and may be non-metaphoric whereas *John blew the roof off the house* receives a metaphoric interpretation in unspecified contexts. In NPs, cause can occur as specifier to N' (*the wind's erosion of the cliffs*), or as $_{BECAUSE\ OF/BY/WITH}$NPs (*the erosion of the cliffs by the wind*). (WH = WHAT)

Coding: The wind CAUSE eroded the cliff.

4.3.5   Experiencer – sentient entity that reacts to, knows or perceives phenomenon

Experiencer does not allow intention and cannot take a +intention adjunct. For instance, *John likes Fred deliberately* with *John* as Experiencer is at best peculiar. The distribution of Experiencer varies with the subcategory of predicate as follows.

(1) **Experiencer** may be realized by Subject NP, or by $_{BY}$NP in passives, in 'experiencer oriented' reaction predicates as in *The guests liked/enjoyed the show, The show was enjoyed by the guests*; in 'perception' predicates (*The guests saw/heard the show, The show was heard/seen by the guests*), and in 'cognition' predicates (*John knows/understands/believes the answer, The answer is known/understood/believed by John*). There are the expected related NP realizations for reaction predicates (*the guests' enjoyment of the show, the enjoyment of the show by the guests*); cognition predicates (*John's knowledge of/belief in the answer, knowledge of/belief in the answer by John*) although the $_{BY}$NP phrases in the second in each of these pairs may potentially be construed in relation to the adjacent N (as in *the show performed by the guests, the answer provided by John*). NP realizations of perception predicates are also possible if awkward: ?[*the guest's seeing/hearing of the show/the sight/hearing of the show by the guests*] *before the dress rehearsal was a mistake.*

(2) **Experiencer** may be realized by Direct Object NP, or by Subject NP in passives, in 'phenomenon oriented' reaction events. (*His behaviour disgusts/ revolts me / I am disgusted/revolted by his behaviour.*) Nominalizations are peculiar: (*my disgust at/with his behaviour, John's revulsion to/for work*) seem OK but there do not appear to be any $_P$NP realizations (**the disgust of/by me*, ??*the revulsion of John/John's*). Note that Experiencer here shares distributional (and semantic) properties with Thematic roles (see below) and thus might be regarded as a subtype of theme.

(3) **Experiencer** may be realized by $_{TO}$NP with copula verbs of perception such as *seem/appear/look/sound* (*It seems/appears to me that John is sick, John looks sick to me*). (WH = WHO)

> Coding: The guests EXPERIENCER liked the show.

4.3.6   Stimulus

The Stimulus is the entity or event or state which is reacted to in 'phenomenon oriented' reaction predicates realized by NPs, or by finite or non-finite clauses as Subject in active clauses as in *mushy peas disgust me / that they were late annoyed her / John's being early surprised Mary*. There are the expected related passives as in *I am disgusted by mushy peas / Mary was surprised by John's being early*. (The analogue for the finite clause in subject position is not passive but extraposition as in *she was annoyed that they were late*). (WH = WHAT)

Coding: Mushy peas STIMULUS disgust me.

4.3.7   *Source – the entity from which motion takes place*

In motion processes, Source is typically realized by $_{FROM/OUT OF}$NPs as in *John came from Toronto / John ran out of the kitchen*. In transfer processes Source may combine with Agent as a Subject NP or a $_{FROM}$NP Complement as in *John sent the book to Mary / Mary received the book from John*. (Note that the second example is optionally a modifier of *the book*.) Within NPs, Source may be realized as $_{FROM}$NPs (*John's departure from Toronto*), or, with predicate NPs that allow Source to combine with Agent, as a Possessive NP Determiner (*John's gift of the book to Mary*), and as a $_{FROM}$NP (*the gift of money from the bank*) and (in some dialects) also as a related $_{BY}$NP construction (*?the gift of the money by the bank*) (WH = WHERE/WHO).

Coding: Mary received the book from John SOURCE.

4.3.8   *Goal – the entity towards which motion is directed*

Goal requires subclassification as:

(1) **Goal: location** – a spatial destination in motion and transfer processes realized by an NP (*John went home/south*) or $_p$NP as (*John went to Toronto / John put the roast in the oven*), or by a complement particle (preposition) (*John went out / John put the dog out*), or by the 'deictic adverbs' *there/here* (*put it there*). In NPs, only $_p$NP constructions (with optional *there/here* substitution) seem possible as in *the placement of students in senior courses / his departure for home*.

Coding: John went to Toronto GOAL-LOC.

---

(2) **Goal: recipient** – the recipient in non-locational transfer processes. In active clauses it is realized by NP as Subject where it combines with Agent as in *Mary received the book from John*, or NP as Indirect Object (*John sent Mary the book*), or by a $_{TO}$NP Complement as in *(John sent the book to Mary)*. The related passives are (i) *The book was received by Mary / the book from John was received by Mary / The book was received by Mary from John; (ii) Mary was sent the book by John.* 'Verbalization' predicates such as *tell, write, say, relate, report* and so on typically behave as non-locational transfers insofar as they take the role of Goal: recipient as in *John told Mary the story.* The distribution of Goal: recipient in NPs varies predictably with the head N. Nominal *receipt* allows either possessive NPs or a $_{BY}$NP realization of Goal (*Mary's receipt of the letter / the receipt of the letter by Mary*). Nominalizations corresponding to clauses in which Goal: recipient appears as an indirect object NP or $_{TO}$NP only allow a $_{TO}$NP realization as in *John's telling of the story to Mary, sending of the letter to Mary.*

Coding: John sent Mary GOAL-REC a letter.

---

(3) **Goal: beneficiary** – the entity for whom the process is carried out.
Goal: beneficiary is realized by an Indirect Object NP (*Mary built John a house*), or by a $_{FOR}$NP (*Mary built a house for John*), and (for some varieties) may be realized as Subject NP in a passive (*John was built a house by Mary*). Within NPs, Goal: beneficiary may only be realized as a $_{FOR}$NP as in (*John's building of the house for Mary*). (WH = WHERE/WHO/WHOM)

Coding: John built Mary GOAL-BEN a house.

Note: The status of beneficiary and Instrument as argument versus circumstantial roles is ambivalent. They both share adjunct-like (circumstantial) properties insofar as they are not required by any predicate and can combine with a wide variety of predicates. However, they both also can occur in 'argument positions' and thus syntactically behave as though they are arguments. For discussion of the issues see for instance Huddleston and Pullum (2002); van Valin (2001).

4.3.9   Theme

The standard definition describes Theme as the 'entity in motion' in motion and transfer processes, and as the entity located in locational relations. In active clauses, Theme is realized by a complement NP in transfer processes (Theme: transferent) as in *John gave Mary the book / John gave the book to Mary*. It combines with Agent and is realized by a Subject NP in motion processes as in *John went to Toronto*. And it occurs as Subject NP in locational relations (Theme: located) as in *John is in Toronto*. In practice Theme is often used as a term for any argument that does not fit any of the designated roles above. Thus it may be given a broader gloss to include not only the motion, transfer and location readings but also the entity affected by, resultant from, or designated by an event or state. Some grammars refer to a 'macro-role' of 'undergoer' to characterize this configuration of roles (e.g. Pike and Pike 1982; van Valin 2001). What unites all these different meanings is that Thematic arguments are never realized as syntactic adjuncts in English clauses. They are always realized as either Subjects or complements of the verb. Since Theme is used for such a variety of arguments it requires further subclassification as follows.

Theme: patient   Theme: patient is the entity that pre-exists the process and undergoes a change of state in the process. Patient is realized by an NP Direct Object in active clauses as in *John killed Mary / John cooked the carrots* or as Subject in the related passives *Mary was killed by John / The carrots were cooked by John*.

Coding: The carrots THEME: PAT were cooked by John.

Theme: resultant – the entity or event resulting from a process.   Resultant is realized by either an NP as Direct Object (*John built a house*), or by a finite or non-finite complement clause as in (non-finite) *John makes Mary cut her hair*. Note that the much discussed three argument predicates such as *persuade* and *teach* take both Theme: patient (realized as an NP complement) and Theme: resultant (realized as a clausal complement [CP] as in *John persuaded them that they should leave / he taught them that they should be polite*). See also the related non-finites as in *John persuaded them [PRO to leave] / he taught them [PRO to be polite]*.

Coding: John built a house THEME: RES.

Theme: percept   Theme: percept is an entity or event which is experienced or perceived, realized as either an NP or a finite or non-finite clausal complement of 'perception' predicates such as *see, hear, feel*; 'cognition' predicates such as *know, believe, understand*; and 'processor oriented mental reaction' predicates (*like, enjoy, want, seem, appear*) as in

- perception: *Mary saw John / Mary saw that John was running the marathon / Mary saw John running the marathon*;
- cognition: *Fred understands the problem / Fred knows that the solution will be difficult / Fred believes the solution to be difficult*;
- reaction: *Mary likes John / It seems to me that they are leaving / I want them to leave.*

> Coding: Mary saw John THEME: PERC.

Theme: message   What is communicated in message transfers (verbalization predicates) is realized by non-finite complement clauses (*The demons told me PRO to leave*), or by finite complement clauses (*John said that he would be here by six and to have dinner ready*). Theme: message is distinguished from Theme: transferent in that the former, but not the latter, may be realized by a clause.

> Coding: John said that he would be here by six THEME: MESS.

Theme: range   Theme: range is an entity that designates the nature of a process realized by complement NPs (*Mary plays tennis/piano/chess / John runs marathons/the 100 meters / Mary told them a story/a lie*).

> Coding: Mary plays tennis THEME: RAN.

In addition, by analogue with Theme: located in locational relations, the Subjects of relational clauses (those that have a form of BE as the main verb) are treated as subtypes of theme and may be classified according to whether the 'complement' identifies, classifies or attributes properties to the Subject which may be realized by an NP or, in some cases by a finite or non-finite clause.

Theme: identified   *Obama is the president of the US/The president of the US is Obama/That they are starving is the problem.* The defining characteristic for Theme: identified is that the predicate NP should be definite and that the relations be reversible. (Note that 'reversibility' implies that predicates in identificatory relations can be realized by clauses as in *The problem is that they are starving.*)

> Coding: Obama THEME: IDEN'D is the president of the US.

Theme: classified   Clark was a Prime Minister / John is a murderer / People are bi-peds / To be truly free is an impossibility. Theme: classified requires an indefinite specifier for the predicate NP and is not reversible outside of poetry. (**A Prime Minister was Clark* is ungrammatical, and although *bi-peds are people* is grammatically acceptable its default interpretation is false.)

> Coding: People THEME: CLASS'D are bipeds.

Theme: identified and Theme: classified can also occur in appositional constructions in NPs as in *Obama, the president of the United States* ... or *John, an opera singer* ....

Theme: attribuand   Mary is clever/silly/pretty / That they are in trouble is obvious. Theme: attribuand occurs with a 'predicate' AdjP. In NPs, the adjective usually precedes the noun as in *They are in obvious trouble.*

> Coding: Mary THEME: ATTR is clever.

Theme: possessed   Cosmo has a toy monkey / Michelle owns a Vespa. Theme: possessed occurs with a small subset of lexical verbs indicating possession such as *have, own, possess.* The possessed element is an NP complement. The possessor is subject in the unmarked case. In NPs, theme: possessed can appear as a possessive determiner as in *Cosmo's monkey.*

> Coding: Cosmo has a toy monkey THEME: POSS'D.

Theme: existent   There is a rabbit / I think, therefore I am. Theme: existent occurs as complement in a clause with an existential *there* subject or as subject for the 'existence' predicates *be* and *exist.*

> Coding: There is a rabbit THEME: EX.

Theme: ambient   It is snowing. Theme: ambient occurs as predicate with expletive *it* as subject.

Coding: It is raining THEME: AMB.

A summary chart for argument roles is presented in Figure 4.6.

Circumstantial roles   Circumstantial roles correspond broadly to adjuncts of TIME, PLACE and MANNER. Adjuncts are not 'projected' by a predicate, but rather add additional information about the circumstances surrounding an event or relation. Syntactically, circumstantial roles are always adjuncts regardless of the constituent that they modify. In most grammars, all circumstantial elements except sentence adverbs are treated as Adjuncts within the VP.

4.3.10   Time

Time may be realized by NPs (*last night, three days ago*), ₚNPs (*on Tuesday, at three*), ADVPs (*never, always, usually, now, then etc.*), and by finite or non-finite clauses with *when/for/while* and so on. All but the adverbial class of temporal circumstantials are arguably modifiers of clauses insofar as tense and aspect selections for the clause are governed by reference to semantic Time (past, present, future) and Perspective (whether events are construed as beginning, ongoing, or completed), and it is precisely this sort of information that the temporal circumstantials make explicit. The adverbial realizations of Time seem to be V′ adjuncts. McCawley (1988) presents an insightful discussion of the relationships between Time adjuncts and tense and aspect selections (WH = WHEN).

Coding: They ate last night TIME.

4.3.11   Place

Realizations of Place include ₚNPs (*They ate dinner on a rocky hillside*), ADVPs (*somewhere, anywhere, elsewhere, outside*), and finite and non-finite clauses with an appropriate complementizer. Again, Place adjuncts seem to modify whole clauses rather than just VPs and are thus clause adjuncts rather than VP adjuncts: Place circumstances can modify conjoined clauses as in [*They ate, they worked and they played*] *in the kitchen*; they are readily realized by separate tone groups (i.e. don't necessarily constitute a single tone group within a VP constituent) and they have no relation as arguments of a predicate (WH = WHERE).

Coding: They ate in the kitchen PLACE.

AGENT – the 'doer' of an action.
  e.g. [JohnAGENT] killed the ducks.

INSTRUMENT – an entity used in the performance of an action.
  e.g. [The coat-hangerINSTRUMENT] opened the door.

CAUSE – the inanimate cause in events.
  e.g. [The windCAUSE] eroded the cliff.

EXPERIENCER – sentient entity that reacts to, or perceives a phenomenon.
  e.g. [The guestsEXPERIENCER] liked the show.
  Mushy peas disgust [meEXPERIENCER].
  It seems [to meEXPERIENCER] that John is sick.

STIMULUS – the entity or event or state which is reacted to in 'phenomenon oriented' reaction predicates.
  e.g. [Mushy peasSTIMULUS] disgust me.

SOURCE – the entity from which motion takes place.
  e.g. Mary received the book [from JohnSOURCE].

GOAL – the entity towards which motion is directed:

(1) **GOAL: LOCATION** – a spatial destination in motion and transfer processes.
  e.g. John went [to TorontoGOAL:LOC].

(2) **GOAL: RECIPIENT** – the recipient in non-locational transfer processes.
  e.g. John sent [MaryGOAL:REC] a letter.

(3) **GOAL: BENEFICIARY** – the entity for whom the process is carried out.
  e.g. John built [MaryGOAL:BEN] a house.

THEME – the 'entity in motion' in motion and transfer processes, or the entity located in locational relations, or the only argument in relations.

PATIENT – the entity that pre-exists the process and undergoes a change of state in the process.
  e.g. John cooked [the carrotsPAT].

RESULTANT – the entity or event resulting from a process.
  e.g. John built [a houseRES].

PERCEPT – an entity or event which is experienced or perceived.
  e.g. Mary saw [JohnPERC].

MESSAGE – what is communicated in message transfers (verbalization predicates).
  e.g. John said that [he would be here by sixMESS].

RANGE – an entity that designates the nature of a process.
  e.g. Mary plays [tennisRAN].

IDENTIFIED – subject NP in identificatory relation (should have a definite specifier and relations are reversible).
  e.g. [BushIDEN'D] is the president of the US.

CLASSIFIED – subject NP in classificatory relation (should have an indefinite NP and relation is not reversible).
  e.g. [PeopleCLASS'D] are bipeds.

ATTRIBUAND – occurs with a 'predicate' AdjP.
  e.g. [MaryATTR] is clever.

POSSESSED – occurs with lexical verbs indicating possession.
  e.g. Cosmo has [a toy monkeyPOSS'D].

EXISTENT – occurs as complement in a clause with an 'existential *there*' subject or as subject for the 'existence' predicates *be* and *exist*.
  e.g. There is [a manEX] we know.

AMBIENT – occurs as predicate with expletive *it* as subject.
  e.g. It is [snowingAMB].

Figure 4.6 Argument roles

4.3.12   Manner

Realizations of Manner include ADVPs (*carefully, quickly, slowly*), $_p$NP (*in a careful manner, with care/courage/fortitude*), the NPs (*this way, that way*), and clauses with an appropriate complementizer. Within the general category of 'manner' are circumstantial modifiers of clauses (so called 'sentence' adverbs such as *unfortunately, frankly, hopefully*), VP modifiers (such as *quickly, sadly, slowly*) and modifiers internal to V' (*barely, hardly, nearly*) (WH = HOW).

Coding: He chewed in a careful manner MANNER.

There are also logical circumstances which occur as syntactic adjuncts to clauses.

4.3.13   Reason

Realized by a complementizer phrase [CP] with *because* (*they stayed home because it was raining*) WH = WHY.

Coding: They stayed at home because it was raining REASON.

4.3.14   Purpose

Realized with (*in order*) + marked infinitive/*that* or *so that* (*they stayed home in order to keep dry / she stay up in order that she might finish her work, she read so that she would understand*) WH = WHY.

Coding: They stayed at home in order to keep dry PURPOSE.

4.3.15   Condition

Typically realized by *if* clauses (*they'll stay home if it is raining*) (WH = ? (only composites e.g. *under what conditions*)).

Coding: They'll stay at home if it is raining CONDITION.

4.3.16   Concession

Typically realized by *although* clauses (*they stayed home although it was nice out*) (WH = ?).

> Coding: They stayed home although it wasn't raining CONCESSION.

These 'logical' circumstantials are usually treated as adjuncts within the verb phrase. They may be represented as either VP Adjuncts or as adjuncts of a complementizer phrase. Circumstantial roles are summarized in Figure 4.7.

The combination of an articulated set of features and distributions for English argument roles and circumstances together with the possibility of representing lexical selections as feature arrays allows for rich coding of both literal and figurative ideational values in discourse. If one adds to this the semantic values

---

TIME – may be realized by
- NPs
- pNPs
- ADVPs
- finite or non-finite *when/for/while* etc. clauses
  e.g. They ate [last nightTIME].

PLACE – may be realized by
- pNPs
- ADVPs
- finite and non-finite clauses with an appropriate complementizer
  e.g. They ate [in the kitchenPLACE].

MANNER – may be realized by
- ADVPs
- pNP
- the NPs *this way* and *that way*
- clauses with an appropriate complementizer
  e.g. He chewed [carefullyMANNER].

LOGICAL CIRCUMSTANCES occur as syntactic adjuncts:

REASON
Realized by a complementizer phrase with *because*.
  e.g. They stayed at home [because it was rainingREASON].

PURPOSE
Realized with (*in order*) + marked infinitive/*that* or *so that*.
  e.g. They stayed at home [in order to keep dryPURPOSE].

CONDITION
Typically realized by *if* clauses.
  e.g. They'll stay at home [if it is rainingCONDITION].

CONCESSION
Typically realized by *although* clauses.
  e.g. They stayed home [although it wasn't rainingCONCESSION].

Figure 4.7 Circumstantial roles

associated with tense and aspect selections, a fairly complete picture of the ideational information made explicit in a discourse can be coded and analysed. Below are three examples of clauses coded for argument roles (Examples (44)–(46)).

(44) *The male robin*Agent/Theme *flew*Action *in to the bushes*Goal: location.
(45) *Max*Agent/Theme *flew* Action *into a tizzy*Goal: location.
(46) *Max*Agent/Theme *flew*Action *away*Source Goal: location.

As can be seen, the coded analyses are a kind of shorthand for inheritance of semantic features associated with predicates and their argument roles and with features of the actual arguments in particular examples. Table 4.4 presents a possible predicational and feature analysis for the same examples (44–46). There are default interpretations which are respectively, literal for example (44) and metaphorical and idiomatic for Example (45). The third Example, (46), is potentially ambiguous. It has possible literal, metaphorical and idiomatic interpretations.

As may be seen from Table 4.4, the default literal interpretation arises because there is a match between the features for FLY and its argument roles and the features of the actual arguments filling these roles. The default metaphorical interpretation for (45) is based on the mismatch between the features for the Goal associated with FLY (that it be a location) and the features for TIZZY (a mental state). To successfully interpret the metaphor, speakers must allow the features of both the argument role and the argument to be inherited in the instance. The ambiguity of the third example is based on the possibility that MAX refers to a non-human participant and the indefiniteness of AWAY which indicates a spatial orientation from an unspecified source to an unspecified goal. Literally, Example (46) could mean either (a) or (b):

a. MAX is the name of a bird. The bird flew away.
b. MAX is the name of a person. The person got on a plane which flew away or Max flew the plane.

Alternatively, the clause could have the metaphoric interpretation in (c):

c. Max is the name of a person. He left (quickly).

The metaphoric possibility is again based on the indefiniteness of AWAY, which allows Example (46) *Max flew away* to be interpreted in relation to the idiom *the bird has flown* where flight to an unspecified destination is understood as 'hasty departure' or 'escape'. The general points here are that (1) in interpreting Examples (44)–(46) the features of predicate and argument role relations and those of lexical and grammatical selections instantiating arguments are inherited; and (2) that coding predicate argument relations functions as a shorthand for such inheritance relations.

We present detailed analysis of ideational representation in the sample Text (5.1a) in Chapter 5, where lexical and conceptual information is also mapped.

Table 4.4. *Example of predicational and feature analysis*

	Predicational Analysis	Event	+ Theme: transferent +/- Agent	FLY	+/- Goal: Location +/- Source
	Features of predicate and inherent arguments		+ entity in motion + doer of action + intention	+ Action + Motion + travel through the air	Spatial location + Destination (motion towards location in space) + Source (place motion begins from)
(i)	Features of arguments	PAST	The male robin DEFINITE MALE BIRD (+WINGS, CAN FLY)	Flew	into the bushes IN: spatial relation, containership TO: spatial relation, destination THE: definite BUSHES: LIVING THING, PLANT, can function as 'container' LOCATION since it defines an area with a periphery and interior
(ii)			Max MAX: name (for person or animal) + CAPACITY FOR INTENTION	Flew	into a tizzy A: indefinite TIZZY: mental state: disturbed, excited, state unwarranted by circumstances
(iii)			Max	Flew	Away AWAY: indefinite spatial orientation: motion from source to unspecified destination

4.4   The grammar of message organization

'Ideational grammar' has to do with what a text is 'about'; the 'grammar of interaction' has to do with the role relationships between speaker/writers and addressees and the expression of attitude to what is predicated. The grammar of message organization, the 'textual function' of language in Halliday and Hasan's work (1976; 1989), has to do with the organization of texts as both cohesive and coherent within their contexts of text production. There are three general ways in which linguists have addressed these issues: through the study of presupposition relationships in discourse (cohesion), the study of syntactic and prosodic resources for signalling information as given or new (focus and prominence), and the study of the relationships between discourses and contexts (discourse coherence and intertextuality). We discuss coherence in Chapters 5 and 8. The discussion of cohesion is based on the foundational works of Halliday and Hasan (1976; 1989) and the terminology used is largely theirs.

4.4.1   Cohesion

The study of cohesive features of texts involves isolating those linguistic features which create relationships of **presupposition between sentences**, allowing us to interpret one sentence in relation to preceding and following sentences, and between sentences and the **extra-textual contexts in which they are produced**. This initial distinction gives a binary contrast between reference internal to a discourse (or **endophoric reference**) and reference external to a discourse (or **exophoric reference**). Within endophoric reference there are the further contrasts between **anaphoric reference** (which is reference 'backwards' to information assumed to be already available), **cataphoric reference** (reference to information yet to be presented), and **homophoric reference** (reference to 'self' or to a head element). Within exophoric reference there is also a possible binary distinction between **situational reference**, reference to objects, events and so on present in the immediate perceptual or shared conceptual environment of speaker/hearers, and **intertextual reference**, reference to other discourses presumed to be known by addressees. All of these relations can be summarized as a system as in Figure 4.8.

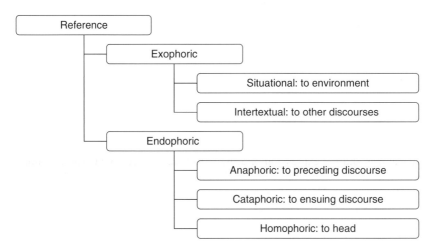

Figure 4.8 Referential relations

Within these broad categories of types of reference, five more or less distinctive subtypes of cohesive relation are recognized. They are reference, substitution, ellipsis, conjunction and lexical cohesion (Halliday and Hasan 1976).

Reference handles items whose specific function is to index referential relationships, that is items whose interpretation depends, in part, on the presence of other elements. There are three general types. The first is called **personal reference**. This involves the use of personal pronouns such as *I, me, mine, you, yours* and so on and possessive deictics as in ***my** hat, **her** elephant*. Personal referencing items are definite, referring to known or given information, and thus are typically used for situational or anaphoric reference. The second type is demonstrative reference with demonstrative pronouns (*this/that, these/those*) and spatial and temporal 'pro' words (*here/there, now/then*). Demonstratives are also definite and frequently used exophorically as well as being used endophorically. Halliday and Hasan (1976) include the articles *the/a* within demonstrative reference. We find the notion of an indefinite demonstrative (*a*) anomalous and prefer to think of the articles as an independent two-item class indicating only definite/indefinite + singular reference. Comparative reference includes all items which can be used to establish qualitative or quantitative comparisons between entities. Thus, the comparative forms of adjectives and adverbs (e.g. qualitative: *easier, cleverer, more sweetly, more cleverly,* quantitative: *more, fewer, less* and so on), deictic adjectives and adverbs expressing identity (*same, equal/ly, identical/ly*), similarity (*such, similar/ly*), and difference (*other, else different/ly*) may form cohesive ties insofar as the interpretation of any comparison requires a reference 'point of comparison' as in *Sam is a very clever linguist. However, Mary is cleverer when it comes to syntactic theory*. The domain for the interpretation of *cleverer* in the second sentence is the predication A VERY CLEVER LINGUIST: Classified [SAM]. Normal conventions for coding reference relations are to assign indices of some sort to the referents and then track them through the discourse as in the coding below. However, if the reference type needs to be recovered from the coded data without inspection, more detailed codes may be used (e.g. R1/RP1 for *he* in the example).

Coding: Sam1 is a very clever linguist.
He1 is especially clever when it comes to syntactic theory.

Substitution of one element for another is cohesive insofar as substitutes require textual antecedents. Nominal, verbal and clausal substitutions are recognized. Nominal substitutions are the items *one, ones* and *same*. The verbal substitute is *do*. Clausal substitutes are *so* and *not*. Examples are *John bought a new hat. Mary bought one too* where the item *one* is a nominal substitute for *a new hat* in the preceding sentence; *Does he know? He may do* where *do* substitutes for the verb *know*; *Does he know the answer? I think so* where *so* substitutes for the clause *he knows the answer*.

> Coding: Does he know the answer2?
> I think so SUB2.

Ellipsis can be thought of as a variant of substitution (substitution by 0 if you like) and, like substitution, requires an antecedent in a preceding sentence. It also can be nominal, verbal or clausal. Examples are *I haven't the slightest idea. Nor have I* – where the noun phrase *the slightest idea* is ellipted; *Don't move! Why shouldn't I?* – where the verb *move* is ellipted; and *Did you see anyone? Yes – John* where part of the clause (*I saw*) is ellipted.

Note that substitution and ellipsis are like reference in that they may be thought of as PRO forms (including 0) for clausal and verbal elements. The nominal substitutes *one, ones* and *same* seem to be treated as substitutes on the grounds that they involve nominal reference which is not personal or demonstrative. However, unlike demonstrative, comparative and personal reference, ellipsis and substitution only work anaphorically within a text. They require antecedents in preceding sentences for their interpretation.

> Coding: Don't look3!
> Why shouldn't IEllip3?

Conjunction as a type of cohesive relation has to do with logical and temporal relations between sentences which are overtly marked by 'sentence conjunctions' such as *however, moreover, nevertheless, consequently, therefore, meanwhile, afterwards* and so on. Such relations are cohesive insofar as they presuppose other propositions which are temporally or logically related.

> Coding: [The view is magnificent.]1 HoweverCONJ1 you shouldn't look because the drop will make you dizzy.

The final type of cohesive relation is lexical cohesion. **Lexical cohesion** involves the occurrence of lexical items which have some kind of semantic relation to each other. Halliday and Hasan (1976; 1989) and Hasan (1985) discuss three types of lexical cohesion. The most obviously cohesive use of lexical items is simple **repetition** of an item or items. The occurrence of the lexical item may be distributed through different word categories and still be treated as repetition. For instance, our use of the noun *cohesion* and the adjective *cohesive* in the preceding sentences, and indeed throughout this text exemplifies cohesive repetition. Note that a good deal of intertextual coherence is established by repetition as well. That is, the use of lexical items which have high salience in other discourses may activate references to those discourses if they are known.

Coding: Don't look4.
Why shouldn't I lookLC-REP4?

A second type of lexical cohesion has to do with **synonymy** where items are interpreted in relation to each other because they share some semantic components. For example, in this text our use of *cohesive relation, presupposition* and *cohesive tie* are close synonyms and form cohesive ties. Halliday and Hasan (1976) include within the category of lexical cohesion synonymy relations of **superordination** and **antonymy**. Superordination has to do with categorial structure in taxonomic hierarchies. Here, *lexical cohesion* functions as a superordinate term that is cohesive with the subtypes introduced (*lexical repetition, synonymy* and *collocation*). The use of antonyms functions cohesively insofar as word pairs such as *dead/alive, white/black, awake/asleep, moving/still* or for that matter *synonym/antonym* exhibit tendencies to co-occur. If you think of a conversation, say, in which a speaker reports that they have been *feeling sick*, it is likely that they will be asked if they are *feeling better* or that there will be some expression of hope that they are soon *well*.

CODING: **Collocation** is the third broad type1 of lexical cohesion2 ... As a cohesive L-REP2 category L-CSYN1, this is a sort of rag-bag L-CSYN1.

Collocation is the third type of lexical cohesion recognized by Halliday and Hasan. As a cohesive category, this is a sort of rag-bag insofar as it is a general term used to cover anything not dealt with under repetition and synonymy. Moreover, repetition and synonymy involve collocation since items which are cohesive in these ways are also collocated. The category is useful though as a gloss for underspecified types of semantic relation. For example, items such as *smoke/fire, ice/cold* and so on are often collocated and are cohesive. (The semantic relation in these examples is effect/cause and attributive respectively.) Similarly, items such as *shoot/snap* have a high probability of occurring with collocates such as *film/picture* (where *film* and *picture* might be expected to appear as result). Figure 4.9 summarizes the options for relations of this type.

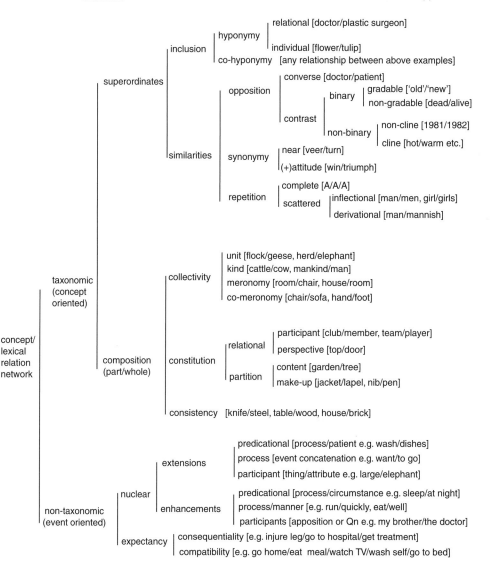

Figure 4.9 Conceptual/lexical relations network[2]

In the box below, the collocational relation between kettle and cup of tea could be characterized as event-oriented compatibility based on purpose.

Coding: Sam put the kettle5 on.
He made a nice cup of tea LC-COL5.

Table 4.5. *Errors in use of cohesive devices*

Cohesive tie	Criterion of error	Example
Reference	Referent is not in text, referent is ambiguous or wrong pronoun is used	Baseball or soccer. I I used to do that for sportsnight.
Substitution and ellipsis	Ellipted or substituted word or phrase cannot be explicitly identified	Would you like to go to a movie? I don't have **one**.
Conjunction	Semantic relation that conjunction is signifying is wrong	There's a fourth person. I **But** there are four people.
Lexical cohesion	The second word of the pair occurring in the adjacent sentence does not contribute to the cohesiveness, or does not follow from the previous sentence.	What happens if you go on a **pass**enger train? I You **pass** the test.

Lastly, items which are collocated but do not entail any overt semantic relation that would lead you to expect them to co-occur can be reinterpreted or recoded simply by virtue of the fact that they are collocated. For non-linguist readers of this book, for instance, the items *agent, patient* and *argument role* may well not have entailed any overt semantic relationship. However, we hope that having introduced the notion that *argument role* is a superordinate term in relation to *agent* and *patient* non-linguist readers will begin to expect these to co-occur.

Investigating the way in which cohesive devices are used by particular speakers may also involve identifying errors or non-conventional use of cohesive devices, determined on the basis of a clear breach of linguistic rules (McKenna and Oh 2005). Reference, for example, may not be recoverable. Unrecoverable references do not form cohesive ties with a reference point of comparison but can still be coded. We follow McKenna and Oh's criteria for scoring erroneous ties, including unrecoverable reference (Table 4.5).

The significance of cohesion in relation to the interpretation of particular discourses is perhaps best illustrated in relation to different varieties of text. If for example one considers discourses which vary with respect to the medium and mode of communication, it is apparent that different modes entail different types and different degrees of cohesive relation. Spontaneous face-to-face dialogues will be different from telephone conversations because in the former, but not the latter, a physical environment is shared so that situational exophoric reference is both more likely to be used and has a better chance of succeeding. Spontaneous spoken monologues might be expected to exhibit more internal cohesion than conversations, and monologues which are distinctly lacking in cohesive relations are often understood as signs of fatigue, distraction, mental illness or other disorder. Within written modes note that, for example, texts which are written to be spoken as if not written (e.g. plays) can exhibit all the types of cohesive relation available for ordinary spoken modes although invariably they will be more tightly structured than spontaneous speech. Similarly, some texts are 'written to be read as if thought'. One of the things this mode 'licences' are fragments of text which do not have any overt cohesive relation to the rest of the text (as in 'stream of consciousness'). Such 'deviations' are licensed by the mode because we can interpret them as coherent with the presentation of a participant's thoughts. Similarly, the same mode licences the use of partial or complete exophoric reference because, as presented from the perception of the 'knower', such reference makes sense. Journals kept only for personal use may present similar features. The general point then is that, on the one hand, certain modes presuppose or entail certain types of cohesion and, on the other, that different cohesive relations can in fact be signifiers of modes. The relevance of this in relation to the interpretation of particular discourses is that a discourse may be expected to have cohesive features that are appropriate to its function.

Halliday and Hasan's (1976) description of cohesion was largely developed with reference to written texts and was focused on making presupposition relations with overt signifiers explicit. As Figure 4.10, an extract from a semi-structured interview between a caregiver and a researcher, illustrates, analysis based on the possibilities they describe does help to make local presupposition relationships explicit. The text is densely cohesive, with demonstrative

---

IV; Can you tell me a little bit about **[the way$_1$ her$_2$ memory$_3$ has changed]$_4$**?

CG; As far as like I said **the pills$_5$**.

She $_{R-P2}$'s very **forgetful** $_{LC-C3,4}$ in **those things** $_{R-D5}$.

[It $_{R-P4}$'s a lot of **[little things** $_{LC-R5}$]]$_4$,

um **[it** $_{R-P4}$'s **not so much names or faces$_6$]$_4$**,

she $_{R-P2}$ doesn't tend to **forget**$_{LC-R3,4}$ **those** $_{R6}$ **things** $_{LC-R6}$.

She$_{R-P2}$'ll tell me **[stories of long ago]$_7$** which I don't know

um **[but then again she** $_{R-P2}$'ll tell me the $_{R-D7}$ **same**$_{R-D7, 7}$ **story**$_{LC-R7}$ maybe three days later

and things have **changed** $_{LC-A7}$ within **the** $_{R-D7}$ **story**$_{LC-C7}$]$_8$

IV; umhum

CG; **[So CONJ she**$_{R-P2}$'s **forgetting**$_{LC-R4, c3}$ **those** $_{R-D8}$ **things]$_{4,8}$** ah.

For [right now it's really just a [memory $_{LC-R3}$ **loss]**$_{LC-C4}$ for **her**$_{R-P2}$]$_4$.

Figure 4.10 Cohesive analysis

and personal reference, lexical repetition and collocation used extensively. It is also evident that the extended turn taken by the caregiver must be read as a response to the researcher's question, *Can you tell me a little bit about the way her memory has changed?* This means that not only does the adjacency pair, question–response, contribute to the coherence of the interaction, but also that there are relationships, not just between 'words', but between the interviewer's prominent *the way her memory has changed* and the propositions the caregiver offers to elaborate *the way her memory has changed.* We have indicated relations between presupposing constituents by bracketing and assigning an index to the constituents.

4.4.2   *Focus and prominence*

The second major way in which members of the London School have addressed message organization has to do with the resources available to present parts of a message as being focal (points of departure, backgrounded information) and other parts of a message as being prominent (informationally salient [new] and/or marked). Two major types of phenomenon are often considered in these contexts. The first is the theory of THEME/RHEME for sentences, which is a development of the Prague School linguists' work on Functional Sentence Perspective (Halliday 1967; Danes 1974; Firbas 1992). The second is the theory of Given and New (Halliday 1967). We use Gregory's terms FOCUS/PROMINENCE for these to avoid confusion with the argument role called theme (Gregory 1988; Watt 1990).

The basic idea of FOCUS/PROMINENCE is that there is a statistically high probability that certain types of element will occur as the first element in a clause and that any departure from such normative probabilities will be in some degree *marked.* Thus, statements in which the first element is subject are said to involve FOCUS only. That is, they are UNMARKED, since statistically this is highly probable. Similarly, questions beginning with WH words or an auxiliary verb only involve FOCUS (although in many types of text, especially written modes, questions themselves are 'more marked' than statements). Also, in commands, the unmarked thematic element would correspond with either a main verb in Neutral ('bare infinitive') form or the 'let' auxiliary verb. Which one you get depends on the type of command, and note that the same proviso holds for commands as for questions, viz. that commands may overall be more marked than statements and, perhaps, questions. However, the variety of text being considered really does matter here. The language used by drill sergeants ordering troops, by directors rehearsing actors for performance, as well as the language of cooking recipes, and instruction manuals of all types share a feature which is that there is a predictably high frequency of command realized by jussive imperatives. That is, command is the unmarked choice of speech function in these varieties.

FOCUS elements interact with the creation of PROMINENCE insofar as prominence is established in part by the location of the major pitch movement in a tone group. Usually, the major pitch movement coincides with the last lexical item in a clause and thus the constituent of which that element is a part is prominent. Thus in *//1 I like/ coffee//* we would say that the subject *I* is the unmarked focus of the clause and the complement *coffee* is prominent because that is where the major pitch movement occurs. If one moves, say, the complement to initial position, the effect is to break the sentence up into two tone groups (and hence two chunks of information) with a major pitch movement occurring both on the moved element and on whatever is the remaining, 'last lexical item'. Thus, the statement *Coffee, I like* is MARKED. The first element is both FOCUS and PROMINENT (it is site of a major pitch movement) and the verb *like* is the locus of the second major pitch movement and so is also prominent.

Somewhat similar effects can be created by other strategies. For instance, it is possible to simply shift tonicity 'forward' to the middle or beginning of a clause without changing the syntactic structure of the clause. If the initial element is selected as tonic, it is both focus and prominence for the message but, barring other effects, there will not be a second prominent element as there is in the case of pre- or post-posed elements.

In general, the importance of focus in relation to texts is that the elements that regularly occur as focus establish the 'back-grounded' or 'given' information for the discourse (and may reflect aspects of the text type). For example, in a story the protagonist might well appear as FOCUS in successive sentences about their activities, whereas in a logically structured argument we may find that what appears as the prominent element in one sentence will be focus in the next and so on. Contrastively, those elements which are prominent in individual sentences can, cumulatively, create prominence for the discourse as a whole. They may effectively mean that an aspect or aspects of a message are foregrounded. Focus and prominence are thus semantic functions with a variety of discoursal, syntactic and phonological realizations that interact with each other. The morphosyntactic resources enabling marked selections for focus and prominence are listed below where focus is coded with underlining and **prominence** with bold face. (The example is originally from Halliday 1967.)

Coding: Peter left his luggage **at the station**.
(Focus = UNDERLINE; Prominence = **BOLD**)

4.4.3   *Morphosyntactic resources for marked focus and prominence*

Topicalization   A topic element (TE) may be adjoined to the beginning of a clause to explicitly mark its topic. It usually refers anaphorically to preceding discourse or exophorically to context.

(47) **Speak**ing of luggage [TE], Peter left his at the **stat**ion.
(48) According to **Pe**ter [TE], he left his luggage at the **stat**ion.

Preposing   An element of clause structure may be preposed [PreP]. The topic and preposed elements are both focus (starting place for the message) and prominent (they occur as a separate intonation unit). Within the clause, the last lexical item is prominent.

(49) **Pe**ter [PreP], he left his luggage at the **stat**ion.
(50) His **lug**gage [PreP], he left at the **stat**ion.

Post-posing   Elements of clause structure may be post-posed [PosP] as in (51). The post-posed element occurs in a separate tone group and is prominent.

(51) Peter left it at the **stat**ion, his **lug**gage.

Cleft and **pseudo cleft clauses** allow prominence to occur on a single marked constituent:

Cleft

(52) It was **Pe**ter who left his luggage at the station.
(53) It was at the **stat**ion Peter left his luggage.
(54) It was his **lug**gage Peter left at the station.

The constituents *Peter, at the station* and *his luggage* are made prominent in these constructions, while the focus of cleft clauses is the speech function itself. (Compare 52–54 with the corresponding polar questions.)

Pseudo-Cleft

(55) What **Pet**er did was leave the luggage at the station.
(56) What **Ell**ie likes is chocolate.

Clauses with preposed, post-posed, or topicalized elements are similar in that they each require two tone groups and therefore two points of prominent (new) information. Clauses with cleft or pseudo-cleft constructions allow markedness with a single point of prominence.

A related set of systems are those which allow the emphasis or omission of an argument. Among the most commonly described are passivization, ergativity and nominalization.

Passivization   Passivization reorders the elements of a clause so that a thematic argument appears in the focus (subject) position and an agent, cause or experiencer is either deleted (backgrounded) or made prominent in a final position as in (57), (58), and (59) respectively:

(57) a. The luggage was left at the **sta**tion.
      b. The luggage was left at the station by **P**eter.
(58) a. Point Pleasant was de**stroyed**.
      b. Point Pleasant was destroyed by Hurricane **Juan**.
(59) a. The idea was thought ri**dic**ulous.
      b. The idea was thought ridiculous by most **fac**ulty.

Ergative Verbs Verbs of motion and change of state (ergative verbs)
allow inclusion or omission of Agent or Cause without the need for passivization.
When Agent or Cause are present and clauses are active, they are focus as in (60a)
and (61a); when absent, the thematic argument is focus as in (60b) and (61b).

(60) a. Peter rolled the **rock**.
      b. The rock **rolled**.
(61) a. The water changed the **shore**line.
      b. The shoreline **changed**.

Nominalization refers to processes which incorporate predicational information into noun phrases. These processes include changing word class from verb
to noun as in destroy > destruction; employ > employment; realize > realization. Such nominalizations of verbs can allow backgrounding of processes and/
or participants because they can be presented within the noun phrase as 'given'
information (through use of definite articles for instance); they can occur in non-
prominent positions, and the arguments required by the verb are not required by
the noun. For example the use of *destroy* as a verb requires an Agent/Cause and
Patient as in (62a). The nominalization of destroy allows Agent in (62b) and
Patient in (62c) to be back-grounded or deleted altogether (62d).

(62) a. The Americans destroyed **Khabul**.
      b. The destruction of Khabul was **sad**.
      c. The destruction by the Americans was **sad**.
      d. The destruction was **sad**.

Other nominalizing processes incorporate clauses into NPs which can have
similar effects as in

(63) The destruction which occurred in Khabul was **sad**.

The importance of morphosyntactic resources for these features in clinical discourse analysis is that, while they are all resources which enable speakers to
select focus and prominence and therefore presumably increase the potential
for effective communication, with the exception of ergatives, some of them
also increase information processing loads in both speech production and
speech reception. Processes which re-order clause constituents increase their
syntactic complexity, while those which incorporate predicational information

---

Topicalization – topic element adjoins to the beginning of a clause to explicitly mark its topic

Preposing – an element of clause structure may be preposed

Post-Posing – an element of clause structure may be post-posed

Cleft and Pseudo Cleft Clauses – allow prominence to occur on a single marked constituent

Passivization – reorders the elements of a clause so that a thematic argument appears in the focus (subject) position and an agent, cause, or experiencer is either back-grounded through deletion or made prominent in final adjunct position

Ergative Verbs – verbs of motion and change of state allow inclusion or omission of Agent or Cause without the need for passivization

Nominalization – predicational information is incorporated into noun phrases allowing for back-grounding of processes and/or participants. Processes for nominalization include:
- changing word class from verb to noun as in destroy > destruction
- incorporating clauses into NPs

Figure 4.11 Morphosyntactic resources for marked focus and prominence

into noun phrases increase their lexical density (cf. Halliday 1987, 1989). Both syntactic complexity and lexical density have implications for the evaluation of language in clinical settings (e.g. van Dijk and Kintsch 1983; Snowdon *et al.* 1996; Kemper *et al.* 2001).

English morphosyntactic resources for marked focus and prominence are summarized in Figure 4.11.

5   Phase and contexts of culture and situation

5.1   Contexts of culture and situation

All discourse is produced in context and interpretation depends on contexts of production and interpretation being, in some measure, shared. Early ethnographic work addressed context dependency by positing contexts of culture and context of situation (Malinowski 1923; 1935; Firth 1957). Context of culture accounted for sets of culturally specific beliefs, expectations and practices in terms of which people interpret events around them. Context of situation referred to patterns of behaviour and talk which appear so regularly in association with a particular activity that they are understood as (abstract characterizations of) the function of the situation type. Behaviours which do not reflect some expected pattern can be interpreted as irrelevant, and behaviours which appear totally unrelated to the contexts in which they occur may be judged uninterpretable.

Later work by Halliday, Hasan, Gregory, Martin and others refined and developed ideas of context. Our view is once again a hybrid, informed by Halliday's ethnographic perspective (e.g. 1977; 1978; 1984; 1994), by our awareness that contexts are significantly matters of what speakers know (e.g. van Dijk 1977; 2006; van Dijk and Kintsch 1983; Gregory 1988), and by work in AI, psychology and discourse analysis on top-down cognitive models as to what 'contextual knowledge' might be like. The latter approaches (and ours) differ from traditional functionalist and ethnographic approaches in explicitly situating context in neurocognitive domains of semantic and episodic memory (see also van Dijk 2006). Any and/or all neurocognitive systems involved in information processing may be engaged when processing physically and/or temporally present situational information. Which systems are engaged will depend both on the nature of the information presented and the processors' capacities for processing it.

Taking this perspective, context of culture which in Gregory's (1988) formulation referred to known parameters of cultural variation in terms of temporal, geographical, social and individual provenances of speakers, can be construed as referring specifically to semantic and episodic memories speakers have that are conditioned by and in these environments (van Dijk 2006). Similarly, context of situation in this framework refers to configurations of ideational, interactional and medium information which are encoded episodically and semantically represented in generic patterns of function, meaning and use. They are limited by our contexts of culture.

5.2   Frames, schemas, scripts and scenarios

A good deal of the information represented in memory systems is not inherently linguistic or even discoursal. For example, we have more or less elaborated knowledge (that varies in different contexts of culture) about what to do if we feel unwell. Our knowledge can include information that lets us make judgements about whether the feeling is minor, temporary and likely to go away without help, or sufficiently severe and persistent as to require attention from a medical professional. Should we decide that help is required, we have knowledge about where to go and who to see, about the types of role relationship we might expect to have with the healthcare professional and about what they may do to help us. Such knowledge may be described in **frames**, **schemas**, **scripts** and **scenarios**. **Frames** are representations of (culturally specific) knowledge and belief associated with events, states or things. In early versions of frame theory, knowledge was assumed to be propositionally represented and relatively static (e.g. Minsky 1975; van Dijk 2006). **Schemata** are similar representations but include abstract elements in different modalities such as visual schemata for faces or houses, or discourse schemas for narrative such as those articulated by Propp (1928), Barthes (1968) and Labov and Waletzky (1967), as well as conventional and/or stereotypic conceptual organizations (Tannen and Wallat 1993). **Scripts** are representations of highly abstract generic structure potential associated with events – they delineate the inherent elements of events and their sequences (Schank and Abelson 1977). **Scenarios** were developed to refer to characteristic properties of situations that were not necessarily represented in propositional form (Sandford and Garrod 1981). They cover some of the same ground as frames and schemas but focus on identifying multi-modal aspects of situations such as features of the setting.

Thus, in the situation 'being unwell', if one makes a decision to seek help rather than wait, frame knowledge might include information about options to make an appointment, go to a walk-in clinic, go to an emergency unit at a hospital, or call an ambulance.

Which option is chosen will depend on other frames/schemas (e.g. what we know about the services available at the different settings) together with an assessment of how urgent the need for medical attention is, which requires integration of proprioceptive experience with (yet more) frames/schemas about sickness. Choosing 'go to a walk-in clinic' suggests an evaluation including 'not immediately life threatening', 'not requiring immediate surgery or resuscitation', but sufficiently disturbing as to need 'same day' assessment and/or treatment. (There are, of course, other considerations that might motivate such a decision such as access, whether one sees any doctor regularly and so on.) Going to the walk-in clinic evokes not only frames/schemata, but also features of the setting (scenarios) which might include: a waiting room which will have seating and may have other people waiting to be seen; a receptionist at a desk; a nurse, doctors, consulting and examination rooms; and so on. Even the quality of the light (often fluorescent) and the type of decor and furniture may be anticipated. A script for 'going to the walk-in clinic' might include getting there, entering the clinic, talking with the receptionist about the problem, filling out health insurance and diagnostic forms, establishing a wait time, being told to go to a consulting/examination room, removing any necessary clothing and so on.

The relevance of such cognitive models for discourse becomes apparent if one considers a telephone conversation in which a speaker says 'I had to go to the walk-in clinic yesterday.' This statement immediately evokes not only frame information about possible severity of the problem motivating the action, but also associated script and scenario models which condition expectations about what the speaker might say next. If the speaker reports 'Yah, I got hit by a car on my bike and dislocated my shoulder and broke my arm in two places' an addressee might be disconcerted since, outside war zones, walk-in clinics are not usually equipped to deal with injuries of this nature. At this point, our hypothetical addressee will need to suspend expectations and wait (or ask) about what happened next. An account in which the bone is set and the shoulder relocated at the walk-in clinic will require a modification of the frame for 'walk-in clinic'; an expected one in which the speaker is sent on to an emergency unit is likely to have the addressee wondering whether the speaker didn't also hit her head. The general point is that simple mention of an event such as 'I had to go to the walk-in clinic yesterday' sets up a whole range of expectations about what the speaker might say next, based on shared knowledge of why one goes to walk-in clinics, what walk-in clinics can do, what happens when people go there and so on.

Frames, schemas, scripts and scenarios are useful insofar as they help to articulate the mental models which characterize the cultural and generic information we use to make sense of what is going on in situations and to construct relevance and coherence in discourse. There is evidence, which we discuss in Chapter 8, that people actually do use such mental models in constructing relevance and making assessments of coherence. Some of these, particularly highly abstract models for event and discourse schemas appear to have universal relevance. For example, the schema for stories appears always to involve a 'complicating event' (Labov and Waletsky 1967) and a schema for buying and selling does involve exchange of goods/services for some medium (currency or other). But the details of what counts as a complicating event or what can be bought or sold for what medium of exchange vary across cultural contexts and entail generic models of the kind represented in frames, scripts and scenarios. It is also important to acknowledge the extent to which such models are provisional and open to revision when the instance supplies information that conflicts with properties of the known model (Hudson 1984; 2007). New learning is not possible if features of models cannot be altered by experience. Finally, it is worth emphasizing that discourses usually do not explicitly instantiate top-down models. Rather, the linguistic signals within a discourse provide indexical signs of such models (Barthes 1968; 1994). Consequently, we follow van Dijk and Kintsch (1983) in assuming that relevance and coherence are not properties of texts, but rather achievements of discourse processors in integrating linguistic input with contextually available information.

5.3   Coherence

Coherence itself is a term for the complex of inferential processes that enable us to produce discourse that others can make sense of and to interpret what others say. Coherence thus depends on linguistic information instantiated in discourse, inferences we draw from this information, presuppositional relations involved in linguistic cohesion, our situational knowledge (represented in models such as frames, scripts, scenarios, and schemas), and our attitudes and evaluations of these. The study of discourse in clinical contexts is a study of the breakdown, at some level, of discourse coherence. Imaging studies over the last few years have made the development of a model of discourse coherence for which the neural substrates are understood begin to seem like an achievable goal (see e.g. Stowe *et al.* 2005; Ferstl *et al.* 2008; Mason and Just 2007 for suggestive reviews). However, given the wide range of phenomena involved in producing and interpreting discourse as coherent, and the potential configurations in different disorders that could lead to impairment, isolating particular features contributing to perceived coherence or incoherence is highly relevant in clinical settings.

5.4   Registers and dialects

In addition to background knowledge that informs discourse production and interpretation, speakers' knowledge of language, including functional varieties (registers), associated structural knowledge, and dialect varieties, is acquired in and conditioned by their contexts of situation and culture. So, a speaker of English will know at least one dialect variety which can be identified in terms of the temporal, geographical and social provenances in which it was acquired (such as contemporary, middle class, Toronto English). Of course, they may also know other English dialects as well as other languages. Depending on the contexts of culture and situation which speakers have experienced, they will also know a variety of registers. Pursuing our medical motif, an example is the register of medical interview which involves an expert medical person, a patient and some reason (often illness) for the patient's presence and the interview occasion. These interviews are normally face-to-face. The medical interview situation results in linguistic selections in which the experience referred to will have lexis associated with illness, symptoms, diagnosis, prognosis and treatment and interactional patterns which reflect the medical professional's role as expert and the patient's role as advice/aid seeker. For instance, the professional asks questions about the patient, may make statements about the patient, and may give commands to the patient (*take these three times a day and call me if you experience any dizziness*). The patient may ask questions and make statements but these are unlikely to be about the healthcare professional's personal life. Other interactional systems reflecting the social role of the expert and their relationship to the patient may result in differential use, for instance of address terms (*Dr. X/Sarah*) and politeness markers (*lift up **please***). Organizationally, the face-to-face interview will result in spoken discourse, dependent on instantial context, and therefore is likely to be highly exophoric (*Does it hurt **here** or **here**? Do you feel that **now**?*). If there has been previous interaction there may be shared and therefore underspecified reference.

5.5   Phase

Phase is the construct used here to link context and discourse and track relevant information (e.g. Gregory 2002). A phasal analysis maps the changing contexts of situation at different levels of delicacy based on coding and interpretation of shifts in linguistic patterns. One does this by analysing the grammatical and discourse features presented, and identifying patterns of regularity in one or more functions. Transitions between phases, when they occur, are marked by presence of both anaphoric and cataphoric reference, signalling how discourse to come is to be interpreted relative to what has already been said. We illustrate phasal patterns in Text 5.1, which is a slightly more extended fragment of the caregiver–interviewer Text 4.1 in Chapter 4.

Text 5.1 How her memory has changed

(1) IV: Can you tell me a little bit about the way her memory has changed?
(2) CG: As far as like I said the pills. She's very forgetful in those things. It's a lot of little things # um it's not so much names or faces # she doesn't tend to forget those things. She'll tell me stories of long ago which I don't know um but then again she'll tell me the same story maybe three days later and things have changed within the story.

(3) IV: umhum

(4) CG: So she's forgetting those things ah. For right now it's really just a memory loss for her.

(5) IV: What did her daughter pick up that

(6) CG: Um just repeating

(7) IV: Just repeating?

(8) CG: Repeating constant repeating. Ahm # I'm trying to think of what else ahm # I don't know you'd have to speak to her what changes she might of found in her. But I find the repeating is yeah.

(9) IV: She doesn't get sort of balled up in the kitchen or anything like that?

(10) CG: No: no: If she's concentrating on doing the dishes # she'll do the dishes. She's not jumping from one thing to the next. No I haven't seen her do that. Like ah no.

(11) IV: And she does do the dishes? That is something.

(12) CG: Yeah yeah yeap.

(13) IV: How about the paper?

(14) CG: Does she read the paper? Ah they don't generally get the paper but when they do yeah I think she picks it up. Um I've noticed too now when she she likes to read. I did take notice this one one time she had a book mark in it where she had stopped reading and I came back the next day the next morning I came back and I noticed that the bookmark had moved but it went backwards instead of forwards. Like she started more to the beginning of the book and started reading there.

Consistent selections from experiential, interactional and organization functions will correspond with a single primary phase and its associated generic situation. For example, this bit of discourse is part of a home-visit interview, the goal of which is to establish a phenomenologically realistic baseline evaluation for the patient's memory and ability to participate in activities of daily living (ADLs) (Rockwood *et al.* 2002). This situation is reflected in the medium (face-to-face semi-structured talk) and in turn and topic patterns instantiated by speech function and predicational selections. The researcher asks questions which direct topic selections – here about memory (1)–(8), household chores (9)–(12) and reading (13)–(14). For each topic, the caregiver responds, stating details that elaborate on particular abilities and deficits, and then links the observations back to the researcher's more general questions with a summary statement. There is thus an overall consistency of roles as represented in the speech function and turn-taking patterns of speakers. The discourse is also cohesive as elaborated above and there is a global coherence of ideation insofar as what is talked about is the patient's cognitive well-being as reflected in her memory and ability to stay focused. So in terms of the generic function of the situation we might treat this as a single primary phase.

Secondary phases within it are marked by the shifts in ideation from memory, to household chores, to reading. Within each of these secondary phases, we see the caregiver taking extended turns at talk, moving into a monologic mode in order to fulfil the role of 'giver of information', the speaker responsible for topic development. The organization of information within these

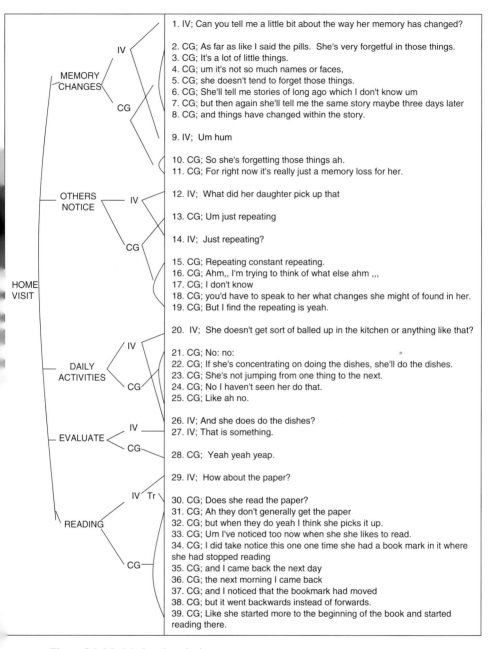

Figure 5.1 Model phasal analysis

mini-monologues also differs in that, after initial responses which are often elliptical, clauses are full (not elliptical) and there is internal cohesion as subtopics are introduced and developed. As noted, the caregiver also links specific topics back to the interviewer's questions, in effect telling the interviewer how to interpret the details offered and at the same time signalling the end of each phase. The phasal pattern of this text is laid out in Figure 5.1.

Phase is a heuristic for showing patterning of information in discourse by which we can interpret people's ongoing understanding of the context of situation relative to the topic at hand and their knowledge of the addressee. It also helps to make explicit current information, on the basis of which people infer what they should say. Such choices and inferences are typically made in terms of the speaker's cultural and situational knowledge in semantic and episodic memory systems relative to the information available to them in the current situation and whatever goals they may consciously or unconsciously be pursuing in the interaction. In this sense, phasal analyses differ from van Dijk and Kintsch's (1983) microstructural analysis of a text base primarily insofar as they are developed from an inherently multi-functional view of language so that interactional and organizational features form part of the base and can inform inferential processes (as can ideational information). Moreover, because what phasal analysis does is aid the identification of patterns in functional linguistic selections, it has the potential to show patterns that are not otherwise obvious but may nevertheless influence the sorts of inferences speakers make.

Neurocognitive disorders can interrupt or make unavailable any of the resources necessary to process texts: ability to encode, monitor, plan, select or maintain information online, access semantic or episodic memory, infer from current and contextual information what might come next, integrate currently available information with existing models, or figure out the needs of the addressee. All or any of these can be compromised, as of course can more obviously linguistic systems, and affect discourse production and comprehension. Discourse analysis lets us design studies which can help us investigate such effects. Clinical discourse analysis seeks also to contribute to understanding them.

6   Study design

6.1   Introduction

The abilities to talk, to carry on a conversation, and to tell stories are central to us; they are constitutive acts through which we create, embody and perform our selves. Conversation is ontogenetically prior to narrative, developing in tandem with language: two and three year olds can carry on simple conversations: story telling develops around four years of age, co-incident with the emergence of episodic memory and theory of mind. Because of their centrality in our social and cognitive lives, narrative and conversation tasks are increasingly used in study designs to investigate linguistic, discoursal and cognitive patterns. Narrative and conversation tasks provide naturalistic, ecologically valid data which can be used to identify both positive and negative features in discourse.

In this chapter, we explore narrative and conversation tasks for three commonly investigated areas: linguistic structure, narrative and memory. We outline issues in study design based on the models presented in previous chapters. Linguistic structure is commonly investigated in contexts of language development and in speech disorders and is central in the evaluation of speech performance in educational and clinical settings. We discuss morphology and syntax as two areas of linguistic structure in interaction with information processing load as represented in the conversation of speakers with AD and an ASD in Section 6.2. Narrative occurs universally and is important in our cognitive representation of events (van Dijk and Kintsch 1983; van Dijk 2006). Narrative tasks are used not only to investigate linguistic structure and discourse, including narrative skills, but also to evaluate cognitive abilities such as comprehension and recall. In Section 6.3 we outline classic structural definitions of narrative elements and describe the types of narrative tasks used for research in clinical settings. We then characterize the spontaneous narrative abilities of a speaker with an ASD. In Section 6.4 we examine performance of speakers with Alzheimer's disease and mild vascular dementia on controlled narrative recall tasks. In Section 6.5 we discuss the design of research questions and the corpora required to address them.

6.2   Linguistic structure: morphology and syntax

6.2.1   Morphosyntax

For clinical populations, there are two kinds of structural questions researchers
ask about morphosyntax. The first is 'what kinds of errors and/or omissions
occur in the speech of a particular group or in an individual?' The second
is 'what kinds of complexity are there in speakers' language?'. Omissions
and errors in morphological form are assessed by frequency and type. The
misuse or omission of determiners, pronouns, number, case, gender, tense,
verb auxiliaries, aspect and prepositions are standardly investigated morphological features. Morphological features are used both to track language
development in children and to identify problems for people whose speech
is affected by neural trauma or disease. In cases of trauma or disease, morphological deficits may be associated with damage or dysfunction in particular regions. However, which areas are implicated depends on the nature
of the morphological deficit so assumptions about regional specificity cannot be made with confidence without reference to the specific deficit and
diagnosis.

Inability to use morphological features appropriately can have obvious
syntactic consequences such as lack of agreement between subject and predicate (e.g. *They sings*), omission of all morphological inflections and function words (e.g. *John – store – shop* for *John went to the store to shop*) or
pragmatic consequences such as problems of cohesive reference. Argument
structure problems are also possible, either through omission of arguments or
prepositions required by a head (sometimes called 'incomplete predication'),
inclusion of arguments which are not projected by the relevant head (these are
sometimes called 'faulty predication'), or inability to use a head element either
at all or appropriately:

(1) Argument omitted: *They put the milk*
(2) Preposition omitted: *They put milk __the fridge*
(3) Wrong argument: *she ate the bread **to Sam***
(4) Predicate omitted: *she___ bread*
(5) Wrong predicate: *she **was** bread*

6.2.2   Argument structure

Argument structure problems can be a function of not knowing what arguments are required by a head, essentially not knowing (how to use) a word.
Or they can be caused by specific neurocognitive dysfunctions affecting,
singly or in combination, phonological, syntactic and semantic systems. For
instance, while the nature and causes of these differences are not yet clear

(and indeed are hotly debated), a number of studies suggest that agrammatic and fluent aphasics differ in their predicate–argument structure abilities from normal speakers and from each other. Agrammatic aphasics appear to have difficulty with non-canonical dependency relations but are comparatively able to process argument roles in canonic positions (see Drai and Grodzinsky 2006a; 2006b for meta-analysis of data for agrammatic aphasia). Fluent aphasics on the other hand are apparently more impaired in the interpretation of argument roles (Shapiro *et al.* 1993). (For the range of views in this area, see, for instance: Bird *et al.* 2000; Shapiro and Caramazza 2000; Collina *et al.* 2001; Webster *et al.* 2001; Druks 2002 for review; Black and Chiat 2003; Thompson 2003; Lee and Thompson 2004; Nankano and Blumstein 2004.)

Alternatively, argument structure problems may occur as a consequence of information processing load. We use 'information processing load' to refer to situations in which there is evidence that a speaker is struggling to access, maintain and/or monitor information online. We evaluate information load in terms of signs of processing difficulty presented by the speaker: for instance, a speaker who shows frequent hesitation, long pauses, false starts and incomplete utterances will be presumed to be experiencing some difficulty in discourse production. In such contexts, argument structure problems are also likely to occur as speakers fail to monitor, or cannot access lexical selections, or lack working memory capacity to complete their utterances. Most speakers will be familiar with how multi-tasking and fatigue can affect their own and/or others' discourse so that cognitively undemanding tasks can become challenging, discourse less coherent, and well-known lexis unavailable.

Particular neurocognitive disorders may influence the experience of information load, resulting in patterns associated with the dysfunction. In AD for instance, information processing load is partly associated with verbal working memory deficits (e.g. Kemper *et al.* 2001b). This may result in incomplete sentences, where the speaker begins a sentence and stops part way through because they cannot retrieve lexis, have forgotten what they meant to say, are interrupted, or are distracted by new information as in Example (6).

(6) Incomplete sentence:

IV: = would would that be a hope for you uh, that you would be able to uhm, go and do
      things like you used to be able to do, around the farm
P: yeah, *there's maybe a few things that,
IV: mhmm
CG: and be able to go and do things without, me sort of being there to help him, and
      show him what to do and what not to do

In *They put the milk __, *she ate the bread **to Sam**, the speaker produces sentences as though they were complete, but they lack an argument or include an inappropriate one. In Example (6) above, the patient who has AD just stops part way through the utterance and pauses. This may be an effect of working memory deficit and/or other systems since the structure that he begins is complex, requiring a dependent clause complement for the *that* which he does not supply. Other speakers wait and when he doesn't complete his turn they take the floor. If the patient started again and corrected or completed the utterance, it would be treated as a false start as in Example (7):

(7) False start:
It was um, it sounded like, i, it was a new, re- recent one.

False starts appear to signal planning problems, but the repairs indicate that the speaker is monitoring and so does successfully complete the utterance. Thus, information load processing problems can arise from multiple causes but do tend to be overtly marked by features such as hesitation, false start and incomplete utterances. The latter can of course affect argument structure. Information processing load also increases with increases in grammatical complexity (e.g. Stowe *et al.* 1995; 1998; Caplan *et al.* 2001; Michael *et al.* 2001).

The simplest measures of **morphosyntactic complexity and diversity** assess presence or absence of simple or complex units and their frequencies expressed as proportions of some relevant constituent or text. Thus, one can look at the proportion of morphologically complex words in a text sample according to length. Length can be specified by number of words, clauses, predications, utterances or turns. It is also valuable to record time of speaking. Measures of syntactic complexity are evaluated in the same domains, and assess the number of words per clause, the number of predications per clause or sentence, or the number of simple versus complex and/or compound clauses per sentence. Syntactic complexity evaluations may also address types of clause constructions and so refer to embedding of clauses functioning within the structure of other clauses or phrases, their distribution to the left or right (where left embedding is more complex than right), and dependency relations in passive, relative, unaccusative and WH constructions which entail processing arguments or adjuncts in non-canonical positions relative to their traces. Thus, although the clauses in Examples (8a) and (8b) are predicationally similar, (8a) is simpler than (8b) because (8a) consists of two independent clauses coordinated with the alternative conjunction *but* whereas in (8b) the predications in the first independent clause of (8a) are relativized within the subject noun phrase of the main clause [[*Sam* [$_{RELATIVE\ CLAUSE}$]] *eats heaps of chocolate every day*].

(8) a. Max says Sam is supposed to be on a diet but he eats heaps of chocolate every day
    b. Sam_i, who_i Max says t_i is supposed to be on a diet, eats heaps of chocolate every day

The relative clause requires that *Sam* and *who* be co-referential with the relative gap t_i and that *Sam* be kept in working memory until the verb of the main clause (*eats*) occurs. Both the working memory demands and the co-reference demands make (8b) more complex and so more challenging to process. While (8b) is demonstrably more complex than (8a) and increased complexity generally has the effect of slowing processing speed (Kemper and Herman 2006), it is worth noting that 'not all complexity is equal'. Cognitively healthy older speakers are more likely to produce (8a) than (8b) (Kemper *et al.* 2001a), but may be as accurate, if slower, than younger speakers in processing (Saxton *et al.* 2001; Grossman 2002). (But see Kemper and Herman (2006) where older speakers made more efforts because of effects of increased memory load and increased syntactic complexity.) An AD speaker might have serious difficulties with (8b) presumably because of the working memory demands, but would process the active and passive in Examples (9a) and (9b) similarly (Almor *et al.* 1999). However, for an agrammatic aphasic speaker, (9b) might be challenging because of its non-canonical presentation (e.g. Shapiro *et al.* 1993; Thompson 2003), though whether the grammatical structure itself or the need to maintain grammatical information online for processing is the real source of the problem is currently unresolved (see Stowe *et al.* 2005 for discussion).

(9) a. The guests devoured all the food in the first hour
     b. All the food$_i$ was devoured t_i by the guests in the first hour

Other factors which may increase clause complexity include textual re-ordering for focus and prominence with resources such as preposing, postposing, cleft formation and topicalization which were illustrated in Chapter 4. These structures increase syntactic complexity; however, in normal speakers they also appear to increase, rather than reduce, processing efficiency for prominent elements (e.g. Sturt *et al.* 2004; Sandford *et al.* 2005).

Lexical density and richness may also affect information processing. Lexical density in a discourse is evaluated by averaging the number of lexical (as opposed to form) words per clause in samples of a specified length (Halliday 1987; 1989; Bucks *et al.* 2000). Lexical richness is evaluated similarly but in terms of the number of lexical items relative to other words. A Type–Token Ratio (TTR) is the most commonly used formula for evaluating lexical richness. TTR is the total vocabulary words V as a ratio of the total number of words in N. Thus, TTR $= V/N$, where a higher value for V reflects a richer (more varied) vocabulary. A limitation of TTR is that it is sensitive to length. Brunet's Index is a length insensitive version of TTR. Brunet's Index W is calculated as $W = N^{V-0.165}$. The value for W is the index, lower values are richer (Brunet 1978; Bucks *et al.* 2000). Finally, there is the notion of idea density which evaluates the amount of information in a discourse in terms of the average number of propositions per ten words in a specified sample (Kintsch and

Keenan 1973; Small *et al.* 2000; Kemper *et al.* 2001) and processing capacity (Kemper and Sumner 2001). Syntactic complexity and lexical density are modelled in Chapter 7.

Morphosyntactic features can be investigated either through discourse tasks, or through sentence completion tasks which require participants to supply correct forms or to correct errors. This we illustrate with conversational text between an interviewer and a young man with an Autism Spectrum Disorder. The first topic is bowling, the second is a film.

Text 6.1 Bowling

(1) CHI: I'm on a bowling team.
(2) RES: oh I don't know much about bowling.
(3) RES: I haven't bowled a lot.
(4) CHI: ((laughs))
(5) CHI: this is about this is about five-pin we do.
(6) CHI: I used # I used to even bowl ten-pin too.
(7) RES: uhhuh?
(8) CHI: I was pretty good at ten-pin.
(9) CHI: I'm also pretty good at five-pin too as well.
(10) RES: good.
(11) RES: how many are on a team in bowling?
(12) CHI: um I'd say about five or five or six I would say.
(13) RES: umhum?
(14) CHI: five or six.
(15) RES: yeah.
(16) CHI: well sometimes if there's a smaller team there's four is an exception too as well.

The young man is very responsive. He chuckles when the interviewer says she knows little about bowling. He tries to inform her about the topic, answering her questions with careful detail, and taking turns appropriately. When he is uncertain, he uses hedges appropriately as in *um I'd say about five or five or six I would say* (12). His use of *I'd say* and *about* indicate uncertainty about the number of players, as does his presentation of alternative numbers (*or five or six*). However, the way he organizes his text here and later shows some difficulties in information processing, which he tries to compensate for by adding redundant information. Here, he repeats the modalization *I would say* in final position. Other information processing features are reflected in common dysfluencies such as false starts (*I used, I used* (6)), and hesitation markers (*um*).

There are also problems with two of his morphosyntactic constructions. In lines (5) and (16) he completes a predication successfully but then adds predicative content that creates an error as in *well sometimes if there's a smaller team there's four is an exception too as well* (16). Here there are three possible interpretations. In one reading, *is an exception too as well* appears without an external argument (there is no subject for the verb *is*). Alternatively, *four* can be interpreted as the subject of *is* in which case we could say the existential clause is incomplete (has no predicative complement), or that *four is an exception too as well* is the predicative complement of the existential clause in which case we might suppose that a relative clause was intended. There is also redundant repetition, most obviously in the two occurrences of *too as well* (9, 16), *five or six* (12, 14), and *I would say* (12). Normally, intonation would disambiguate a structure like this but this speaker structures information using fewer tone groups: *there's four is an exception too as well* is spoken as a single tone group (de Villiers *et al.* 2006).

Text 6.2 Transvestites

(1) CHI: <it's> [<] about these three men that dress up as females.
(2) CHI: they're like um.
(3) CHI: what do they call them?
(4) CHI: they call # transvestites.
(5) CHI: that's what <they're called> [>].
(6) RES: <uhhuh> [<]?
(7) CHI: sexual transvestite.

In Text 6.2, there is a missing argument (*they call # transvestites* (4)). *Sexual transvestite* (7) lacks number agreement with its apparent antecedent (*they* in *they are called transvestites*). In isolation one might conclude that the speaker has difficulty with linguistic structures. However, examination of a 1,000 word sample of his conversation suggests that problems of argument structure and agreement are infrequent. There are seven including the four described here: one sentence has added predicative content; there is one missing relative pronoun and one wrong preposition. However, problems associated with information processing and perhaps lexical retrieval are pervasive. This can be shown by giving the ratios of the number of words used to construct complete predications as a proportion of the total number of words. The rest of the words are processing features such as false starts, repetitions, ums and uhs. Such features occur in all spoken discourse relative to the difficulty the speaker experiences in text production (Clark and Wasow 1998). However, the frequency of features here, 254/1000, approximately 25% of the speech, is unusual. Here, in examples (10–11), we see the speaker struggling:

(10) there's it also delivers to to places in Saint Catherine's as well and also the um and also places like in um like s like international places like Germany and England and stuff like that.

(11) and then and then we then we work then we work um something like uh nine-thirty to nine-thirty to twelve.

In (12), the speaker actually refers to his own word finding (fluency) and cognitive processing difficulties.

(12) um.
      guess to s uh sort sort out um sort out uh mail and stuff.
      put them into little um # categories and stuff.
      and it's um # and uh um #.
      well # it's hard to think now.
      …
      god I forgot all these machine names what they've called them
      …
      I forget what they call them
      …
      I found that I find those names sort of a bit greek to me sometimes
      … uh I'm trying to think now
      … I'm trying to think of it.

The features of repetition, false starts and hesitation fillers clearly reflect processing difficulties which may involve planning, monitoring, retrieval and/or flexibility. Those morphosyntactic problems that do appear may be an effect of such processing difficulties and simultaneously reflect the speaker's attempts to compensate for them. His efforts to provide accurate and detailed information are characteristic of ASDs and the challenges he faces are in some senses constructed by the tension between his attempt to give detail and his ability to retrieve appropriate lexical items. It is possible, given this, that some apparent grammatical 'errors' are in fact other kinds of constructions serving different discourse functions. For instance, the lack of agreement cited for Text 6.2 (*transvestites…transvestite*) may be serving a textual function of 'recap', comparable to the other repetitions such as *too as well*.

It may of course also be the case that this speaker's processing difficulties are simply signs of fatigue or distraction in the interview situation. Collecting more data from a range of different situations at different times would allow one to evaluate the extent to which such features are constant in his discourse, or occur only in specific situations. If it were established that these features are constant in his discourse, that would be indicative of information processing load difficulties, the specifics of which could then be investigated.

6.3   Narrative

Narrative as distinct from other generic text types such as dialogue or report has a number of conventional features. Classic descriptions (e.g. Propp 1928; Labov and Waletsky 1967; Barthes 1968) identify:

• title (*now I'm going to tell about the time …*);

Table 6.1. *Narrative performance features*

Formal elements of narrative structure	Other commonly considered aspects	Other possible considerations
Title	Themes	Lexical density
Setting/orientation	Evaluation and causation	Narrative voice
Participant(s)	Character	Syntactic complexity
Events	Cohesion and coherence	Fore- and backgrounding
Initiating event	Reported speech	Prosodic organization
Complicating event	Episodes	
Resolution	Gist/recall	
Coda	Morphosyntactic features	

- setting/orientation (time, place, participants);
- events (including an initiating event and at least one complicating event – the complicating event is surprising in some way and requires a protagonist to act);
- resolution (an action or event which alters the situation created by the complicating event);
- coda (a comment on narrative significance and/or termination).

Most elements may be omitted but the complicating event sequence is defining of narrative: it is what makes a story a story rather than, say, a simple report. Narratives are commonly evaluated both in terms of the presence, absence or accuracy of story elements, and also in terms of themes, evaluation, characterization of attitudes, cohesion and coherence. Narratives may also be used to assess morphosyntactic features, lexical density, recall, gist formation, fore- and backgrounding and prosodic organization. Table 6.1 summarizes features used to evaluate narrative performance.

Narratives may be spontaneous or they may be elicited through a narrative task. A common task is picture description, where pictures without texts are used to elicit narrative discourse. Picture description as study design is informative about language organization and comprehension and has the virtue of controlling topics of speech. However, picture description does not tell you about the effects of memory loss in the discourse of patients with Alzheimer's, nor about interactive conversational skills of people with autism. Moreover, as a consequence of controlled topic selection, the information picture description can provide about topic management and development is limited in any group (Duong *et al.* 2005). Other common tasks include narrative recall tasks and cued narratives (e.g. *what's the most exciting/frightening thing that ever happened to you?*). Conversational tasks, interviews, semi-structured interviews and/or spontaneous conversations may be examined for spontaneous narratives. (Spontaneous conversations can be acquired by, for instance, giving

.. Narrative task scale

	Controlled	Prompted	Spontaneous
ɪo demand on memory	Picture description, cartoons puppets, films	Cued narrative (semantic, episodic, prospective)	
Maximum demand on memory	Read aloud, read to self		Non-elicited narrative occurring spontaneously in conversation

participants something to do and recording the conversation that occurs while they are doing it, or by asking about something.)

One could think of narrative tasks on a graded scale with controlled elicitation using story stimuli and spontaneously occurring narratives on opposite ends. Picture description requires speakers to construct a narrative sequence from supplied material. It controls for topic, participants and event sequence but other elements are determined by the speaker. There is no demand on memory. Films similarly require speakers to encode and recall event sequences from supplied visual and auditory representation. They control for topic, participants and event sequence. Other elements are determined by speakers and demand on memory is quite high. Cued narrative controls for topic but not event sequences unless the cue is for semantic events (socially known, public/historical events). That is, cues can be focused to place demands on episodic, semantic or prospective memory (see Chapter 2 for definitions). Read aloud or read-to-self recall tasks may assess comprehension, verbatim and/or gist recall of a story. They are the most controlled narrative tasks. Table 6.2 summarizes narrative tasks on two dimensions: memory demands and speaker production demands.

Evaluation of narrative can include not only accuracy relative to story elements and language features as described above, but also narrative patterns associated with particular disorders. For instance, ASD speakers may spontaneously offer narratives about subjects of particular interest to them.

Text 6.3: Creature from the Blue Lagoon
This is a story retell of a film, the original title of which was 'Creature from the black lagoon'. The speaker has retitled it 'The Blue Lagoon', although he refers to the 'black lagoon' as the origin of the monster.

(1) CHI: I made it.
(2) RES: what is it?

(3) CHI: ever seen The Blue Lagoon?

(4) RES: um: I don't remember if I have.

(5) RES: I don't think so.

(6) CHI: uh the monster that comes from the black lagoon.

(7) CHI: and he has webbed fingers and webbed toes and webbed things.

(8) CHI: and this is supposed to be his hand.

(9) RES: what's the story about?

(10) CHI: um: these explorers go out into the rainforest.

(11) CHI: and they find fossils of # of the the # the monster from the black lagoon.

(12) RES: umhum?

(13) CHI: they find clay mo they find skeletons and stuff f from the.

(14) CHI: and they find one that's living still that was caught in ice.

(15) RES: and then what happens?

(16) CHI: and they uh killed all of them.

(17) CHI: they all get killed.

(18) CHI: and then there's number two.

(19) CHI: and then they had to go catch er the thing.

(20) CHI: and bring it back to America.

(21) CHI: and then he tries to kidnap a beautiful woman.

(22) RES: does it succeed?

(23) CHI: no.

(24) CHI: he gets shot.

(25) CHI: and he falls into a a lake.

(26) RES: uh.

(27) CHI: and then uh # in number three they go down there.

(28) CHI: and uh they accidentally torched him.

(29) CHI: and uh he and then they wrapped him up like a mummy.

(30) CHI: and uh done surgery and stuff.

(31) CHI: and uh he transformed into a kinda like a man.

(32) RES: hm.

(33) CHI: but still he was an amphibian.

(34) RES: umhum.

(35) CHI: they put one of those things that people get put in their throats so then they can breath.

(36) RES: oh right.

(37) RES: umhum.

(38) RES: they usually talk funny after that don't they?

(39) CHI: they don't he doesn't talk at all.

(40) CHI: ((laughs))

(41) RES: no?

(42) CHI: and then they put clothes on him.

(43) RES: umhum?

(44) CHI: and then wa runs away.

(45) CHI: and breathes in the swampy area.

(46) RES: do you like movies like that?

(47) CHI: umhum.

(48) RES: with monsters and things?

(49) CHI: that's right.

In Text 6.3, *Creature from the Blue Lagoon* a young man with an ASD is asked about a film and responds with real enthusiasm, giving plot summaries for the original (*Creature from the Black Lagoon*) and two sequels. He initiates the topic as a response to the researcher's question about a model he has made of the creature's hand. When asked what the story is about, he supplies all three plot summaries, with prompting only for resolving events. For the first one, he gives the setting and participants, and the event sequence including the complicating event (*they find one that's living still that was caught in ice*) and, when asked, supplies the resolving event (*they uh killed all of them*). He volunteers a title in *and then there's number two* (18) and gives the initiating event (*go catch thing and bring it back to America*), complicating event (*thing tries to kidnap a beautiful woman*) and, with a prompt (*does it succeed?*), he offers the resolution (*no he gets shot and he falls into a lake*). Similarly, in the third story he offers a title (*and then in number three they go down there*), supplies initiating (*go there, accidentally torch him*) and complicating events – those surrounding the transformation of the creature through surgery into something *kind of like a man, but still ... an amphibian* (31–33), who when clothed runs away back to the swamp. In the third story, the resolution is not stated. The only element of evaluation of the film, apart from his very evident interest, occurs when the researcher asks:

(13) RES: do you like movies like that?
    CHI: umhum.
    RES: with monsters and things?
    CHI: that's right.

What we see here then is a well-formed set of narratives, with conventional narrative elements, spontaneously produced with minimal prompting. The absence of evaluative comments and resolving events is perhaps part of a disorder specific pattern.

For instance, there is a lack of attention to the movie's emotional elements in the young man's narratives. He never mentions that the creature loves the woman in the film. He also does not say that the creature dies at the end, an implied outcome that is a key dramatic element of the movie. The creature is unable to survive in the water because, following his operation, his lungs rapidly evolved and he lost his gills. Dramatic music and contextual clues (proceeding directly to the ocean after his escape as he has done repeatedly before; standing longingly by the water's edge; a slow but steady march into the water) inform the audience of the unfortunate creature's fate. The speaker does not appear to make use of these clues of context to infer the story's outcome or the mental state of the creature at the end of the film. Failure to use contextual clues to interpret and predict behaviour is a characteristic feature of ASDs (Baron-Cohen 1995; Frith 2003).

6.4   Narrative tasks designed to investigate memory

In contrast with spontaneously produced narratives occurring in conversation or interview, some narrative tasks may be designed to make specific demands on memory. Participants are read or asked to read short narratives and to remember them as they will be asked to repeat them verbatim. Repetitions can occur immediately or after a delay (the latter task is typically referred to as a delayed recall task). The sample texts below are examples of delayed recall of a single narrative. The recall task in the study was the WMS III, logical memory (Weschsler 1997). The stories have been modified here to protect the source narrative. The first (Text 6.4) is produced by a participant with a diagnosis of subcortical ischemic vascular disease (SIVD), and mild vascular dementia (VaD). Texts 6.5 and 6.6 are produced by speakers with clinical diagnoses of mild AD. The speaker of the fourth text (Text 6.7) is an older adult with no cognitive impairment. These texts are from a small study which evaluated gist, verbatim recall, confabulation and modalization on narrative recall tasks for participants with diagnoses of mild AD, mild vascular dementia (VaD), and older adults with no cognitive impairment (NCI) (Klages 2006; Asp *et al.* unpublished[1]). Verbatim recall and confabulation distinguished the participants with mild VaD from participants with mild AD. AD participants confabulated more and had poorer verbatim recall than VaD participants on two out of three repeats. VaD and AD participants did not differ significantly from each other on any neuropsychological or cognitive measure.

Text 6.4 Delayed recall (SIVD)

(1) P: // the what//
(2) IV: the second story //and start at the beginning//
(3) P: // the second story// what was it about//
(4) IV: The story was about a road report
(5) P: //oh yes// this chap was uh getting to ready uh to go out // around breakfast time// and he listened to the uh the uh news the road report// there had been a big accident and whatever whatever// so he changed his plans// and he put away the keys // and he went into the yard // and he uh worked // and worked in the garden//

In Text 6.4 the speaker provides a very accurate gist based on the narrative event structure, including orientation (*this chap was uh getting to ready uh to go out around breakfast time*), initiating (*and he listened to the uh the uh news the road report*), complicating (*there had been a big accident and whatever whatever*) and resolving events (*so he changed his plans and he put away the keys and he went into the yard // and he uh worked // and worked in the garden*). However, there is limited detail supplied about participants and circumstances. For instance, the speaker uses indefinite and general references as in *the chap* instead of a proper name, *around breakfast time* instead of the actual time and *whatever whatever* instead of the accident details. The absence of lexical specificity is characteristic of the delayed recall performance of the SIVD participants. Nevertheless, 29% of the lexical items were repeated verbatim from the source narrative and his excellent gist contrasts markedly with that produced by the speaker of Text 6.5.

Text 6.5 Delayed recall (AD)

(1) P: // what was the second story//.
(2) IV: the story was about a road report
(3) P: // oh yes// can't remember it dear//
(4) IV: any little detail?
(5) P: //aah //had there been an accident//
(6) IV: umhum
(7) P: // yeah// a crash//
(8) IV: ye
(9) P: // (I) don't know anything else// (accident) (15)//1 can't think//
(10) IV: **ok**
(11) P: //oh you poor thing//do you have many like me//
(12) IV: oh, you're doing fine
(13) P: ((laughs))
(14) IV: you're doing your best. [Instructions]
(15) P: oh, I see. that's good

The only event that the speaker recalls is the complicating event *had been an accident* and this is a question. *Accident* and *crash* are also the only words repeated verbatim. The speaker is very aware of her recall difficulties, saying that she can't remember, and doesn't know anything else. She also comments on her cognitive state (*I can't think*) and appears to believe her performance is cause for commiseration with the interviewer (*oh you poor dear. Do you have many like me?*). So while her recall is very limited, her awareness of deficit and perception of it as burdensome is acute.

The third text (Text 6.6) is also produced by a speaker with mild AD. He is similar to the second speaker in that he comments directly on his performance (*I can't word it word for word*) and his cognitive ability (*there's no way the old brain'll*). He differs in that his delayed recall is a significantly more detailed gist (similar to the one produced in Text 6.4), but much of the detail is confabulated.

Text 6.6 Delayed recall (AD)

(1) P: // the second story was the fella who got up at dawn to go on a trip// fishing// and the road report came on// and gave him a bad accident report// an that there'd been a huge pile up, and roads closed and traffic all rerouted// and that was the advisory to people not to go out// and he did// and it was a very disastrous day// that's what I got out of it//(laughter)//1 but that's about the gist of the whole story//

(2) IV: (laughter) yeah
(3) P: // I can't word it word for word//
(4) IV: ok
(5) P: // there's no way the brain'll ()//
(6) IV: Not a problem. Just what you can remember.

Story elements are judged to be confabulated when processes, participants or circumstances (or entire predications) which are intended to represent story elements are reported but are not present, nor synonymous, with the control narrative. This speaker confabulates entire predications representative of story elements. Specifically, the setting (*the second story was the fella who got up at dawn to go on a trip fishing*) and an added element of the complicating event (*that was the advisory to people not to go out*) as well as the resolving event (*and he did*) are all confabulated. The speaker also offers a narrative coda (*and that was a very disastrous day for him*) which, though potentially coherent with his version, has no relationship to the control narrative. In the control narrative there is no mention of a fishing trip or an advisory for people not to go out, although this is a reasonable inference to draw from a major accident report. The setting is nine, not dawn, and the participant stayed at home. The only two elements that are accurately represented from the control narrative are the initiating (getting ready to go out) and the complicating event (the bad accident report). 17% of lexical items are repeated verbatim from the source narrative.

There are three types of confabulation recognized (Kern *et al.* 1992; Dalla Barba *et al.* 1999). The first is error of recall as in mistakenly asserting that one has heard something from an individual when in fact it was on a news broadcast. The second type is sometimes referred to as 'fantastic'. Typically, it involves statements about personal past which are entirely imaginary (and often grandiose). The third type of confabulation involves replacing one set of experiences or reports with others (Berlyne 1972; Kopelman 1987). The examples in Text 6.6 appear to be largely of this type. It is also worth noting that the speaker assesses his performance as personal *that's what I got out of it* and appears unaware of the confabulated elements *but that's about the gist of the whole story.*

The amount of confabulation can be straightforwardly modelled in narrative recall tasks as counts of words referring to processes, participants or circumstances which are intended to represent story elements but are not present in the control narrative, nor synonymous with the control narrative. All words are counted when the entire predication is confabulatory: *Uncle Thomas got up at dawn to go fishing* as a representation of a story in which no such event or participant occurs counts as 9 words. *He heard it on the television* in a story where the participant has heard something on the radio counts as 1 (confabulation of source *television* for *radio*).

Verbatim recall	Narrative recall (read or listen to a story)	Match to control (percentage of words repeated verbatim)
Gist	Narrative recall (read or listen to a story, watch a film etc.)	1) Percentage of story elements accurately repeated 2) Predicational analysis of percentage of participants, events and circumstances accurately repeated
Confabulation	Narrative recall (as above)	Match to control (word counts and/or gist elements)
	Report of activities	Check with caregiver

Figure 6.1 Evaluating confabulation, gist and verbatim recall.

The last delayed recall sample (Text 6.7) is produced by an older adult with no cognitive impairment. The text differs markedly from all others not only in the accuracy of gist recall but in the amount of participant and circumstance information incorporated verbatim from the control narrative.

Text 6.7 Delayed recall (No cognitive impairment)

(1) P: //It was nine o'clock on a Saturday morning// and Gino Costa was, getting ready to go to market// and listening to the radio// and the program was interrupted by a road report //to say there had been a multi-vehicle accident on the main highway // the highway was closed to outbound traffic, and secondary routes were at a crawl // so Gino decided he wouldn't go to the market // he put away his keys // and he went out to work in the garden//
(2) IV: um terrific

This speaker reproduces a verbatim account, including all story elements and high lexical specificity (52% of lexical items from the source narrative). In the first two repeats, the speaker even reproduces the intonation patterns occurring in the read-aloud original story. We might call repetition of intonation 'prosodic verbatim'. None of the other speakers represented does this.

What we have done here is illustrate different kinds of narratives, taking examples from opposite poles of the Narrative Tasks Scale. We looked at a speaker who has an ASD who produced well-formed narratives spontaneously, highlighting the role of clinical discourse analysis in looking at abilities as well as deficits. We then showed how performance can vary on a single narrative delayed recall task. The speaker with no cognitive impairment differs from the speakers with AD/VaD both in accurate production of story elements and verbatim lexical recall. This is unsurprising given the diagnoses. AD and VaD participants differ from each other in that the VaD speaker produces a very good gist, while gist is poor in the AD participants, verbatim lexical recall minimal and confabulation high. Figure 6.1 summarizes the features investigated, the sort of tasks that may be used to investigate them, and possible ways of evaluating the results.

6.5   Designing research questions

Research questions can be narrowly targeted or open ended and clinical discourse analysis may play a role in either case. When addressing a clinical group whose discourse patterns are not well established or described in the existing literature, a first step would be to develop full characterizations of a representative sample of texts produced by speakers diagnosed with the disorder in question. This step may seem extravagant insofar as full characterizations take time. However, the initial full characterization of sample texts functions rather like taking a medical history, and can inform the process of developing research questions and study designs that focus on particular diagnostic groups. In Table 6.3 we give four sample research questions and possible study designs, and indicate some positive and negative features associated with each design.

These study designs illustrate that there are different ways to address specific research questions and that depending on the nature of the pathology and the research questions being asked, study designs will be more or less structured. Semi-structured tasks are less natural, but can be thought of in relation to context of situation and functional varieties, determining what is relevant given the nature of the disorder. The choice of register and context of situation should be informed by the nature of the pathology.

Decisions also must be made about whether or not a control group is needed and if so what kind(s) of controls are most suitable. A variety of statistical methods (e.g. regression, analysis of variance, chi-square) may be used. Bridging the gap between qualitative approaches to discourse analysis and research which uses statistical methods may present an initial hurdle for some humanities researchers. Statistical methods books in the health sciences may be consulted, but a team-based approach or working with statistical consultants can also reduce the divide.

6.6   Corpora design

Any discourse study requires the development of some sort of corpus. In its simplest sense, a corpus is a collection of language samples. Corpus-based studies of discourse skills present comparable sampling issues of power as occur in epidemiological studies. Thus, an issue that clinical discourse analysts

Table 6.3. *Four research questions with* pros *and* cons *of study designs*

Research questions	Approaches to study design	Pros	Cons
1. Is pedantic speaking characteristic of all subgroups within the autism spectrum?	Unstructured or semi-structured conversation with inter-rater reliability on rating pedantic speech in different subgroups and/or identify specific linguistic characteristics of pedantic speech and code in different subgroups	– quite naturalistic, spontaneous – ecological validity – can use measures (e.g. lexical density) for other questions – more detail	– large number of participants needed – hard to measure degree replicably – hard to compare patterns with other disorders – costly for coding and can't be used by clinicians as a rating tool
	Control group is optional since the question addresses variation within the autism spectrum	– measures may have known neurocognitive bases	
2. Do people with ASDs express attitude and evaluation comparatively less than a control group?	Elicit favourite topics in interview (semi-structured or open question/with family input) or	– may be informative for developing interventions for individuals	– topic not controlled – heterogeneous data – requires sophisticated coding and analysis
	Elicit narratives using picture book stimulus. Look for presence or absence of evaluation of narrative in discourse + control group	– picture description is a well-established elicitation method – controlled for topic – can look at particulars of evaluation without distraction	– less informative about recurring individual behaviour – less naturalistic
3. Do low lexical density and syntactic complexity scores correlate with high/low modalization values in AD?	1000 word samples from variety of discourse types Code for patterns + control group	– small corpus – naturalistic – some results may be scalable	– data requires sophisticated coding and analysis
4. Is confabulation associated with disease phase in AD?	Narrative recall or	– controlled – simple scoring	

Table 6.3. (*cont.*)

Research questions	Approaches to study design	Pros	Cons
	Episodic memory task (e.g. 'what did you do last weekend')	– may target personal state/experience more directly – may be informative for developing interventions for individuals	– needs a greater number of participants – heterogeneity of data – sophisticated coding and analysis

will need to be concerned with is sampling size, both for the number of partici-pants and the amount of discourse produced by each participant, relative to the research questions being asked.

The number of participants needed varies, ranging from a single participant case study or small group case study to large groups. Limitations imposed by time demands of data transcription and analyses can be issues if the aim is full characterization. Coding and analysis, even using good programmes, take time. In the case of smaller case and group studies, it is simplest if those small groups are clinically both very well defined and very homogeneous since it then becomes possible to see whether participants with similar diagnoses and demographic profiles exhibit the behaviour. (This of course, though, begs questions as to whether other participants with other profiles behave similarly. It also presents the rare case from the clinician's perspective, where heteroge-neity is the norm.)

The amount of text needed can also vary depending on research questions. A standard thousand-word sample may be adequate to provide information about grammatical structures for speakers, but is unlikely to provide information about specific highly salient features of discourse which may be characteristic but comparatively rare. For example, it is widely recognized that people with autism are known to be literal, including having difficulty in both producing and understanding metaphor (Frith 2003). But the frequency with which such cases arise is not sufficient to ensure an occurrence of difficulty with metaphor or other figurative language in any given task. The rare case is only likely to be observable in corpora when there are large amounts of data. Thus, a thousand-word sample is suitable for observing some language features. Longer sam-ples may be necessary for discourse features and spontaneous performance. If specific genres are addressed (e.g. narrative), there is a possibility for shorter sampling. Other important considerations in corpora design are whether to

Table 6.4. *Research design and text type*

Type of analysis	Text type	Considerations
Cohesion analysis	100 sentences from a speaker (McKenna and Oh 2005)	Requires continuous prose – tasks such as prompted narrative, story retell and picture description could be used
Grammatical structures and/or fluency	1,000 word sample (Bucks *et al.* 2000)	Prompted narratives or spontaneous conversation can be used for continuous sample
	15 independent clauses from 2 different sections of an individual's text, or 30 clauses where texts are collected from multiple settings (Rochester and Martin 1979)	The advantage of this type of sampling is that a speaker's discourse can be characterized in different registers. More clauses will be necessary for some questions.
Type token ratios	100 words from at least 3 different parts of a speaker's discourse, or 350 word samples (Hess *et al.* 1986), or 250 words segmented into 10 samples (Bradac 1988)	Widely used as measures of lexical density, although requires attention to contexts of use for representative sampling, and has been shown to be less stable and sensitive than other measures. (See e.g. Watkins *et al.* 1995; Owen and Leonard 2002; Chipere *et al.* 2004 for discussion and alternatives.)
Metaphor, homograph or other comprehension	Task specific samples (Happé 1997)	– Allows investigation of particular areas of discourse comprehension and production, including rare phenomena – Difficulty can be an issue relative to the disorder being investigated – Samples from multiple language varieties may be required where evaluation (scoring) depends on pronunciation
Discourse features and spontaneous speech	Longer samples in multiple settings (Fine 2006)	Registerial variety required for fuller characterization and generalizability of findings
	Specified parameters for full characterization	Prompted, structured, semi-structured and spontaneous spoken and written discourse in a range of generic situation types: – with family – with peers – with schoolmates – in jobs – in the clinic – in typical situations for individuals – narratives – conversations Cross-sectional studies are useful for developing a characterization and for specific questions. Looking at change over time requires longitudinal studies.

look at different time periods (to investigate stability and change) and whether to collect data from multiple contexts for full characterization and variation.

It is usually possible to design corpora for specific questions. In Table 6.4 we suggest some sampling considerations in relation to areas of inquiry and text types. There are corpus linguistic techniques and technologies, including corpus collection software (for audio and video), standard concordancing and search tools, parsers, taggers, tools for data extraction and phonetic and prosodic analyses and speech-to-text software for transcription. These make the development of disorder specific corpora more than feasible. In addition to specialized corpora developed to investigate particular questions or disorders, it is also invaluable to have access to corpora which are broadly representative of the speech community at large. Such corpora can inform investigators about normative patterns and be resources for checking hunches both about what is typical and what may be rare for the speech community.

7   Differential diagnosis and monitoring

7.1   Introduction

We noted in Chapter 1 that experts have often internalized patterns of discourse behaviour characteristic of neurological disorders and their phases which inform their clinical judgements. However, these internalized patterns may not be explicitly recognized and consequently appear as 'intuitive' responses. Just as people can often recognize regional or social dialect variation without being able to say precisely what it is they recognize, so the patterns informing clinicians' impressions may not be explicit. Descriptions of discourse can make experts' tacit knowledge about discourse patterns associated with diagnostic groups explicit, in the same way that descriptions of dialect variation can aid dialect recognition. Such descriptions can also be used to model characteristic patterns for healthcare workers and families who may not have experts' breadth of experience.

Beyond explicitness, one role of clinical discourse analysis is to add tools to existing diagnostic resources where diagnosis is still a clinical decision. Another is to provide characterizations for diagnostic categories which are under-investigated. These may help with diagnostic clarification and planning for treatment. A third role for description of discourse is to track change over time both intra-individually and for group applications. There is potential for monitoring developmental and degenerative processes and tracking responses to treatments and interventions. There is also a fourth role which is to improve understanding of relationships between everyday discourse behaviours and neurocognitive function.

In relation to these roles, in this chapter we model study designs which address discourse correlates of diagnoses and monitoring. Except where primary signs and symptoms of neurocognitive dysfunction are linguistic, descriptions of discourse patterns in these contexts are neither abundant nor widely available. There is thus an a priori value in the descriptions as descriptions. They may also be used to develop rating scales for assessing categorical and continuous variations and, in conjunction with other assessments, to improve understanding of the neurophysiology of disorders and the effects of treatment and intervention.

7.2   Pedantic speech in ASDs

Pedantic speech is a recognized characteristic of ASDs (Ghaziuddin and Gerstein 1996; de Villiers 2006). It has been described as an area of difficulty in ASDs because of its pragmatic and functional effect on social communication. Descriptions highlighting attributes of pedantic speech include that it may seem mechanical, formal or more technical and detailed than the context demands (Baltaxe 1977), that it resembles written speech (Asperger 1944), and may be more literal and include redundancies which are not necessarily cohesive (de Villiers *et al.* 2007). Such characterizations are based on behavioural observation but do not articulate the specific discourse features that are signs of pedantic patterning. One unanswered question is the extent to which pedantic speaking characterizes different subgroups in the spectrum. Having a comprehensive characterization of pedantic speech may help clarify this question and can lead to development of clinical diagnostic practices and research tools.

Here we operationalize the patterns for pedantic speech using a case study approach. We look at lexical and syntactic patterning and message organization in a conversation between a young man with Asperger syndrome, Jay, and an interviewer. We then present a novel battery for analysis of pedantic speech.

The conversation consists of three primary phases. The opening is informal chat. Then later in the conversation, Jay uses pedantic speech to talk about a meal (phase 2) and then about the weather (phase 3), a favourite topic. Text 7.1 is an excerpt from the weather phase:

Text 7.1 Weather

(1) CHI: um: what month was this?
(2) RES: that was in # July.
(3) CHI: that might have been the uh time of the severe thunderstorm outbreak.
(4) RES: I think so.
(5) CHI: with the # six tornadoes.
(6) RES: umhum.
(7) RES: I think it was.
(8) CHI: cause they were saying that was the worst severe thunderstorm outbreak to ever occur in cottage country.
(9) RES: uhhuh?
(10) RES: <I think there> [>].
(11) CHI: <there were> [<] six tornadoes.
(12) RES: umhum?
(13) RES: I think there was just too much hot weather at once eh?
(14) CHI: yeah.
(15) RES: and that caused it.
(16) CHI: yeah.
(17) CHI: when you get temperatures of ninety-five the # the air sometimes rises itself.
(18) CHI: and then # causes a storm without a cold front.

(19) RES: umhum?

(20) CHI: so you can get severe storms either from # hot air rising up so high that it cools off or # a hot air mass actually colliding with a different cold air mass.

(21) RES: umhum?

(22) CHI: and I'm sure it must o been a cold front if the storms were that bad # with tornadoes.

For the three primary phases in the text, lexical density and syntactic complexity are compared. The analyses are based on a transcript which has been cleaned for false starts and hesitations, but which is otherwise a verbatim record of an audio-recorded interview. (Note that cleaning transcripts in this way is not essential, or even desirable insofar as leaving such features in means that scores reflect actual performance (Clark and Fox Tree 2002; Sampson 2003). We cleaned transcripts here in order to model standard practice.) Two standard measures of syntactic complexity are used: mean length of utterance (MLU-w) defined as the average number of words per independent clause (Thordardottir and Weismer 1998; van Dijk and van Geert 2005), and clause complexity defined here as the ratio of dependent clauses (all types) to independent clauses. The third measure, lexical density, (LD), is calculated here as the number of open class lexical items (as opposed to closed class 'form words' such as 'a' and 'up') occurring per independent clause (LD = [lex/Cl]). Lexical density measures give a rough guide to how much information is packed into a clause or text. In general, the greater the lexical density, the more information per clause.[1] Lexically dense clauses demand more information processing and consequently are more common to writing than speech. Similarly, more complex clause patterning is characteristic of formal written (rather than spoken) English because, again, it may require greater planning on the part of a speaker and places higher demands on listeners for processing (van Dijk and Kintsch 1983; Sampson 2001; 2003; and cf. Halliday 1987; 1989).

The overall pattern of these three measures, indicated in Table 7.1, suggests that the speaker's conversation has grammatical and organizational properties which make it more similar to written or 'expert' prose than to ordinary adult casual conversation. For example, Sampson (2003) gives length and complexity means for an 80,000 word speech sample and a 63,500 word published writing sample from the British National Corpus (BNC) as a way of measuring comparative 'wordiness'. He calculates length somewhat differently (averaging the number of words over each immediate constituent in a construction that dominates more than one word), but the results appear comparable to other measures. Mean length for the speech sample is 4.62 and for the published writing sample it is 9.45. These means are roughly parallel to the contrast between the first conversational phase of Jay's discourse in which the participants are discussing recent personal events (shopping, a visit to the doctor and so on) where his average independent clause length is five words, and subsequent

Table 7.1. *MLU-w, lexical density and syntactic complexity in the weather text*

	Words (N)	Lexical words (N)	Sentences (N)	Clauses (N)	Independent (N)	Words per independent clause (MLU-w)	Clause complexity (N clause/ N independent clause)	Lexical density (lexical words per IC)
Phase 1 Casual	125	42	18	27	25	5	1.08	1.68 (0.34)
Phase 2 Recipe	106	63	8	13	11	10.47	1.18	5.73 (0.59)
Phase 3 Weather	1000	442	92	182	100	10	1.82	4.42 (0.44)
Continuous	1231	547	118	222	136	9.05	1.63	4.02 (0.44)

phases where he moves into a pedantic speaking style and his average clause length doubles to ten. Similarly, in the same corpus Sampson gives clause complexity means (evaluated in terms of depth – the extent of clause embedding for words in subordinate clauses) for published (adult) writing in the same corpus as 1.857 and for speech as 1.365. The pattern seen in this young man's three phases parallels this, although the syntactic complexity measure cannot be directly compared. Jay's weather phase is much more complex (1.82) than his casual conversation phase (1.08).

Lexical density scores follow the same pattern. In the conversational phase, Jay's lexical density score (1.68) is quite close to the sample presented in Halliday (1987: 329) as characteristic of adult spontaneous speech (1.8). And this contrasts markedly with the second and third phases. In the second, when asked about a meal by the interviewer, he actually supplies the whole recipe for the meal he plans to prepare. Here, the lexical density increases by more than two thirds (5.73), again following written language patterns. In the third phase, when he shifts to a favourite topic, there is a slight decrease in lexical density (4.42), but this is still very much in the 'written' range (Halliday 1987), and is offset by increased syntactic complexity.

The pattern exhibited highlights two points: first, the sorts of differences suggested by descriptors such as 'wordy' and 'formal' appear to be associated with specific properties in the speaker's discourse. Longer sentences and comparatively complex syntax can translate into 'wordiness', and greater lexical density does sound more 'formal' and like written prose because (published) writing generally is lexically more dense than speech. Second, the analysis of phases shows that the speaker is not limited to the use of pedantic speech. He is quite capable of producing the simpler, less lexically dense syntactic constructions more typical of adult conversations, but moves into 'pedantic speech' when possible.

7.2.1   *Lexical repetition and collocation*

Patterns of lexical repetition and collocation bind text and help to create cohesion and coherence. However, frequent repeated lexis or marked textual or collocational patterns can create redundancy. Jay's discourse is cohesive and coherent but may appear verbose. A prominent feature of the third phase of this discourse is the lexical repetition of items relating to weather. In Table 7.2, the highlighted lexical words referring to weather occur and are often repeated. For all repeated items, the number of occurrences is included.

Collocations of verbs from the register of weather report are also prominent, contributing to an impression of 'expert discourse'. The verbs themselves occur in a range of registers, with potentially different argument structures and associated meanings. For instance, in *they're calling for more beer, calling*

Table 7.2. *Lexical items and repetition counts in the weather text*

18 occurrences **thunder** (thunder 7 thunderstorm 7 thunderstorms 3 thunders 1)	13 occurrences **lightning**	8 occurrences **severe** (severe 7 severest 1)	7 occurrences **tornado** (tornadoes 5 tornado 2)	6 occurrences **clouds** (clouds 3 cloud 2 cloudy 1)
5 occurrences **wind** (wind 4 winds 1) **storm** (storms 4 storm's 1) **power actually**	4 occurrences **hot high fall rain** (rains rainstorm rain rainy) **shower** (shower 3 showers 1)	3 occurrences **strikes cold mass bolt** (bolts 2 bolt 1)	2 occurrences **front downpour conditions temperatures hurricane threaten** (threatening 1 threatened 1) **brew** (brewed 1 brew 1) **rise** (rising 1 rises 1) **cool** (cools 1 cool 1) **knock** (knocked 1 knocking 1) **streak** (streak 1 streaks 1)	1 occurrence **flashing, cracks, growing, gusts, loud, sounds, gear, activity, humid, forecasting, breaks, calm, bang, continuous, line, strokes, chain, ground**

takes three arguments and is synonymous with *ask*. However, given the collocations here, they are stereotypically associated with weather reports where *to call for x* takes only two arguments and is synonymous with *predict*. Collocates of 'weather' verbs are in italics in the list below.

- they're still **calling for** *showers* today and tonight maybe.
- and if conditions are right that could **trigger** *off a thunderstorm* later.
- we're **getting back** *into fall temperatures.*
- I'm surprised though today with that *big cloud mass* that **formed** it didn't fully **develop** *into a thunderstorm.*
- <the> *storm* didn't fully **develop**.
- and I watched it as it **brewed**.
- <and> then it **blew over**.
- well today they were **forecasting** *cloudy and rainy*.
- cause they were saying that was the *worst severe thunderstorm outbreak to ever* **occur** in cottage country.
- that must o been scary when *the lightning* **knocked** *the power* out.
- so it wasn't like *a continuous storm* that never **ceased**.

- so you can get severe storms either from # *hot air* **rising** up so high that it **cools** off or # *a hot air mass* actually **colliding** with a different *cold air mass*.
- when you get *temperatures of ninety five* the the *air* sometimes **rises** itself and then **causes** *a storm without a cold front*.

The three most commonly occurring lexical bases are *thunder, lightning* and *severe*. Below are listed three sets of sentences in which they occur. Many of the sentences are found in more than one list since they contain the lexical item from more than one set (e.g. 'thunder' and 'severe'). In most cases, the sentences listed are not adjacent to each other, but the lexical features of repeated items and their collocates combine to connect the discourse, making it very cohesive and, at the same time, giving the speech a formal, and in some cases repetitive quality.

Collocations of the three most frequent lexical items
Thunder

today it threatened to uh **thunderstorm**.
there was # a little bit of distant **thunder** I think I heard in the distance.
I could tell from the clouds that it was a **thunderstorm** and not just a shower.
and if conditions are right that could trigger off a **thunderstorm** later.
I'm surprised though today with that big cloud mass that formed it didn't fully develop into a **thunderstorm**.
I'll tell you that uh # I think the hot weather and the severest **thunderstorm** activity is over now for this year.
I don't think we're gonna get any more **thunderstorms** of the severe nature that we got this summer.
that might have been the uh time of the severe **thunderstorm** outbreak with the six tornadoes.
cause they were saying that was the worst severe **thunderstorm** outbreak to ever occur in cottage country.
there was severe lightning and **thunder**?
and you hear this big bang of **thunder** after the lights come on again.
it's amazing that a line of **thunderstorms** can come through in a half hour.
was it right after was the **thunder** right after the lightning?
so how many miles was this one away from the lightning the **thunder**?

I woke up when I uh heard wind and a tiny bit of **thunder** and heavy rains.

no **thunder** in it?

hearing the distant **thunders** growing tends to relax me somehow.

in the **thunderstorms** I've seen usually we have gusts around maybe eighty kilometres an hour.

Lightning

was there any severe **lightning** in the storm you were at at your cottage?

<there> was severe **lightning** <and> thunder?

what's chain **lightning**?

some people call them streaks of **lightning**.

<was> this during **lightning** strikes?

that must o been scary when the **lightning** knocked the power out.

the **lightning** wasn't that close I guess.

when your lights went off uh how far away was the **lightning**?

was it right after was the thunder right after the **lightning**?

<so> how many miles was this one away from the **lightning** the <thunder>?

several areas of Niagara were without power after several **lightning** strikes.

there were several **lightning** strikes.

and there was **lightning** flashing every two seconds.

Severe

was there any **severe** lightning in the storm you were at at your cottage?

<there> was **severe** lightning <and> thunder?

during a **severe** morning electrical storm.

I'll tell you that uh # I think the hot weather and the **severest** thunderstorm activity is over now for this year.

I don't think we're gonna get any more thunderstorms of the **severe** nature that we got this summer.

that might have been the uh time of the **severe** thunderstorm outbreak with the six tornadoes.

cause they were saying that was the worst **severe** thunderstorm outbreak to ever occur in cottage country.

so you can get **severe** storms either from # hot air rising up so high that it cools off or # a hot air mass actually colliding with a different cold air mass.

There is register-specific lexis and a high frequency of co-occurrence of particular lexical items such as *severe lightning, severe thunderstorm, severe storm(s)*. Selections from the grammar in other areas such as quantification are also markedly consistent. Jay uses *several* three times (e.g. *several lightning strikes; several areas of Niagara*) and repeatedly questions the interviewer about the details of a storm she mentioned as in *was there any severe lightning…?; how far away was the lightning?; how many miles was this one away from the lightning…?*. An examination of the internal structure of noun phrases (NPs) provides further information about the interaction of high frequency items. In *they were saying that was the worst **severe** thunderstorm outbreak, severe thunderstorm* is treated as a compound (with *severe* categorizing storm type in weather report register), since *worst* and *severe* would not otherwise occur together in this kind of construction.

7.2.2   *Message organization*

It has been suggested that in ASDs there are problems recognizing relevance in context (Happé 1993; Frith 2003). This can also be reflected in how relevance is marked in discourse (de Villiers and Szatmari 2004). Marked use of relevant and irrelevant information can be a contributing factor to a pedantic quality in speech, since the inclusion of known information can make speech appear detailed or verbose (Baltaxe 1977; de Villiers and Szatmari 2004). So, in pedantic speech it is likely that examination of linguistic backgrounding and foregrounding of information will be revealing since the linguistic and discoursal resources for organizing information as new and relevant or as known are aspects of how relevance is constructed in talk and text. In addition to the kinds of lexical pattern already discussed, this involves consideration of reference type, syntactic constructions and prosodic features that background or foreground relevant information. Here we present a battery for message organization. It consists of resources for the description of a whole system of patterns associated with information structuring.

Reference   Participants are represented by noun phrases. Typically, when a speaker introduces information about participants that they want to present as new, indefinite articles and full noun phrases are used. Where information is already known, anaphoric pronominal reference and definite articles would be expected. Known information may be established through mention in the specific context of situation/discourse, or known information may be presupposed in a given context of situation and context of culture. Relevance construction is in part dependent on knowing and negotiating what may be textually and contextually presupposed as known and what must be introduced as new.

Below are the frequencies of reference type in Jay's text. (Pronominal reference here includes only pronominal reference to non-human participants and events. Personal pronoun reference is excluded because these referents are always definite and the context of situation here involves only two speakers so inclusion is uninformative. In other situations, personal pronoun referents could be highly salient and one would want to include them.) Included are only pronominal *it* and *that*. Indefinite NPs are those which occur with indefinite articles as in *a severe thunderstorm*, or if the head noun is plural, with no article as in *severe thunderstorms*. Definite NPs include those with proper nouns *(Niagara)* as head, and those with definite articles, quantifiers or possessive articles as in **the** *lightning,* **six** *tornadoes,* **your** *lights* respectively.

> Indefinite reference: 39% (59/151)
> Definite reference: 42% (64/151)
> Pronominal reference: 22% (33/151)

One observation that can be made is that Jay's use of pronominal reference is relatively infrequent (22%) as compared with his use of definite and indefinite noun phrases (42% and 39% respectively). Limited pronominal reference might suggest a text in which many participants are introduced as new, and perhaps not referred to again. However, in this text Jay introduces 59 participants as new using indefinite NPs, and refers to them 97 times. Two thirds of his referencing, though, is in full, definite NPs. Here, the use of full noun phrases instead of ellipsis or pronominal anaphora adds a pedantic redundancy. For instance, in the complex sentence in Example (1), the noun phrase *the severe thunderstorm outbreak* is fully specified when it is repeated in the dependent clause, although it is given information:

(1) that might have been the uh time of **the severe thunderstorm outbreak** with the six tornadoes cause they were saying that was **the worst severe thunderstorm outbreak** to ever occur in cottage country.

In the second mention it would be quite possible to either ellipt *severe thunderstorm outbreak* or substitute *one* for it, as in **the worst** or **the worst one**.

Syntax and prosodic features Consideration of **syntax** and **prosodic features** is also involved in a full characterization of message organization. Relevant syntactic constructions include the systematic options for clause rank alternative sequences and embedding listed and exemplified below.

Cleft constructions Cleft constructions can mark information that is to be presented as news. In *it's amazing that a line of thunderstorms can come through in a half hour*, Jay highlights the attribution *amazing* by placing it in the complement position of the *it is* _____ *that...* construction.

Sentence topic constructions   Sentence topic constructions serve to orient an addressee to a topic shift as in **speaking of the weather**, *they're calling for rain tomorrow* where the topic element is highlighted. Jay does not use such constructions. He introduces the topic of the conversation with a comment on the weather: *today it threatened to uh thunderstorm.*

Ellipsis   As noted, ellipsis refers to the deletion of elements. It is normally used when information is redundant as a type of zero anaphora. Jay typically does not delete where deletion is possible. There are certainly cases of ellipsis, as in the Example (2) where the subject (marked with t_i) is ellipted in the third clause:

(2) when you get temperatures of ninety five the the air$_i$ sometimes rises itself. and then t_i causes a storm without a cold front.

However, more typically, Jay repeats the subject in coordinate clauses where ellipsis would be possible, as in Example (3).

(3) I've read a bit.
     and uh I've learned a bit from tv.

Here it would be possible to ellipt the second mention of subject (*I*) and the operator (*have*) as in *I've read a bit and learned a bit from tv.*

Relative and other subordinate clause types   Relative clauses can be used to background information within NPs. Other subordinate clause types such as content clauses can serve to move information out of given positions such as subject into positions after the complement (which typically receives tonic stress). In Jay's *I'm surprised though today with that big cloud mass* **that formed** <u>that it didn't fully develop into a thunderstorm</u> there is a relative clause (in bold face) and the second *that* clause (underlined above) provides the content for the adjective *surprise*. High frequency of these constructions increases the overall syntactic complexity of the discourse. Additionally, the proportional use of logical and temporal conjunctions for subordination (e.g. *because, if, although, consequently*) versus coordination adds to relative syntactic complexity of message organization. Another speaker might have produced the propositional information in Jay's sentence above as a sequence of simple independent paratactically linked clauses as in *A big cloud mass formed today but it didn't fully develop into a thunderstorm. That surprised me.* The complexity of Jay's style is partly created by his habitual selection of hypotactic rather than paratactic relations between clauses. This is in part perhaps an effect of his interest in the weather and what causes events like storms and tornadoes, but also results from his foregrounding of his reactions to meteorological events as in this instance.

Preposing   Preposing moves an element to initial position so that it is fore-grounded and lets the final element also take tonic prominence. Preposing is used quite regularly in Jay's discourse. In Example (4) temporal information (*when you get temperatures of ninety five*) and conditional information (*if conditions are right*) are foregrounded:

(4) [**when you get temperatures of ninety five**]ᵢ the the air sometimes rises itself *t*ᵢ.
and [if conditions are right]ᵢ that could trigger off a thunder storm later *t*ᵢ.

Passive and ergative   Passive voice as in *the tea was brewed by Sam* is rare in weather report registers presumably because weather is culturally construed as happening or being caused by inanimate forces and thus there is limited possibility for agency deletion or emphasis. Ergative use, where an affected entity appears as subject in an active clause, is more frequent as in *and I watched as it brewed* where the storm, the referent of *it* is construed as 'brewing'.

Prosody   The syntactic constructions illustrated change the potential distribution of tonic prominence such that information can be marked as new and salient, or known.

Example (5) marks the high frequency lexical item *actually* as salient:

(5) CHI: <uh> [<] ninety mile an hour winds <can be a tornado> [>].
RES: <is that right> [<]?
RES: is <that right> [>]?
CHI: <yeah> [<].
RES: oh.
CHI: anywhere from ninety to one hundred and twenty.
RES: I see.
CHI: **act**ually it's anywhere from ninety to **two** hundred and twenty.

Here, the probability adverb *actually* was given emphatic contrastive stress, which its preposed initial position permits. In the last element *two hundred and twenty*, *two* is the site of contrastive stress.

Unsurprisingly, in pedantic speech we find features typical of speech in general such as the use of cleft, topic and pre- and post-posing to organize focus and prominence, but also features which are either more characteristic of written modes such as the use of embedded clauses, or, in the case of frequent full lexical repetition of known information, perhaps unique to pedantic speaking in ASDs.

A message organization battery can be combined with other features that are characteristic of pedantic speech to create a 'pedantic battery' as in Table 7.3. Calculations of the proportion of pedantic speech relative to total speech in conversation might add to this characterization.

Table 7.3. *Pedantic battery*

favourite topic
- pedantic speech is more likely when favourite topic is the topic
- speaker is more informative than might be expected in context

lexical repetition of given information
collocational patterns associated with the (often technical) lexis of the registers of the favourite topic
syntactic complexity – as for written norms
lexical density – as for written norms
syntactic aspects of message organization
- reference (through lexical repetition more than pronoun reference)
- theme marked constructions
- sentence topic constructions
- limited ellipsis
- embedding: relative and other clause types
- preposing and postposing
- passive and ergative constructions

While the lexical repetition is a marked and characteristic element of pedantic speaking, other kinds of lexical and syntactic patterning contribute to the pedantic quality. As has been shown, these features cannot be adequately addressed without consideration of registers and register variation. With pedantic speech, lexis associated with specialized registers is a partial sign of special interests.

7.3   Monitoring and change over time

If one or more discourse behaviours are clearly associated with particular diagnoses, stages, or levels of severity, it may be possible to use the behaviours as clinical signs of stability or change. Especially in contexts where new treatments and/or interventions have been or are being developed and biomarkers are absent or not widely available, establishing behavioural correlates of responsiveness to treatment can be valuable. In such situations clinical discourse analysis can function as a way of discovering and tracking how treatment affects discourse patterns. In this section, we give an example of the use of clinical discourse analysis to discover behaviours associated with drug treatment response for patients with Alzheimer's disease, and then present a battery for examining interactional aspects of discourse as a means of monitoring treatment.

7.3.1   Monitoring change over time

A number of researchers have observed that pragmatic, interactional and highly automatized aspects of language may be preserved in the discourse of speakers with significant impairments in left hemispheric regions classically associated with linguistic competence (Cardebat *et al.* 1993; Nespoulous *et al.*1998) and in speakers with AD (Ulatowska and Bond-Chapman 1991; Duong *et al.* 2003). Nespoulous *et al.* (1998) characterize discourse with preserved highly automatized lexis, preserved syntactic structure and capacity to express attitude, evaluation and probability as 'modalizing discourse'. They contrast this with 'referential' discourse which has fully lexicalized propositional content. In research on AD, Duong *et al.* (2003) found that participants with AD produce more modalizing discourse relative to referential discourse than a group of older adults with no cognitive impairment. Duong *et al.* (2003) suggest modalization reflects participants' efforts to maintain their communicative role while faced with referential difficulties and their awareness of processing deficits.

7.3.2   Tags in Alzheimer's disease

In work describing the discourse of patients participating in a clinical trial for donepezil, a cholinesterase inhibitor widely used to treat patients with AD, Asp *et al.* (2006a) identified a particular use of tags as characteristic of patients' speech. The first example of this tag use, which we called the checking 'self-referential tag', is one in which people with AD use tags with statements that refer to their own daily routines and activities. Thus if asked 'what time do you get up in the morning?' a patient might respond with a tagged statement such as *I get up at six, don't I?* or they might check a response about their age (*I'm 83, aren't I?*). The tag checks the certainty of the proposition, typically with caregivers who participate in interviews. What is unusual about checking self-referential tags is that they check information normally available from the speaker's own episodic memory. A second kind of self-referential tag is used to monitor information flow (*I told you that already, didn't I?*). These are common to speakers without AD. We paid attention to them because we were interested in what speakers with AD were doing with self-referential tags.

Examination of interviews with one hundred patients and caregivers showed that tag frequencies differed hugely between patients and caregivers, that they used them differently, and that the type of tags patients used correlated with their response to treatment. In brief, more patients (71%) than caregivers (21%) used self-referential tags and used them more frequently: patients produced 93% of all self-referential tags in the corpus. Moreover, more patients used a greater percentage of episodic checking tags than caregivers: 80% of patients' tags are checking tags and most of these (72%) are singular – the sort used to check episodic facts about oneself as in *I don't have a dog, do I?* More than half of caregivers' tags were monitoring (54%) and their episodic checking tags were mostly plural (77%). Qualitative analysis of this difference suggested that caregivers tended to use plural episodic checking tags to engage patients in the interaction (*We went out for dinner last night, didn't we?*) rather than as expressions of uncertainty about episodic information. Among patients, the 31 who used monitoring tags with or without checking tags had significantly better scores on standard neuropsychological measures of cognitive function after twelve months of treatment than patients either only using checking tags (40) or those not using tags at all (29) (Asp *et al.* 2006a).

We hypothesized that ability to monitor information flow reflects preserved and/or up-regulated prefrontal function which may occur endogenously or as treatment response in AD and that, while the frequent use of self-referential tags generally is a sign of episodic and information processing deficits, awareness of these deficits as reflected in tag use by patients with AD is more positive than lack of such awareness. We are currently in the process of checking another corpus from a recently completed double-blind placebo-controlled trial with 120 patients to find out whether this is indeed the case. This work, as well as the research mentioned above, suggests that a 'modalization battery' might be helpful as a general index of processing difficulty and of monitoring abilities. If tailored for a specific group, such as AD patients being treated with cholinesterase inhibitors, it may have the further benefit of providing another way of evaluating treatment response for individual patients.

A model for such a modalization battery is offered in Table 7.4, and its use illustrated in a single text. The modalization battery consists of resources for the description of a system of patterns associated with modalizaton as suggested by Nespoulous *et al.* (1998) and as suggested by the sociocognitive model. It thus includes interactional, ideational and organizational selections which may be relevant.

If the battery were being developed specifically to evaluate monitoring capacity relative to episodic and semantic memory deficits in AD, other features such as the frequency of self-initiated repairs, incomplete utterances and syntactic complexity might be included in the initial investigation on the grounds that these may function as positive or negative signs of discourse monitoring abilities. Below we analyse a single text of an interview with a speaker with AD to illustrate the modalization battery.

Text 7.2 Memory problems

(1) IV: Mmhm.
(2) So can I ask you to tell me a little bit about the time when your health changed.
(3) When you started noticing you were having memory problems.
(4) P: Well I I guess it would only be {(laughs)} recently and not very long ago.
(5) IV: Mmhm
(6) P: Um I suppose # in the past year.
(7) IV: Mmhm.

Table 7.4. *Modalization battery*

(1) **Speech functions**

   (i) proportion of the number of statements, exclamations, questions (WH/polar), commands (jussive/optative) relative to the total number of independent clauses

   (ii) number of questions used to check self-referential episodic information or monitor discourse as a proportion of independent clauses

   (iii) number of minimal responses as a proportion of the number of speaker's turns

   (iv) number of minor clauses relative to total number of independent clauses

(2) **Tagged statements** in terms of the tag types, intonation contours, number of tags in proportion to the number of statements by speakers, and the number of these which are self-referential (monitoring or checking)

(3) **Checks** and **intonation contours:** code for checks (e.g. *you know*) and proportion of statements with rising tone

(4) **Modal verbs, adjectival** and **adverbial modulations:** code for likelihood, capacity, hypothesis, obligation, habitual action and assess their frequency in relation to the number of statements and minor clauses. Include alternatives, when these limit the certainty with which a statement is offered (e.g. *I went shopping or something*).

(5) **Cognition predicates:** (e.g. *think, believe, suppose, know*) assess their frequency in relation to the number of statements and minor clauses. Note the proportion of cognition predicates which are negative (i.e. deny knowledge or express doubt about episodic or semantic information).

(6) **Automatization of lexis**

   (i) proportion of **high-order taxonomic reference** relative to basic or subordinate level categorization in N/V/A/Av selections

   (ii) **indefinite reference** relative to definite reference

   (iii) **lexical density and/or richness measures**

---

(8) What sort of things started happening that made you aware?

(9) P: Um # well um of course I would think that I had said or done something

(10) and someone would tell me I hadn't and that sort of thing you know.

(11) IV: Mmhm

(12) P: Nothing nothing very drastic but ah just,

(13) CG: The little everyday things wasn't it?

(14) P: Little little things.

(15) IV; : Mmhm

(16) and what sort of took you off to the doctor the first time to check it out?

(17) P: Ah well just what other people were saying to me

(18) that I was getting forgetful and so on.

(19) IV: Mmhm.

(20) P: But ah of course ah just the ordinary doctor that doesn't # have much of a remedy for that. ((laughs))

(21) But ah I I went to my doctor anyway

(22) IV: And and did your doctor refer you to the clinic?

(23) P: Ah # # did he?

(24) CG : Yes

(25) P: Yeah

(26) CG: Yes Dr Smith did Dear.
(27) P: Yes Dr Smith yeah.
(28) CG: He wanted the Geriatric assessment test done.
(29) IV: Umhum.
(30) And how was that for you?
(31) Was that was that test ah
(32) P: I I I ah I don't know.
(33) IV: Guess you went through it
(34) and maybe didn't
(35) P: Didn't even know it ((laughs))

Text 7.2 is a fragment of a home-visit interview with a patient, Doris, and her caregiver. The patient has moderate, untreated AD. As can be seen from the interview, Doris participates actively. She takes almost half (12/25) of all turns, attempting responses to every question addressed to her. She is obviously attentive, even successfully (if ironically) completing the interviewer's final turn. Her lexical density score in this fragment, calculated here as the proportion of non-repeated lexical words per independent clause, is 2.6 (24/9). This is in the normal range for spontaneous spoken adult discourse. However, there is some evidence represented in pauses, hesitations, false starts and incomplete utterances (21 altogether) that she has some processing difficulties. Examination of modalization features and lexical patterning (summarized in Tables 7.5 and 7.6) suggest the source of some of these problems may be episodic memory – that is, since she is being asked about when her memory problems started, what she personally noticed, what sent her to the doctor and so on, the questions make demands on her recall of her own recent past experience.

As Table 7.5 indicates, half of Doris' responses to questions are statements. Otherwise, she uses elliptical polar responses, minor clauses and one polar question to respond to questions. One of her statements is checked with a monitoring *you know,* but otherwise they are untagged and have falling tone (so tags and *you* are not represented in Table 7.5). Her only question (about referral) is addressed to her caregiver (*did he* (23)), indicating that she doesn't know who referred her to the memory clinic. Three of her other responses are hypothetical: she uses a modal *would,* (*It would only be recently* (4)), and lexical verbs, (*I guess* (4) and *I suppose* (6)). In full independent clauses, the proportion of lexical verbs referring to mental cognition processes is 71% (5/7). If minor clauses are included , the proportion of mental cognition predicates is lower at 41% (5/12). In addition to *guess* and *suppose,* there is the habitual past cognition (*I would think* (9)) and two negative mental cognition predicates (*I don't know*) in response to questions seeking episodic information about her visit to a specialist.[2] Elliptical responses following her episodic polar question echo her caregiver's responses and thus add no new information. The sense that she speaks well but not very informatively is thus partly a consequence of the hypothetical modalization, and in some cases frank denial, of knowledge about

Table 7.5. *Modalization features in the discourse of a person with AD*

Element	Category	Feature(s)	Number	Value
Speaker turns			12/25	48% of all turns
	Independent clauses	(include elliptical responses to polar questions)	9/12	75% of patient's turns
	Minor clauses		3/12	25%
Speech functions	Statements	Full	6/9	66% of patient's independent clauses
		Elliptical (positive)	2/9	22%
	Polar question	Episodic check	1/9	11%
Modalizations	Statement check	(monitoring – *you know*)	1/9	11% of patient's statements and minor clauses
	Modal verbs	Hypothesis (*would*)	1/9	11%
	Mental cognition	Hypothesis (*guess, suppose*) *Not know* (2) *Think*	5/9	55%

her past: leaving out the habitual *would* and the monitoring check, it is the case that 58% of her clauses are modalized in ways that limit episodic certainty.

The lexical patterns displayed in Table 7.6 augment this impression. For example, of the nouns she uses, only two (*remedy* and *Dr Smith*) could be classified as subordinate level and *Dr Smith* is an echoic repetition of her caregiver so would be excluded in a count. Of the others, half are superordinate and half are basic level and one of these is repeated. None of her other lexical selections are subordinate, except perhaps the adjective *drastic*. Excluding personal pronoun reference, Doris uses nine noun phrases (NP). Five (55%) of her NPs are indefinite. Moreover, three of her definite NPs (excluding the echoic *Dr Smith*) have very general reference: one has superordinate lexis (*that sort of thing*); one gives a time span (*in the past year*) but is attenuated by a mental cognition verb indicating hypothesis, (*I suppose*) as well as by the preposition *in* which makes this a rather underspecified elaboration of *recently*; and one refers to *the ordinary doctor*, rather than the 'family doctor' or 'general practitioner' or the contrastive 'geriatrician' or even 'specialist'. Only *my doctor* refers to a specific, known participant.

The other word categories show a somewhat similar pattern. All verbs (5) referring to actions or states are superordinate, and Doris' basic level verbs (8) refer exclusively to mental cognition and verbalization processes such as *think*

Table 7.6. *Lexical patterns in the discourse of a person with AD*

Reference (n) = number of occurrences		Taxonomic relations			
			Nouns	Verbs	Adjectives	Adverbs
Personal pronouns	I (9) me (2) you (1) he (1)	Superordinate	sort thing people	do get (become) have go		ago
Definite reference	– the past year – that sort of thing – the ordinary doctor – my doctor Dr Smith (echo rep)	Basic level	year doctor (2)	guess suppose think tell say (2) know (2)	long past little (2 – echo) forgetful ordinary	recently
Indefinite reference	– something – someone – nothing (2) – things (echo) – other people – a remedy	Subordinate	remedy Dr Smith (echo rep)		?drastic?	

and *say*. There are no subordinate level verbs or adverbs and only one potential candidate (*drastic*) as a subordinate level adjective. Pooling these patterns, we see that only 8% of Doris' lexical selections instantiate subordinate level concepts. The rest refer to superordinate (36%) and very high frequency basic level (56%) concepts.

Prevalence of indefinite rather than definite reference, superordinate and high-frequency basic level concepts rather than subordinate level concepts, together with discourse which is heavily modalized for uncertainty about episodically salient information all contribute to the overall pattern of speech which is rather uninformative.

The pattern of co-operative but 'empty' speech in AD has been attributed variously to the breakdown of lexical–semantic systems, conceptual systems or to problems with executive function processes which limit access to these systems (e.g. Hier *et al.* 1985; Nicholas *et al.* 1985; Carlomagno *et al.* 2005). Each of these difficulties is progressive in AD so establishing change patterns of modalization and lexical selection over time, and in the context of treatment, may be effective means of monitoring change.

7.4   Steps to usability

Above we have presented descriptive batteries for characterizing pedantic speech in ASDs and modalizing discourse in AD. These may be used in other contexts. For instance, the initial observations about modalizing discourse were made with regard to speakers with aphasia. We suggested that these batteries could provide descriptions which in themselves have an a priori value as descriptions in under-investigated areas. We also are interested in the potential of using the information from such characterizations for monitoring change and as a supplement to diagnoses. Another useful application for discourse characterizations is in the development of rating scales.

A rating scale is an instrument used to diagnose disorders, evaluate severity or subgroup, or track change over time. A rating scale tells you how to interpret an observed set of behaviours by assigning a value to them. Linguistically explicit scales that measure aspects of discourse offer a useful complement to other scales and neurocognitive assessment tools.

Observations allow qualitative and quantitative evaluation of a group (or an individual relative to a group or a baseline state) based on some described, coded set of phenomena. From the initial observations, linguistic descriptions can be used to develop scales. Hypotheses can then be generated to test whether a feature or bundle of features will be present, absent or occur with a specified frequency likely to be associated with the disorder, disease phase, treatment response, or other research question being investigated. Depending on what a scale evaluates, rating scales may be used by clinicians, researchers, families, educators and other caregivers in clinical contexts or a variety of life situations.

Rating scales based on discourse analysis directly and explicitly address discourse features. Insofar as discourse is a readily observable everyday behaviour and reflects neurocognitive states, rating scales that refer to discourse may be quite useful. This is well established as practice in assessing child language development, and of course in aphasia studies. The design of scales can be targeted to specific users and take into consideration their potential linguistic experience, time demands and likely contexts of use. For instance, a general practitioner may need a tool that can help inform a decision to refer. Clinical discourse analysis can also be useful in designing tools that are specific to particular disorders and that are sensitive to register: in assessing AD, performance in the clinic is important because this is where medical personnel see and evaluate patients. A scale for evaluating change from a baseline in relation to treatment would also be useful for assessing AD. Thus descriptions that inform rating scales need to be based on data collected from appropriate contexts of situation and their associated registers. The approval process for rating scales varies in different communities, but the timeline is never short.

We end the chapter with an example of a rating scale developed for use in ASDs. Conversation is an area of particular difficulty in ASDs. Thus a tool for measuring conversational difficulties specific to ASDs might be useful in assessing the degree of impairment, and in evaluating change over time or in response to treatment. In research aimed at understanding social communication difficulties in high-functioning autism and Asperger syndrome, de Villiers *et al.* (2007) developed a preliminary scale for rating conversational impairment in ASDs. Based on a descriptive linguistic approach, this scale identified five areas of conversational difficulty in ASDs:

1) atypical intonation
   Speech has a monotone quality and/or atypical stress selection
2) semantic drift
   Includes abrupt switching of topics and 'disengagement from verbal context'
3) terseness
   Minimally responsive, including short, delayed responses or necessary prompting
4) pedantic speech
   Stereotypic or rehearsed sounding speech with more factual or technical detail than is required for the situation
5) perseveration
   Excessive persistence on a particular chosen topic

These five constructs were derived from a wider set of characteristic discourse features which were then collapsed to create a more useful version of the scale. As it makes explicit the nature of certain social communication difficulties in ASDs, this scale may be usefully applied to measure variation within an ASD population. A full description of the development of the rating scale can be found in de Villiers *et al.* 2007.

8 Cognitive models, inferencing and affect

8.1 Introduction

This chapter outlines approaches to top-down cognitive modelling and inferencing, and addresses functionally grounded work on affect. We describe each area and illustrate its potential for addressing questions in clinical discourse analysis. We also review recent work from neuroimaging and lesion studies to suggest some of the relevant neural systems. As usual, we draw on various disciplinary perspectives and theoretical models. Our practical motivation here is to use what works, and has potential for coding corpora in the various linguistic contexts and situations encountered doing clinical discourse analysis.

Cognitive models in general characterize information bundles of various kinds. Perhaps the most familiar are those used to represent words or word-like concepts. Models for words may be more or less detailed depending on the tolerance for elaboration within a particular framework, but morphosyntactic class, inflection and distribution features are typically indicated. How a word is pronounced – its phonological form and regular phonetic variants – will be spelt out in phonological and phonetic representations. Semantic features are often specified only at superordinate levels as in THING/EVENT or merely indexed through the use of the 'CAPS-for-concept' convention. Thus, the model for the lexeme 'cat' will include the information that it is a common count noun, with the inflectional and distributional features of this class – it can occur as head of a noun phrase and it inflects for plural number /s/. It is pronounced /kæt/. The entry might also include semantic features such as THING, ANIMATE and so on, or just CAT as a shorthand for some presupposed set of features.

Conventionally the semantic features associated with word-like concepts have been presented as modality-neutral conceptual representations in linguistics, either in some sort of algebraic formulation or, less formally, in lists of lexically represented features. Depending on the model, there may be pointers to schematic, modal, functional and encyclopedic information included as relevant. One rationale for such a presentation is that a modality-neutral conceptual system would allow communication between otherwise incommensurable modes such as language, vision and taste (e.g. Jackendoff 2002; in preparation). However, work in cognitive neurology (Mesulam e.g. 1998), cognitive neuropsychology (Warrington and Shallice 1984; Warrington and McCarthy 1987) and neuroimaging (Thompson-Schill 2003; Martin 2007) raises questions about the plausibility of modality neutral concepts and the existence of a modality neutral conceptual system (Thompson-Schill 2003). We do not address these debates here but offer brief synopses of some of the issues as they are relevant for clinical discourse analysis in chapter 9. Here we merely make the point that agreement even on something as seemingly basic as the neural architecture that supports word-like concepts is absent, so all comments about neural substrate need to be read with caution. That said, we favour distributed models which treat modality/functional specificity as central to neural organization and link information across modes through transmodal gateways (e.g. Mesulam 1998). We discuss this sort of model further in the final chapter.

While there is limited consensus about the neural instantiation of concepts, there is robust evidence that we use information represented in cognitive models of concepts. Cognitive models for concepts are ways of characterizing what we know about real and abstract objects and events, relations and attributes.

Top-down cognitive models are similar except that they highlight aspects of generic situation potential. Following van Dijk and Kintsch (1983), we think of top-down models as contributing to the construction of 'situational models' which, as we use the terms, are speakers' mental representations of particular discourses. We assume that conceptual and top-down models have relationships to executive functions on (at least) two dimensions. First, they affect our capacity to maintain and monitor information 'online' by making recurrent features redundant and informing selection and inhibition processes (e.g. van Dijk and Kintsch 1983; Shallice and Burgess 1996; Tinaz et al. 2006). Second, they inform executive control processes (EFC) associated with inferencing, judgement, decision making and action planning (Norman and Shallice 1986; Baddeley and Della Sala 1996; Goel et al. 1997; Royall et al. 2002; Paxton et al. 2008).

Our emotional states and affective responses continuously modulate and are modulated by experience in situations (Frijda 1986; Mesulam 1998). Insofar as the conceptual and top-down cognitive models we bring to bear in the interpretation of experience contribute to shaping what that experience is, positive, neutral and negative evaluations attached to those models (either directly through experience or indirectly as matters of cultural transmission) will influence not only emotional states and affective responses, but also directly or indirectly the judgements, decisions and plans we make (Coricelli, et al. 2007; Rushworth et al. 2007 for reviews). Thus, affect and emotion have roles to play in 'top-down' cognitive processing associated with executive control processes (Bechara et al. 2000; Royall et al. 2002; Coricelli et al. 2007). We include a section on affect in this chapter because of this association. However, from linguistic, if not psychological, psychiatric and AI perspectives, affect and emotion in discourse have been little studied. Thus, our goals here are to index their importance and point to some work where affect and emotion have been the focus of study.

8.2   Top-down models

This section outlines top-down models and their sources and discusses their use in clinical discourse analysis. Specifically, we discuss **scripts**, **frames**, **scenarios** and **schemas** as developed in psychological and Artificial Intelligence (AI) literature as well as in discourse analysis and linguistics. In Chapter 5, we introduced these elements as representations of event and situational knowledge relative to contexts of situation and culture.

Scripts refer to conventional action sequences associated with generic situations (Schank and Abelson 1977). That is, when we do something or plan to do something such as going to a movie, or going to a restaurant, we have expectations about the essential actions that characterize the generic structure potential of the activity and their order (Hasan 1978).[1] Galambos (1986) has distinguished actions which may be more central to a script rather in the way that some features may be more central to a concept, defining its prototype, while other features may be distinctive without being defining. So the script for going to a movie will include going to the cinema, buying tickets, possibly buying popcorn, finding a seat, watching the movie. Here, finding a seat is neither central nor distinctive. We do this at public lectures and entertainments, on buses and so on. Interestingly, although buying popcorn is optional, it is relatively distinctive insofar as one does not, for instance, buy popcorn to eat at plays, concerts or at the opera. Watching a movie is central and distinctive. Order constraints require that finding a seat cannot precede buying tickets nor follow watching the movie. People usually know both the elements and their order.

There is an extensive body of literature associating script knowledge and performance with prefrontal function and medial temporal lobe function (e.g. Luria 1965; Norman and Shallice 1986; Stuss and Benson 1986; Grafman 1989; Godbout and Doyon 1995; Shallice and Burgess 1996; Zanini *et al.* 2002; Godbout *et al.* 2004; Zanini 2008). Specifically, patients with lesions in the prefrontal cortex (Sirigu *et al.* 1995; 1996; Zalla *et al.* 2000; 2003) and with neurodegenerative diseases focally affecting prefrontal systems have difficulty recognizing event sequences and ordering events appropriately (Cosentino *et al.* 2006). People whose primary impairment is in semantic memory have difficulty with event components but not necessarily with sequences (Cosentino *et al.* 2006) and degenerative disorders such as Alzheimer's and Parkinson's disease may impair knowledge of components and their sequences (Godbout and Doyon 1995; Allain *et al.* 2008). In autism, it has been shown that there are problems generating scripts with all the central elements, although participants typically have such knowledge (Volden and Johnston 1999). There is debate as to whether script knowledge is represented *in toto* (e.g. Grafman 1989; 2002; Zalla *et al.* 2003) or separately as knowledge of sequence and component elements. Evidence supporting the latter view comes from studies indicating that sequence and component elements may be discretely impaired by focal lesion damage (Sirigu *et al.* 1995; Sirigu *et al.* 1996; Cosentino *et al.* 2006), and from imaging and lesion studies that suggest that script knowledge is distributed and its activation engages a functional network that includes the dorsolateral prefrontal cortex, temporal and parietal regions and basal ganglia (Godbout and Doyon 1995; Tinaz *et al.* 2008).[2] There is consensus that script knowledge is closely linked to executive function processes supported by the prefrontal cortex and that these processes are especially associated with abilities to plan and carry out activities in daily life (Shallice 1982; Rusted and Shepherd 2002; Royall *et al.* 2005; Allain *et al.* 2008; Zanini 2008).

Frames refer to information associated with situation specific concepts (Minsky 1975; van Dijk 1977). For example, an event frame would include an event structure specification familiar as predicate and participant role relationships and circumstances, and other information such as social evaluations and logical conditions of the event and its participants. Frames are thus a device for characterizing acquired attitudinal, encyclopedic and lexical knowledge. So, within the script of going to the movies, we could postulate a frame for buying a ticket. This will involve a buyer and a seller, a ticket and money (the predicate–argument relationship). It will also include information that the ticket is likely made of paper and is required for admission to the cinema and an expectation of cost. This can be represented in an argument structure type format with typical default features and options included for arguments and circumstances. Depending on the amount of detail one wants for the description, it may also include explicit evaluations and conditions as propositions. An example for buying a ticket might look like Figure 8.1.

Frames have been used to examine how people orient to and within events. In AI and linguistics, the role of frames is the representation of conventional knowledge structures (Fillmore 1976; 1982; Minsky 1975; 1977). In discourse analysis, Goffman (1959; 1961; 1974; 1986), Gensler (1977), van Dijk (1977), Tannen (1993a; 1993b) and others have used framing to explore contextualization processes. Goffman looked at how people (re)position themselves with respect to situation types and each other and at the discourse behaviours that serve to 'reframe' situations. Van Dijk (1977) investigates the role of frame knowledge in inferring unstated information relevant to the interpretation of discourse. Medical discourse is one area where these approaches have been

Buy ticket

Condition: necessary for admission

Source +/– Agent [person/machine]^1

Agent and Goal recipient [movie goer]^2

Theme transferent [TICKET]$^{1\blacktriangleright 2}$

Theme transferent [MONEY: approximate cost]$^{2\blacktriangleright 1}$

Figure 8.1   Frame for 'buying a ticket to the movies' *(The superscripts are indices for the direction of transfer in the BUY process, where the ticket goes from the seller/machine to the movie goer and money goes from the movie goer to the seller/machine.)*

used extensively (e.g. Tannen and Wallat 1993; Coupland *et al*. 1994). Gensler (1977) used frames as abstracts for interpreting anaphora. Framing is also used to study risk-taking behaviour and decision making more generally (e.g. De Martino *et al*. 2006; Kahneman and Frederick 2007). Insofar as frames involve relations between concepts and propositions relative to generic situation types, they are inherently more complex than concepts and therefore present more challenges for neural characterizations. Van Dijk and Kintsch (1983) assume that frames are represented in semantic memory. So long as we allow that semantic memory for frames is likely to be distributed according to the modal and functional values of concepts entailed by particular frames, this seems reasonable.

Frames (or something similar) are used in presuppositional and inferential processing and decision making. Some imaging studies have examined the way particular frames may affect these processes and findings suggest that the anterior cingulate cortex is more activated in making decisions that involve analytic judgements (Coricelli *et al*. 2007) in contrast with decisions which differentially activate the amygdala. The latter are presumed to involve an affective style (De Martino *et al*. 2006; Kahneman and Frederick 2006). (The anterior cingulate cortex is normally involved in 'difficult task' processing since its generic roles are linked to behaviour monitoring, error correction and response selection (Duncan and Owen 2000; Krawczyk 2002; Rushworth *et al*. 2007).)

The orbitofrontal cortex also appears to be involved in decision making and response evaluations. It receives projections from sensory areas and from limbic regions associated with emotion and memory and it feeds back through monitoring and attentional systems (Mesulam 1998; Royall *et al*. 2002; Rushworth *et al*. 2007). It has been suggested that the role of the medial orbitofrontal cortex in decision making relative to frames is that it integrates emotional and cognitive information, so that greater activation in this region may signify more 'rational' than emotive decision making relative to a frame

(De Martino 2006; Coricelli *et al.* 2007; Kahneman and Frederick 2007). For example, Camille *et al.* (2004) report that patients with lesions to the orbito-frontal cortex did not experience the emotion of regret when they lost in positively framed gambling tasks and did not learn from their losses, though they did feel happy or disappointed depending on whether they won or lost. Control participants did feel regret and learnt from the experience of regret so that they modified their behaviour to resist positive frames associated with high gain and risk and selected instead certain modest gain options. Coricelli *et al.* (2005) showed in an fMRI study that heightened regret increased activity in the medial orbitofrontal cortex, the dorsal anterior cingulate and the anterior hippocampus. Coricelli *et al.* (2007) hypothesize that the engagement of the hippocampus in this loop reflects the activation of consciously accessible information, incorporated through the orbitofrontal cortex activity into the decision-making process – allowing the high risk frame to be evaluated and rejected because it leads to the experience of regret. Activation of the anterior cingulate when people attend to emotional information has been observed in other studies (Rushworth *et al.* 2007 for review). Lane *et al.* (1997) suggest that such activity is coherent with increased monitoring and attention needed for response selection. Figure 8.2 shows some of the brain regions associated with this sort of decision-making process.

There is overlap in what frames and **scenarios** describe insofar as they both refer to features of generic situations such as participant roles. However, scenarios were originally posited to address situational knowledge in non-propositional form, whereas frames presupposed relatively fixed propositional knowledge (e.g. Kintsch 1974. But see also van Dijk and Kintsch 1983 where non-propositional knowledge is not ruled out; and Kintsch 1988 where it is assumed though not addressed because of the challenges it presented). Scenarios and frames also differ from each other in that scenarios can be used to describe elements of 'setting' in the generic situation, whereas frames characterize concepts relevant to such generic situations. Thus, a frame can be a model that refers to concrete entities (theatre ticket), processes (buy ticket), abstractions such as GAIN/LOSS, or emotions such as DEPRESSION/HAPPINESS, while scenarios will refer to generic situation types such as AT THE RESTAURANT, AT THE MOVIES, IN THE CLASSROOM. The scenario AT THE MOVIES will include a film and possibly trailers (and increasingly advertisements).

(1) Scenario: AT THE MOVIES

- ticket booth at the entrance
- it will be dark
- it will be public
- there is seating with aisles separating the rows
- people may eat popcorn

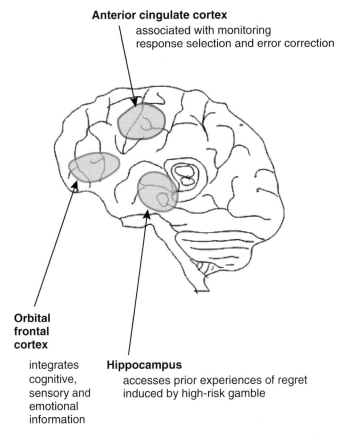

Anterior cingulate cortex
    associated with monitoring
    response selection and error correction

**Orbital
frontal
cortex**

    integrates   **Hippocampus**
    cognitive,   accesses prior experiences of regret
    sensory and   induced by high-risk gamble
    emotional
    information

Figure 8.2 Decisions and brains

- a film will be shown
- other

Evidence that people may use scenarios in processing discourse came initially from a study by Sanford and Garrod (1981) that compared reading times in generic versus non-generic situations: people processed more quickly when the scenario was a generic one suggesting that they used knowledge of the scenario to interpret instantiated information (Sanford and Garrod 1981). A nicely illustrative recent set of examples are two studies investigating the effects of the presence or absence of a title on processing a series of paragraphs (St. George *et al.* 1994; 1999). In both studies, participants read pairs of paragraphs which were identical except that one in each pair of paragraphs had a title which made texts coherent. The paragraphs without titles were quite difficult to interpret. For example, one of the paragraphs describes horseback riding including the facts that it's expensive even if you have the gear, that it can be dangerous and instruction is important, and describes the process of mounting. Without the title, 'horseback riding', from which one can infer the scenario of a first riding lesson, it is incomprehensible, though each of the sentences is well formed. The first study (St. George *et al.* 1994) investigated the electrophysiological response of participants under both conditions and found that the N400 wave (typically associated with semantic processing) was consistently bigger for words in the untitled rather than in the titled paragraphs. Similarly, in the second study, fMRI showed a frontotemporal network of bilateral activation which was much more extensive for the untitled versus the titled paragraphs. These and similar studies suggest that the time course for processing with and without top-down models corresponds to the greater processing demands of the unfamiliar condition.

Brown and Yule (1983) describe **schemas** as models that are operationalized in the interpretation of discourse. They refer not only to narrative and other discourse schemas, but also to concepts that account for stereotypic processing effects in terms of interests, preoccupations and other culturally conditioned expectations of participants. Examples of the operation of schemata include different inferences about the nature of an event type based on interests (where music students and a weight-lifting team interpreted the same text as referring to a musical evening and a card game respectively, in Anderson *et al.* (1977: 372)) and different orientations to events which help to explicate the different discourse acts of participants (Tannen and Wallat 1993).

Like scripts and frames, schemas and scenarios facilitate contextualization and integration processes. The variability and potential complexity of these models suggests that they are likely to have widely distributed representations depending on their contents and the situations they refer to. For example, in talking about the scenario 'at the movies', we used propositions such as 'it will be dark' and 'people may eat popcorn'. This information though, might well be neurally represented in regions associated with darkness and the sound, taste and smell of popcorn. So what the scenario refers to may be a set of episodically encoded multi-modal experiences. We may also know these as propositions but that is not necessary. In this respect, scenarios contrast with frames which are assumed to refer to propositional information associated with semantic memory. Similarly, schemas viewed as stereotypic expectations affecting interpretations of situations may be difficult to distinguish from frames since they can be propositionally represented. However, when the term schema is used to refer to highly abstract structures such as those occurring in narrative or those representing the basic shapes of common objects this is clearly not the case.

The four types of top-down model we have described do show areas of overlap as we have suggested and, indeed, some authors treat them simply as variant labels for situational knowledge (e.g. Fillmore 1982; Bednarek 2005). However, in their original formulations each construct was articulated to address particular aspects of situational knowledge. Research in discourse processes and neurocognitive function over the past thirty years suggests that the nuances early researchers sought to articulate are more than discursive epiphenomena. For example, that we use non-propositional information (scenarios) to process discourses coherently seems to be reflected in recent imaging studies. Ferstl *et al.* (2005) and Ferstl and von Cramon (2007) have shown that activations associated with the representation of spatial information needed for coherent interpretations of stories are very close to activations associated with space perception and object location in general and these activations are distinct from activation patterns associated with processing temporal and emotional information in discourse.

In developmental and neurodegenerative disorders, difficulties in discourse processing can be reflected in problems with top-down models. For instance, Alzheimer's impairs semantic and episodic memory. People with AD may thus have difficulty accessing knowledge of frames, scripts and scenarios. Moreover, cholinergic denervation of the prefrontal cortex and/or other neurotransmitter deficits can limit capacity for the sorts of complex integrative processes that are required in order to integrate top-down models with instantially presented information. These difficulties may be reflected in what people say and how they respond to situations as well as in actual discourse abilities requiring specific generic knowledge. For example in Text 8.1 below a patient with moderate AD responds to questions about an incident in which he got lost while out on a walk close to his home.

Text 8.1 Getting lost

(1) IV: Can you tell me what happened that day.

(2) P: Well # uh it was uh just it it looked different to me,

(3) P: Like I mean # some of them streets # I uh see I been in that place for quite a few years # but I still # I just couldn't quite get them streets figured out # so I just had to keep on walking # slow walking # and just try to figure out where # where I had to go # you see. But uh it took a good part of the day to get it figured out.

(4) IV: So what did you do to find your way back # did you ask someone or call?

(5) P: I did talk to the odd one # like you know # but they were uh kind of uh new too # like the ones I were # was talking to and uh so they didn't really give me any help as far as the directions were that I wanted to go.

(6) IV: Umhum.

(7) P: I wasn't a bit worried about it.

(8) P: I just thought I'll keep on going till I find exactly where to go.

(9) IV: Do you know your address off by heart?

(10) P: Uh it's at uh # well # the one I'm staying at that's at her her uh her place here.
(11) IV: Can you tell me what the address is?
(12) P: Well that's uh # I I should have been able to.
(13) P: I have it written down # too. But
(14) CG: Yeah he has it in his pocket
(15) P: Yeah ( )

The situation (getting lost) might be thought of as generic. Children, especially in cities, are usually encouraged to memorize their home addresses and phone numbers and are taught quite early about what to do in case they get lost. Adults do this learning automatically for new addresses and phone numbers. That is, people learn early on one or more scripts for resolving 'being lost'. Disorientation in space and time is a clinical sign of AD, and the situation in which people with AD get lost close to home is common (Hirono *et al.* 1998b). It is also common for people with AD not to follow generic scripts to resolve the problem. Here the issues actually appear in what the patient says about his experience. The area near his home did not look familiar to him – he was not able to access the relevant episodic experiences to orient himself. His memory is sufficiently unreliable that he carries his home address on a piece of paper in his pocket. However, he did not use this, or find someone who could help him to use it, to get home. He did ask 'the odd one' about directions, but he apparently did not persist until he got help. (He may in any case have been unable to follow offered directions.) The result was that he went for his morning walk but did not arrive home until late evening. The initial problem then of disorientation is here compounded by problems in episodic and semantic memory, and perhaps ineffective use of script knowledge. This situation may also be exacerbated by social conditioning which inhibits elderly people from seeking appropriate help, perhaps because this would require admitting the extent of their dysfunction.

Ineffective use of script knowledge may be a way of characterizing the typically poor responses to direct questions about instrumental activities of daily living in AD, especially those that require some problem solving or calculation (Royall *et al.* 2005). Cosentino *et al.* (2006) report that people with AD differ from people with behavioural dysexecutive syndrome (a neurodegenerative disorder in which prefrontal cortical regions are differentially impaired) in that while the latter have problems recognizing inappropriate sequencing of script elements (e.g. John got dressed and then had a shower), people with AD are more likely to have difficulty with recognizing conceptually impossible script sequences (e.g. John turned the water off and then had a shower) that require information integration and reasoning abilities which rely on both limbic and prefrontal systems. To the extent that semantic systems are impaired in AD, knowledge of scripts, schemas, frames and scenarios may also be impaired. However, semantic impairments are typically progressive and people lose subordinate and basic level concepts before they lose superordinate categories. In discourse terms, this is reflected in patterns such as preserved use of indefinite reference terms, stereotyped idioms and common syntactic structures. It also may be reflected in preserved interactional and social skills that require high-order (over-learned and perhaps multiply represented) scripts, schemas, frames and scenarios but do not make significant demands on online processing and reasoning abilities. Thus, people with AD may know the routines for talking about the weather (though recent episodic details may be missing or confabulated) and can repeat the story that they have told many times before, but may be unable to tell a new story because of the demands it makes for integrating new information into organized event sequences and deciding which events are the most salient, even when that information is supplied as in picture description tasks (Bschor *et al.* 2001).

8.3   Inferencing in discourse

Our ability to make sense of discourse partially depends on our ability to infer relationships between what is said, what is intended and contexts of situation and culture. The input for inferential reasoning includes not only linguistically encoded information, but also information available in the context and retrieved from memory.

The latter kinds of information may include generic knowledge of scripts, frames, scenarios and schemas, as well as instantial information from modalities such as vision, hearing, touch, smell, taste, proprioception and affect. The ability to use all these different kinds of information to produce and interpret coherent texts requires minimally:

(a) that the information is available,
(b) that information from different sources can be integrated and
(c) that there are sorting procedures for selecting relevant information and inhibiting irrelevant information.

Availability of information presupposes integrity of linguistic, sensory and memory systems. Integration of information is mediated by activity in heteromodal and prefrontal cortical regions and includes the ability to maintain and monitor information online. Maintenance and monitoring, together with selection and inhibition are executive function processes necessary to support inferencing (Shallice1982; 1988; Baddeley 1998; Royall *et al.* 2002). Executive processes may also involve explicit (conscious) manipulation of information – what we speak of as thinking, reasoning, planning and judging (Royall *et al.* 2002; 2005). Once again, the neurological substrate for inferencing processes are matters of ongoing research and debate. However, there are a few areas where there is, if not consensus, at least an observable trend toward convergence. We sketch some of these and then discuss the ways in which inferencing has been addressed in the discourse of people with ASDs.

First, it would appear that there is no localized 'inference processor' – rather, as the minimally necessary elements for inferencing above suggest, even the simplest inference may require the recruitment of large-scale networks. Second, there is convergence on the fact that the prefrontal cortex plays an essential role in inferencing processes – and that specific regions may be preferentially recruited for particular tasks. We discussed earlier in this chapter, for instance, the putative role of the medial orbitofrontal cortex in integrating information from emotion and memory systems in the evaluation of risk and reward. In addition to its role in decision making and risk assessment, the orbitofrontal circuit is associated with inhibition of socially inappropriate behaviour and perhaps monitoring of events (regardless of expected outcomes). Lesions in the orbitofrontal cortex result in dysinhibition, and loss of insight and judgement (Royall *et al.* 2002).

Similarly, the anterior cingulate, dorsal and ventral prefrontal cortices each enter into complex circuits which support inferential processes. The anterior cingulate cortex receives information from the amygdala, orbitofrontal and motor cortices, and hippocampus, and appears to be specialized for monitoring, error correction and initiation. People with lesions in this region have difficulties initiating activities, reduced emotional responses and may have attentional problems (Royall *et al.* 2002; Rushworth *et al.* 2007). The dorsolateral prefrontal cortex is linked in a complex network to the basal ganglia and parietal regions, and is centrally involved in verbal and spatial working memory, planning, goal selection, hypothesis generation, sequencing and set shifting, self-awareness and self-monitoring. Lesions are associated with deficits in these areas (Cabeza and Nyberg 2000; Royall *et al.* 2002; Alvarez and Emory 2006). The left ventrolateral prefrontal cortex normally has dense bi-directional links to the temporal lobes and hippocampus and is associated with semantic selection, working memory and episodic encoding and retrieval (Nobre *et al.* 1999; Cabeza and Nyberg 2000; Petrides *et al.* 2002) as well as more generally with linguistic processes (see Bookheimer 2002 for review).

Finally, the functional roles of the more medial aspects of both dorsal and ventral prefrontal cortex are the subjects of very active research programmes in relation to their roles in inferencing and discourse comprehension (see Ferstl and von Cramon 2002 for review). The dorsomedial prefrontal cortex has been associated with reasoning and evaluation, and may be engaged in internally driven evaluation processes. Such processes are potentially self-reflexive and can include affective content which has led some researchers to associate activations here with emotion processing and theory of mind (e.g. Fletcher *et al.* 1995; Frith and Frith 2003). However, comparable activations have been observed in inferencing tasks unrelated to theory of mind suggesting that this region is more generally involved in making inferences associated with coherence (e.g. Ferstl and von Cramon 2001; 2002; Ferstl *et al.* 2005; Seiborger *et al.* 2007; Ferstl *et al.* 2008 for discussion). In contrast, Ferstl *et al.* (2005) found that responses to emotional information about a protagonist's feelings in simple narratives activated the ventromedial prefrontal cortex bilaterally along the supraorbital sulcus and the left amygdaloid complex. Activation of the ventromedial prefrontal cortex does not appear to be replicated by other inferencing tasks and has been associated with emotion processing, decision making and empathy and so may be linked to the ability to infer mental states in others (Bechara *et al.* 2000; Luan *et al.* 2002; Ferstl *et al.* 2005; 2008). One non-frontal region should also be mentioned in this context: there is robust evidence, primarily from fMRI studies, suggesting that the anterior temporal lobes bilaterally are involved in discourse comprehension. Ferstl *et al.* (2008) suggest that this activity is evidence of integration of linguistic and episodic information into a gist of text meaning. Frith and Frith (2003) suggest instead that this activity reflects script retrieval. Given the widely varied text types and tasks in which this activation appears, the latter suggestion seems the less likely of the two.

These circuits are not 'discourse processors' or 'inference generators' *per se.* Rather they each contribute components to processing discourse or other data as input and to generating inferences necessary for coherence. Within inferencing, which systems are most engaged may depend on the type (e.g. inductive/deductive), phase (e.g. evaluation/conclusion) and complexity of the inference process examined, and may also be affected by the ideational or affective content and media related to the inference.

For example, Reverberi *et al.* (2007) have identified a left lateralized fronto-parietal network that is activated in generating simple deductive conclusions. They make the point that variability in activations across studies may be associated with type and stage of reasoning. They suggest that propositional reasoning may differ from relational reasoning. Such a dissociation would explain the left frontal lobe (BA10) and right basal ganglia activations observed in Fangmeier *et al.* (2006) whose study investigated relational reasoning. Similarly, patterns of activation during evaluation of premises may differ from concluding activations, and more complex arguments may result in regionally distinct as well as more widespread activations (Noveck *et al.* 2004; Monti *et al.* 2007).

Kuperberg *et al.* (2006) identify a more widespread temporal/inferior parietal/prefrontal network associated with constructing causal inferences based on intermediately related (as opposed to obviously or unrelated) three-word prompts. They interpret their findings consistently with the above suggestions in that they see the temporal engagement as involving stored semantic information, inferior prefrontal regions are activated for retrieval and selection, and posterior dorsolateral prefrontal regions may be involved with maintenance and manipulation of new information for integration and consolidation. They also suggest that activations in superior medial prefrontal regions may be involved in directed search for sequence relations relevant to inferencing and that activation in the right temporal and inferior prefrontal regions may be associated with monitoring for incoherence.

Chow *et al.* (2008) examine fMRI correlates of inferencing in a reading task. They contrasted reading for understanding with reading with explicit instructions to predict an outcome for sentences such as 'as the plane approached the cliffs the passengers began to scream'. The target prediction is the causally related item 'crash'. In contrast with a baseline task (reading nonsense words), the reading task activated a network in the left hemisphere including the posterior superior temporal sulcus, anterior temporal lobe, the temporal parietal junction and inferior frontal gyrus. The predictive reading task resulted in additional activity prefrontally in the left anterior prefrontal cortex (BA 9/10), left ventral inferior frontal gyrus (BA 47) and left dorsolateral inferior frontal gyrus (BA 44/45). They suggest that these regions each have specific roles – respectively evaluation, semantic retrieval and integration of strategic inferences. Using dynamic causal modelling (Friston *et al.* 2003), Chow *et al.* (2008) also observed that inferential predictions consistently increased interactions between the left dorsolateral inferior frontal gyrus and the left superior temporal sulcus and interpret this as evidence of top-down control of activation and retrieval of lexico-semantic information. Thus, they hypothesize a network for intentional predictive inferencing in which ventral, dorsal and anterior prefrontal cortical regions guide and integrate information selection from lexico-semantic systems in the temporal lobe and evaluate it for coherence. Since the anterior prefrontal activations are seen in the predictive reading task but not in the contrast task (read for understanding), they suggest that the anterior prefrontal activations are specifically associated with the intentional nature of the prediction task.

Den Ouden *et al.* (2005) also suggest that the anterior prefrontal cortex (BA10) (together with the right parietal cortex and precuneus) is specifically involved with prediction or 'prospective memory' and furthermore point to differences in activation patterns depending on what thinkers are thinking about – that is, in their fMRI study activations varied depending on whether participants were thinking about their own intentions versus events caused by the physical environment. 'Intentional causality', where participants were thinking about their own intended actions, activated a wide network that included the precuneus/ posterior cingulate cortex, posterior medial dorsolateral prefrontal cortex, the superior temporal sulcus bilaterally and the temporal poles bilaterally. They associate each of these regions with component aspects of theory of mind, but point to increased activation in an anterior portion of the dorsomedial prefrontal cortex as differentially engaged in intentional causality. Ferstl *et al.* (2005)

and Ferstl and von Cramon (2007) also describe content specific activations during text comprehension. However, as noted above they make the point that the 'theory of mind network' activates the same regions as their general purpose discourse coherence network (see also Ferstl et al. 2008).

Studies such as these consistently suggest complex interactions in functional networks in inference processing – with the type, complexity and context of the inference all affecting the systems involved. They also show some activation in the right hemisphere which has been proposed as being especially important in inference processing and coherence (Marini et al. 2005), as well as being linked to social and emotion processing. However, it is not yet clear what roles the right hemisphere plays in inferencing. One possibility is that prefrontal activity in the right hemisphere may reflect, as Tulving (1983) suggested, an episodic 'retrieval mode' that allows the integration of modality specific information associated with memories and their relation to the rememberer. A second view is that the right hemisphere functions to boost processing capacity, when task demands exceed those of the left hemisphere (e.g. Schacter et al. 1996; Mason and Just 2007). This fits well not only with imaging in healthy populations where right hemisphere engagement appears more often when processing demands are high (e.g. Wagner et al. 2001), but also in aging and demented populations where right hemisphere activity appears to be compensatory (e.g. Dolcos et al. 2002; Grady et al. 2003). Specific roles have also been suggested for particular regions. For example, Henson et al. (1999), Shallice et al. (1994) and others (Rugg et al. 1996; Schacter et al. 1996) have suggested that right-sided prefrontal activity is involved in 'post episodic retrieval processes' such as monitoring. Kuperberg et al.'s (2007) tentative proposal of an 'incoherence detector' is somewhat similar. It should be noted that these are not mutually exclusive possibilities: compensatory activity in the right hemisphere might coincide with an episodic retrieval mode and neither of these exclude monitoring or other processes. It is also worth noting that despite all the interest in identifying specific roles for the right hemisphere in inferencing, theory of mind and discourse processing, recent reviews suggest that language processing is (at least in the right-handed populations studied) predominantly left lateralized. Exceptions appear to be for consistent bilateral activations of the anterior temporal lobes and right lateralized activation of the ventromedial prefrontal cortex for emotional processing (Ferstl et al. 2008). Other activations observed in the right hemisphere, associated for instance with metaphor processing are, so far, inconsistent and might be accounted for in terms of increases in processing load or episodic memory search as a response to processing load demands (Wagner et al. 2001; Stowe et al. 2005; Ferstl et al. 2008).

Just as the neurological picture for inferencing abilities is not complete, so the discoursal signs of impaired inferencing abilities are still under investigation.

In autism, abilities to construct coherence and infer intentions are actively being investigated. Investigations are framed within models such that autism is said to be characterized by inability to imagine the cognitive and emotional states of others (the theory of mind deficit) which is thought to lead to difficulties in inferring the intentions of others (Baron-Cohen *et al.* 1985; Happé 1993; Baron-Cohen 1995). Differences in processing style and ability to integrate information from different sources have also been probed as characteristic of ASDs and have been associated with difficulties in the production and interpretation of discourse. The characteristic processing style is described in central coherence theory (e.g. Frith and Happé 1994; Jolliffe and Baron-Cohen 1999a). Studies have addressed these questions globally from model theoretic perspectives or they have addressed specific aspects of inferential processing and coherence construction.

For instance, Happé (1993) found that there are problems with relevance in social communication: participants could answer questions, but responses were not always relevant to context. She also investigated abilities to understand similes, metaphors and irony and found problems in inferencing. In a small study, Dennis *et al.* (2001) investigated a range of tasks involving inferencing in discourse and found that children with autism had more difficulty with implication than with presupposition. They hypothesize that children with autism make inferences from texts to fixed generic knowledge rather than using instantial information. Happé (1997) also investigated problems of inference from instantial situations using a homograph task where children were asked to select appropriate values for potentially ambiguous words, as in *there was a big tear on her cheek* or *there was a big tear on her dress* (Happé 1997). The study found that children with autism were more likely to make errors because they did not integrate the sentence context in producing their interpretations. These findings were supported in a later study by Jolliffe and Baron-Cohen (1999a) who found that people with Asperger syndrome and high functioning autism performed less well than controls on three tasks requiring use of relevant contextual information, designed to evaluate ability to interpret text as an integrated whole. On homographs and auditorily presented ambiguous sentences, people with an autism spectrum disorder were slower and less accurate than control participants. They also took longer and made incorrect inferences in an interpretation task that required 'bridging' inferences (the inferring of a connection between the current clause and a preceding clause or passage).

More recently, Norbury and Bishop (2002) investigated inferencing and pragmatic abilities in typically developing children, children with high functioning autism, and children with specific language impairment and pragmatic language impairment without autism. In questions about text-connecting and gapping inferences in a story, children with autism had more difficulty with inferencing than others. The 'text-connecting' inferences required children to infer a relationship between two sentences (e.g. that 'juice' and 'the drink', mentioned in different sentences, referred to the same object). In gap-filling inferences, children were required to use general knowledge and textually supplied information to infer facts not stated in the text, such as the location of the seaside based on mention of a swimming costume, sandcastles and water in a story. Again, the children tended to use general knowledge or personal experience rather than the information presented in the story to answer the inferential questions. Norbury and Bishop (2002) suggest that these differences reflect difficulty in incorporating the story information in order to make inferences. These studies may appear to contrast with others such as Saldaña and Frith (2007), who found that sixteen adolescents with autism did not differ from matched control participants in ability to make bridging inferences from world knowledge. However, the inferences in the latter study differ in that they require participants to use generalized knowledge of the world (e.g. that rocks can be big, and that if you drop them on people, people might get hurt), as compared with textually supplied information required for inferences in the Norbury and Bishop (2002) study. (For example, in Norbury and Bishop's study, the story mentioned a clock chiming when some participants were at a pier. Participants were later asked where the clock was. A correct inference would use the story – 'the clock was on the pier'. An incorrect inference would use general knowledge as in the example response from Norbury and Bishop *the clock was in the participants' bedroom*.)

Several studies have looked at humour and found difficulties in ASDs, including interpreting ironic jokes (Martin and McDonald 2004), and explaining the motivations behind story characters' utterances in ways that are appropriate to context (Happé 1994; Jolliffe and Baron-Cohen 1999b). Ozonoff and Miller (1996) found that on tasks measuring humour appreciation, inference and indirect requests in narratives, seventeen high-functioning adults with autism produced significantly more errors in all tasks than a control group. Error analysis of responses to humorous stories showed that the people with autism tended to choose literal or non sequitur funny responses, instead of simply funny or other responses. Ozonoff and Miller suggest: (a) that people with autism do understand that jokes are supposed to be funny, despite the fact that they have significantly more difficulty selecting the 'correct, straight-forwardly funny' punch lines than controls; (b) that the completion of the joke required participants to reinterpret the preceding story in ways that demand a cognitive flexibility which people with autism may have difficulty with; and finally (c) that the tendency for autism participants to choose straightforward story endings or non sequitur funny story endings may reflect problems in set shifting – that is, the straightforward story ending is quite coherent and within the set of the story, while the non sequitur funny ending does not require reinterpretation of the story.

One part of the emergent picture from these and similar studies is evidence that people with autism and Asperger syndrome process information differently, with tendencies to rely on general world knowledge or otherwise given information (from personal experience or from information that is 'old' in the context) in responding to questions and drawing inferences, instead of using new information supplied in the instance. Another fairly robust finding in ASDs is that people often have difficulty with the Gricean maxim of quantity, for example supplying either too little or too much information (Bishop and Adams 1989; Surian *et al.* 1996; de Villiers *et al.* 2007). Loukusa *et al.* (2007) associated the type of information supplied with development stage. In a study investigating the abilities of children with high functioning autism and Asperger syndrome to respond relevantly, they found both younger and older children violated the Gricean maxim of quantity by responding to questions with additional information that created a semantic drift. In the younger children, extra information was about their own experiences, while in older children extra information was more general. Loukusa *et al.* (2007) suggest the speakers with high functioning autism and Asperger syndrome may not stop processing after giving a relevant answer.

The converse of this pattern, where too little information is supplied, is illustrated in Text 8.2 below (repeated from Chapter 2) in which, Patrick, a twelve year old boy with autism, responds to questions about movies and Christmas.

Text 8.2 Free Willy

(1) RES: do you have some movies that you like?
(2) RES: what's the last movie that you saw?
(3) RES: what was it about?
(4) RES: did you see a movie at Christmas time?
(5) CHI: yeah: ## yeah ((faint)).
(6) RES: pardon?
(7) CHI: yeah.
(8) CHI: I did.
(9) RES: what movie did you see?
(10) CHI: Free Willy ((faint)).
(11) RES: pardon?
(12) CHI: Free Willy.
(13) RES: Free Willy.
(14) RES: was it good?
(15) CHI: good.
(16) RES: I've never seen that movie.
(17) RES: can you tell me what it's about Patrick?
(18) CHI: it's Free Willy.
(19) RES : it's Free Willy.
(20) CHI: I watched that show.
(21) CHI: Free Willy.

(22) RES: did you watch it at home?
(23) RES: hm?
(24) CHI: ## yeah.
(25) RES: did you watch it at your house?
(26) CHI: yeah.
(27) RES: tell me about Christmas Patrick.
(28) RES: did you have a good Christmas?
(29) CHI: yeah.
(30) CHI: I have a good Christmas.
(31) RES: what did you get for Christmas?
(32) RES: did you get presents?
(33) CHI: presents.
(34) RES: what did you get?
(35) CHI: I get : toys.
(36) CHI: I should get toys.
(37) RES: get toys?
(38) RES: what kind of toys?
(39) CHI: I : um I # didn't bring it.
(40) RES: pardon?
(41) CHI: I bring it.
(42) RES: you'll bring it?
(43) RES: did you bring it to school?
(44) CHI: ## yeah.
(45) RES: yeah?
(46) RES: what was it?
(47) CHI: Free Willy.
(48) RES: Free Willy hm.

Patrick provides frequent polar responses without elaboration (5, 7–8, 24, 26). He also responds to questions with partial repetitions of given information, repeating parts of questions (tautologies (15, 30, 33)), or previously presented information. So when asked, for instance, what Free Willy is about he simply repeats the film title (*it's Free Willy*), which in Gricean terms is under-informative. This response and *I watched that show* (20) might be delayed responses to the earlier questions about whether he had seen a movie (2, 4) and what it was (9). The repetition of *Free Willy* (21) may be intended to clarify the reference of *that show*, or to emphasize the response, or again, it may be a delayed response to the listed earlier questions which are phrased in a variety of ways. It may also be an attempt to please his interlocutor; Patrick has already received positive reinforcement for saying *Free Willy* several times. Alternatively, it may be a sort of ideational perseveration (Bayles *et al.* 1987). It is also possible that Patrick does not understand what is wanted as a response, and finally, if he does, it may be that he has difficulty organizing his knowledge of the film in ways that allow him to answer the question with sufficient information – that is as a script with an ordered sequence of events.

The exchange from lines (31–47) also deserves comment.

(31) RES: what did you get for Christmas?
(32) RES: did you get presents?
(33) CHI: presents.
(34) RES: what did you get?
(35) CHI: I get : toys.
(36) CHI: I should get toys.
(37) RES: get toys?
(38) RES: what kind of toys?
(39) CHI: I : um I # didn't bring it.
(40) RES: pardon?
(41) CHI: I bring it.
(42) RES: you'll bring it?
(43) RES: did you bring it to school?
(44) CHI: ## yeah.
(45) RES: yeah?
(46) RES: what was it?
(47) CHI: Free Willy.

Patrick's response to the question about what kinds of toys he got for Christmas *I : um I # didn't bring it* (39) appears irrelevant in part because of the pronoun *it* which doesn't have a clear antecedent, but also because the response does not appear to address the question *what kind of toys* (did you get) (38). It is possible that the question *what kind of toys,* which calls for categorization, is too abstract for Patrick. However, assuming that since he does reply he is attempting to be co-operative, it may also be reasonable to infer that his *I didn't bring it* refers to the generic situation type of 'show and tell' in which children bring new toys and experiences to share in school. His response then might be thought of as drawing on his generic knowledge of toy sharing and in this sense is indirectly relevant – it also highlights the patterns noted in Loukusa *et al.* (2007) and others that children with autism may use personal or general knowledge to respond to questions rather than responding to the instantial demands of the situation.

Much of the work on inferential processing in discourse has been directed toward considerations of relevance, as developed, for example, in Grice's model (1975) of conversational maxims and extended in Sperber and Wilson (1986; 1995). Theories of relevance or the Gricean co-operative principle are predicated on models of 'normal' behaviour with the assumption that features such as truthfulness are controlled by the speaker. The context of pathology poses a challenge for some of these assumptions. People who confabulate, for instance, may be quite unaware of the falseness of their assertions, and some disorders, such as autism, can make the demands for relevance quite difficult. What such a framework does help with is in pointing out areas of difference imposed by particular neurological impairments.

Table 8.1. *Gricean maxims in Alzheimer's disease and Asperger syndrome*

Relevance (model presupposes neurotypical function)	Alzheimer's disease	Asperger syndrome
Quality (truthfulness: don't say things you know to be untrue or for which you lack evidence)	– Confabulation – Paranoid suspicions	– Literalness
Quantity: too little information too much information	– Underspecified, deictic reference –Repetition, verbosity	– Poor or linear topic development, terseness – Pedantic, specificity and detail of NPs
Relevance: be relevant (cohesive and coherent), topic sharing assumes mutual interest or at least socially conditioned behavioural norms that allow performance of mutual interests	– Tangential (can't track conversation, so incoherent) – Perseverative ideation: return to same topic despite current one	– Difficulty contextualizing
Manner: be clear, avoid obscurity, avoid ambiguity, be orderly	– Poor planning, information-processing problems lead to fragmented incomplete, unplanned 'disordered' discourse which may affect cohesion and/or coherence	– Difficulty foregrounding and backgrounding information – Sometimes poor discourse planning, though discourse can be very orderly

In Section 8.2 we outlined cognitive models involved in 'top-down' processing of information. These models highlight generic features that people use to make inferences which allow them to interpret what is being said and decide how to respond to it. In this section we have looked at research on inferencing in neuroimaging and in the discourse of people with ASDs and considered some of the ways in which people do not incorporate information from models in ways that let them arrive at an appropriate inference or use it in an appropriate response. We end the section with a presentation of Grice's conversational maxims and their applicability to Alzheimer's disease and Asperger syndrome. As can be seen from Table 8.1, Asperger syndrome does not present problems for Grice's first maxim, Quality or truthfulness, though other conversational maxims may not be followed. In Alzheimer's disease, although observation of turn-taking patterns and responsiveness suggest that people with AD genuinely try to co-operate in conversation (Ramanathan-Abbott 1994; Temple *et al.* 1999), they regularly fail to follow Gricean maxims.

8.4   Affect

In our discussions of top-down processing and inferencing abilities, the primary focus has been on experiential aspects of discourse. In this section we shift focus to affect in discourse. By affect, we refer to the ability to modalize what we say in terms of deontic (obligation) and epistemic (likelihood) values, to express attitudes and evaluations about what is said, and to express emotions. Modalization, attitude and evaluation have been described in terms of interpersonal systems of mediation (Halliday 1994) or interactional systems (Gregory 2009c; 2009d). These resources have been further explicated in appraisal theory (White 1998; Martin 2000; Martin and White 2005). In Chapter 4, we outlined the linguistic elements for expressing modalizations, attitudes and evaluations in detail. Here we illustrate their instantiations in two sample texts and describe how emotion is represented in one of the texts.

In the appraisal framework, speakers are assumed to systematically and continuously orient themselves to others and to what they are saying through expressions of modalization and positive, neutral or negative evaluation and attitude. Such expressions can be unconscious or deliberate. Discourse may also be described as being more or less univocal or 'monoglossic' (White 2000). In monoglossic discourse, speakers may signal positive or negative evaluations and attitudes and express emotions, but they do not modalize in ways that acknowledge other possible states of affairs or interpretations other than their own. Discourse which is monoglossic contrasts with heteroglossic discourse which does make such gestures to others. The following text is a conversation in which an eleven-year-old speaker with autism responds to questions about a potentially emotional and exciting event, Christmas, with a marked absence of expressions of affect and no evident attempts to orient to his addressee except insofar as he does respond to questions. Later in the same conversation the topic shifts from Christmas dinner to favourite foods and then to after-school activities.

Text 8.3 Christmas

(1) RES: it's almost Christmas time Joseph.
(2) RES: it's December.
(3) RES: are you getting excited?
(4) CHI: yeah.
(5) RES: yeah?
(6) RES: what would you like to get for Christmas?
(7) CHI: a Real Talkin Bubba.
(8) RES: what's a Bubba?
(9) CHI: a um oh uh uh a real talking joke playing best friend bear.
(10) RES: oh I see.
(11) RES: do they have them in stores?

(12) CHI: uh uh uh uh: the: uh : they have them on tv.
(13) RES: oh is that where you've seen them?
(14) CHI: yeah.
(15) RES: umhum.
(16) RES: and what did your mom ask for something for Christmas?
(17) CHI: um um he a.
(18) CHI: no no.
(19) CHI: she didn't.
(20) RES: no?
(21) RES: are you going to get her a present?
(22) CHI: uhhuh.
(23) RES: do you know what you're going to get her?
(24) CHI: a Real Talkin Bubba.
(25) RES: oh : .
(26) RES: you're going to get your mom one too?
(27) CHI: yeah.
(28) RES: so that'll mean you'll have two at your house.
(29) CHI: yeah.
(30) RES: wow!
(31) RES: that'll be nice.
(32) RES: so what do you do on Christmas day Joseph?
(33) CHI: I play games.
(34) RES: umhum.
(35) RES: and do you have some friends or family in?
(36) CHI: no.
(37) CHI: I don't.
(38) RES: no.
(39) RES: do you go somewhere for Christmas?
(40) CHI: I don't go anywhere.
(41) RES: no?
(42) RES: hm.
(43) RES: do you have a turkey on Christmas Day?
(44) CHI: uh : .
(45) CHI: I do eat turkey.
(46) CHI: um I do eat turkey.
(47) RES: do you like turkey?
(48) CHI: umhum.
(49) RES: I do too.
(50) RES: I like turkey and dressing and potatoes.
(51) CHI: yeah.
(52) RES: what's your favourite food Joseph?
(53) CHI: ah ah **my** favourite food is rice.
(54) RES: is which?
(55) CHI: my favourite is my favourite food is turkey.
(56) RES: turkey?
(57) RES: mm.
(58) RES: what else do you like what else do you like eating?
(59) CHI: nothing.

(60) CHI: nothing.
(61) RES: mm.
(62) RES: what do you do when you go home from school Joseph?
(63) CHI: ah : I play games.
(64) RES: what kind of games?
(65) CHI: every game.
(66) RES: mm.
(67) RES: can you tell me one of the games that you have at your house?
(68) CHI: I don know what is the games.
(69) RES: hm.
(70) RES: do you have board games or card games?
(71) CHI: uh uh I play board games.
(72) RES: mm.
(73) RES: what board game do you play?
(74) CHI: I pay I pla # I play a card game.
(75) RES: umhum?
(76) RES: and do you watch television?
(77) CHI: umhum.
(78) RES: what's your favourite show on television.
(79) CHI: a card a Real Talkin Bubba.
(80) RES: oh I see.
(81) RES: ((laughter)).
(82) RES: are they on television a lot?
(83) CHI: umhum.

The interviewer unsurprisingly asks all the questions. In doing so, she supplies prompts that might elicit some expression of emotion or attitude. For example, she asks Joseph *are you getting excited* (3) and expresses positive attitude (*wow that'll be nice* (30–31)) about having two *talkin' bubba*s at his house. (A *talkin' bubba* is his desired Christmas present and also apparently what he plans to give to his mother.) Joseph replies only with a *yeah* to the first prompt, without marked intonation that might reflect real excitement, and does not respond to or acknowledge the second evaluation. A speaker who shares the positive evaluation of the interviewer might be expected to at least acknowledge it (*yeah*), and often speakers will reiterate or intensify its value (e.g. 'yeah it'll be great') to show interpersonal alignment. Joseph does not overtly appear to align himself in relation to the interviewer, except where he acknowledges her positive evaluation of a turkey dinner (51) and in that he may also try to provide responses he thinks the interviewer wants. For example, his first vote for favourite foods is rice, but then he switches to turkey, which is given information that the interviewer has already positively evaluated (50–55):

(50) RES: I like turkey and dressing and potatoes.
(51) CHI: yeah.
(52) RES: what's your favourite food Joseph?
(53) CHI: ah ah **my** favourite food is rice.

(54) RES: is which?
(55) CHI: my favourite is my favourite food is turkey.

While Joseph readily provides answers to the questions he is asked, he does not modalize his discourse in terms of possibilities or alternatives. He appears, for instance, to only want one thing for Christmas (a *Real Talkin' Bubba*). He never says things such as 'I might play games' or 'I think we'll have turkey', and provides unequivocal responses to all questions. His discourse is in this respect monoglossic (White 2000).

Similarly, topics are raised which might be expected to elicit some sort of affective response. Joseph is asked what he and his family do on Christmas Day (32–46), whether he likes turkey (47) and what his favourite food is (52–60). To all of these he responds with statements without any expression of evaluation, attitude or emotion. He neither evaluates positively for things he might well enjoy such as playing games at home, nor does he express disappointment or boredom about not having visitors or going somewhere at Christmas. The only place where he appears to offer positive appraisal is in his description of what a *Real Talkin' Bubba* is. In responding to this question he incorporates positively weighted lexical selections (*best friend*), and material from the advertisement (*tells jokes*) into the name of the toy. *Real Talkin' Bubba* becomes a *real talking, joke-telling, best friend bear.* The addition of *best friend* appears to be his own, but may have been part of a television ad.

Joseph does not elaborate his responses. His responses to both questions about what he does on Christmas Day and what he does after school are identical (*I play games*). However, he has real difficulties in classifying the games he plays (*every game),* identifying the games (*I don know what is the games*), and offers no descriptions. He also has some fluency difficulties (12, 74). It may be that the apparent monoglossic style and lack of appraisal features are related to problems with expressive language.

In contrast with the absence of affect we see in Joseph's discourse, people with AD often have conspicuous affect, including emotional responses.[3] As noted in Chapter 6, people with AD often also modalize extensively, reflecting their characteristic epistemic uncertainty. The patient seen in Text 8.4, Julia, is somewhat different in that she has very mild, and successfully treated, AD.

Text 8.4 Travel plans

(1) P: I'm # booked now to go to Toronto on the first of May for fifteen days
(2) IV: nice
(3) P: yeah so I'm looking forward to that
(4) IV: so you're planning that trip
(5) P: um hum yes I'm planning that (8) and that's for my oldest son who works there at the hospital and my daughter-in-law there is a radiologist. I think I've told you that before. So Sarah # that's her name # is busy and I had a great visit with her.

Did I tell you about that IV? I was there for Christmas and into New Year yeah I guess I told you.

(6) IV: this year?

(7) P: yeah oh maybe I didn't. I don't know. When did you last come?

(8) IV: I was here before Christmas

(9) P: yes I probably told you I was going and I did go and we had a really pleasant visit

(10) IV: isn't that great

(11) P: yes and ….

…

(12) P: oh yes and I'm sure there'll be other young people and ah let's see Emily's fourteen and Alice is eleven so they're at a nice age to travel they'll really enjoy that get a lot out of it # I'm glad for Alice who needs a change and ( ) too he works very hard he works for the television company in Toronto and ah ## now where were we IV?

(13) IV: ( )

(14) P: I'm telling you about things that I'm going to do and then you get a picture and what I have been doing

(15) IV: so how about are you planning even longer term like after um in the summer doing something or

(16) P: I haven't made many plans I don't think that we've made any from the time I get back # ah # you know ah # I'll come back from Toronto of course mid May the fifteenth I guess and ah well I like being here a lot of the summer because I love gardening and ah you know that's the time # so when I come back in May I'll enjoy you know ah I'll go with either Carol or Ellen and get some plants and well I usually plant either the last week of May or early June and if it's if there's still a frost warning as there usually is in early June Ellen helps me and I'll still have some of this pine I've got over my gardens for the winter that's for my bulbs

(17) IV: yes

(18) P: she and I had put those in and of course I love ( ) towards the back there and that will be really nice there's something so special about the first flowers springtime

(19) IV: our crocuses are up

(20) P: **oh are they**?

(21) IV: we have a big bed of crocuses and so I picked some yesterday to take to the hospital for mom and dad

(22) P: oh how nice

Julia monitors information in her discourse and does modalize episodic details but her discourse is very informative and comparatively lexically dense with a high proportion of subordinate category references. She orients continuously to the interviewer's needs for information, expresses positive attitude and evaluations both about her own and others' activities and aligns herself with the interviewer's positive evaluations and expressions of pleasure. For example, Julia asks questions of the interviewer to monitor information flow (*Did I tell you about that IV? (5) Now where were we IV? (12)*) and only once asks an episodic checking question (*When did you last come? (7)*). She also monitors information flow through modalized statements about the discourse as in *I think I've told you that before (5), yeah I guess I told you (5), yes I probably told you I was going (9)* and twice expresses uncertainty as in *oh maybe I didn't. I don't know.* Once she appears to monitor an interior (unspoken) question about a participant's name in *So Sarah # that's her name # is busy (5).* Elsewhere in the discourse, she actively clarifies the reference of phrases that might be unclear for the interviewer by supplying relevant information in relative clauses or NP adjuncts as in *my oldest son who works there at the hospital (5)* or *Alex, my husband, was a ...* (ellipted from Text 8.4). She also explicitly comments on her own discourse strategy for the benefit of the interviewer in *I'm telling you about things that I'm going to do and then you get a picture and what I have been doing (14).* In these and similar examples she shows herself to be actively monitoring information for the benefit of her addressee. It is also the case that she supplies details about participants and events so that the interviewer can develop a really complete picture of what and who she is talking about, and share her experience and enthusiasm.

Julia responds to all prompts from the interviewer and aligns herself consistently with the interviewer's evaluations. So for example, when the interviewer offers positive evaluation *nice (2)* of the planned trip, Julia acknowledges with a *yeah,* and then elaborates with another positive evaluation (*I'm looking forward to that (3)*). She contextualizes her anticipation of enjoyment with reference to an earlier visit in which she positively evaluates (*I had a great visit with her (5)* and *we had a really pleasant visit (9)*). She responds to the interviewer's evaluation (*isn't that great (10)*) with a *yes* and then a long narrative about other 'great' activities she's been involved in (omitted from the text). When asked about longer term plans, she modalizes and hesitates a bit initially, but then elaborates a specific plan to stay home in the summer because she likes gardening:

I haven't made many plans I don't think that we've made any from the time I get back # ah # you know ah # I'll come back from Toronto of course mid May the fifteenth I guess and ah.

This passage contains not only explicitly positive statements about her own experiences (*... I like being here a lot of the summer because I love gardening ...(16)*) and evaluations of the phenomena which stimulate these experiences (*... that will be really nice there's something so special about the first flowers springtime ...(18)*) but also again shows her actively engaging and aligning with the interviewer's offer of information (*our crocuses are up (19)*) with another question with marked intonation (*oh are they? (20)*) signalling (perhaps delighted) surprise and then positively evaluating the interviewer's reported action of taking flowers to her parents with an *oh how nice.*

In his work on the language of affect, Downes (2000) points out that emotion shares with language a system of meanings that are categorized. He outlines resources for experiencing and expressing emotional affect including **semantic and lexical resources** and **indexical** or **iconic resources**. We can see Julia making use of these resources. For example, it's expected that people will be excited before a trip. Not surprisingly then, when Julia projects ahead in conversation to her upcoming trip, she expresses affect (*I'm looking forward to it*). In this she exploits semantic and lexical resources for affect in order to show her response to the projected situation. Similar uses of semantic and lexical resources appear in Julia's categorizations of her feelings: she uses both oppositional verbs such as *enjoy, like, love* and gradable adjectives (*glad, nice, pleasant* and *special*), the latter two with intensifiers (*really* and *so*).

Downes also suggests that any linguistic feature or feature combination can indexically or iconically signal affect in real or imagined situations where emotion is evoked. For example, the overall impression that Julia conveys of being happy, thoughtful and engaged might be thought of as iconically represented in her discourse not only through the frequency and repetition of positive evaluative lexis, but also in the amount of information which she volunteers in order to convey her plans and attitudes to her addressee. This elaboration suggests her emotional state and attitude. Finally, as mentioned above, Julia's response to the interviewer's early crocuses (as signs of spring) with prosodic features of increased loudness and rising tone index her enthusiasm.

The affective features of discourse are describable in terms of lexical, syntactic, prosodic and conceptual features which modalize, evaluate or express attitudes. Cognitive models such as scripts and frames describe generic expectations relative to situations. These models may embed evaluations which influence people's judgements in and about instantial situations. (Think of the script for preparing a tax return!) Clinical investigations, especially of framing effects, have shown that patients' judgements and emotional states may be influenced by positive and negative evaluations attached to these models (e.g Everingham *et al.* 2006; Ehrenreich *et al.* 2007; Berg *et al.* 2008). Indeed, the development and use of cognitive therapies to treat affective disorders such as depression and anxiety are predicated on links between cognitive models (especially, but not exclusively, of self) and their relation to emotional states (see Beck 2005 for review).

Here we have shown reduced presentation of affect in one text (8.3) by a speaker with autism, and a display of positive affect in text 8.4 by a speaker with Alzheimer's. In presenting these analyses, we deliberately hedged our descriptions of possible emotional states in the speakers. What discourse analysis allows is merely a description of presented patterns. Inferencing beyond patterns is of course what we all do in our everyday lives. However, in clinical contexts, particularly where speakers' abilities to express affect may be compromised by cognitive impairments, such attribution needs to be guided by neuropsychological and/or psychiatric assessments of emotional states and by patient and caregiver input. The absence, for instance, of emotional prosody is not necessarily evidence of detachment or an absence of emotional involvement – it may reflect an inability to use prosodic resources.

Apart from mentioning the debated theory of mind network and the function of the ventromedial prefrontal cortex in emotional awareness, we have not attempted to articulate neural substrates for affect and emotion. The few areas where there is consensus are well described in the literature. There are some brain regions such as the amygdala, hippocampus and medial prefrontal cortex which are particularly associated with emotional processing (Mesulam 1998; Phan *et al.* 2002; Wager *et al.* 2003; Sergerie *et al.* 2008). There is also some evidence, based in part on impressions from neural trauma, that the right hemisphere may be more involved in emotion and mood. However, the meta-analyses of imaging studies (just cited) do not support greater right lateralization for emotion processing and, in a review of neuropsychiatric disorders associated with brain injury, Cummings (1997) makes the point that while right brain injury is often associated with neuropsychiatric symptoms, most can occur as a consequence of injury to either hemisphere and 'only mania and certain types of personality change are uniquely associated with right brain damage' (p. 33). Cummings suggests that the right hemisphere is important in mood and other disorders because of its role in supporting interaction abilities. There are many observations which associate capacity for expressing and interpreting emotional prosody, facial expression and gesture with damage to the right hemisphere, as well as with pragmatic difficulties in discourse (Mesulam 2000). The relationships of emotion and affect to neurotransmitters such as seratonin, dopamine and noradrenaline have also received extensive attention, perhaps because they are targets for pharmacological interventions (Delgado and Moreno 2006 for review).

There are a great many more areas where research is underway including investigation of relationships between discourse patterns and the neural instantiation of affect and emotional states. However, the work of correlating discourse patterns with neurally, or even neuropsychologically identified or emotional affective states is only beginning. At present, there are some emergent patterns. Just as it seems that ideational components of concepts and models appear to have distributed representations associated with their modal and/or functional values, so emotionally associated words, and indeed discourses appear to differentially activate neural networks linked to emotion processing. For example, Beauregard *et al.* (1997) investigated blood flow in relation to passive viewing of concrete (bear, elephant, rabbit), abstract (ego, purity, rumour) and 'emotionally laden' (sex, murder, sadness) words. They found that the emotional words differentially activated orbitofrontal and medial frontal cortices, compared with abstract or concrete words, or a baseline image. Similarly, Ferstl *et al.* (2005) observed activation in the ventromedial prefrontal cortex associated with participants reading stories with emotional information about the protagonist's feelings. And Goldin *et al.* (2005) observed similar activations in anterior medial prefrontal cortex as part of a network associated with watching sad or amusing film clips. This region has been associated in many studies with different aspects of emotion processing – including imagining emotional events in the distant future (D'Argembeau *et al.* 2008) and viewing emotionally laden negative pictures (Ochsner *et al.* 2002). In a meta-analysis of eighty studies, Seitz *et al.* (2006) associate the region with empathy, but articulate empathy as a collection of processes which are said to be represented in anatomically distinct subregions of the medial prefrontal cortex. The salient point for present purposes is that this region does seem to be involved in networks which process information from a wide variety of emotional stimuli – pictures, films, thoughts about the future, stories and words.

There is also a growing body of imaging evidence which distinguishes activation patterns for different emotions. For example, in the study mentioned above by Goldin *et al.* (2005), amusing films differentially activated subcortical regions associated with positive emotional states (love, happiness) and memory whereas the sad films differentially activated parts of the visual object processing path as well as the amygdala. Two other areas for consideration are emotional intensity (or arousal) and emotional suppression. Dolcos *et al.* (2004) studied arousal for positive and negative emotions (valence) in a picture viewing and rating fMRI task. They found that the dorsolateral prefrontal cortex (generally associated with monitoring) was activated bilaterally, but the left hemisphere was more active for positive pictures and the right for negative pictures. Further, the dorsomedial prefrontal cortex (associated with self-awareness) was more active for more intense emotions, while the ventromedial area (associated with (self-)reflection) was more active for positive emotions. Finally, in an fMRI study designed to address the effects of reappraisal, Oschsner *et al.* (2002) found that appraisal activated a system that included the amygdala and orbitofrontal cortex. Reappraisal deactivated these regions but increased activations in the dorsal and ventral left prefrontal cortex and the dorsomedial prefrontal cortex as part of a more extended network.

The studies described are not intended to create a complete picture of emotion processing in relation to discourse, nor to outline the neural basis for emotion processing – rather, they are intended to make some more modest points that seem to be emerging from current work on emotion. First, the prefrontal cortex seems to function, as Mesulam would put it (1998) like a hub, not for emotions per se but for processing emotional responses and the information that prompts them. Second, specific subregions of the prefrontal cortex appear to be involved with particular parts of this processing. So, as with inferencing, the dorsolateral prefrontal cortex monitors, the dorsomedial region engages for reflection and so on. Third, the prefrontal areas form parts of larger networks that engage cortical and subcortical regions associated with memory, emotion and attention. And just as there is no 'inference generator' or 'coherence generator', so there is no single 'emotion processor', or generator for that matter. Instead, the pattern is of a large-scale functional network, the components of which are differentially engaged according to the content, valence and value of the emotional experience. Finally, the overlap between networks engaged in studies of emotion processing and studies of inferencing and discourse processing suggest at the very least that there is a lot of interesting work to be done.

8.5   Samples analysis

We end Chapter 8 by considering some of the situational models we have explored in reference to a text produced by Will, a 7-year-old speaker with autism. Here he is talking about construction sites in a context where there are toy trucks.

Text 8.5 Construction sites

(1) RES: And then what would it do?
(2) CHI: It would move along.
(3) RES: Where would it move along to?
(4) CHI: The construction site.
(5) RES: The construction site.
(6) RES: And what would it do there?
(7) CHI: Pour cement.
(8) RES: Pour cement?
(9) CHI: Yes.
(10) CHI: And then it hardens.
(11) RES: And when it hardens what happens?
(12) CHI: Then it **dries**.
(13) RES: It dries.
(14) RES: Uhhuh.
(15) RES: And what does it make?
(16) CHI: Um # and it turns that way instead of coming this way.
(17) CHI: That's because they are many machines in the construction site.
(18) RES: there are many which?
(19) CHI: Them there are many machines in the construction site.
(20) CHI: Be careful.
(21) CHI: There might be danger.
(22) CHI: Okay.
(23) CHI: Uh okay bye bye!
(24) CHI: That was great.

Will has a script for what happens in a construction site (a cement truck moves along, it pours cement, cement hardens). When prompted, he offers these actions (2, 7), and in one case he adds an action, in proper sequence, without a prompt (*and then it hardens* (10)). He provides additional generic information about the truck's actions (*it turns that way instead of coming this way* (16)), though this response is not directly relevant to the question posed by the interviewer. Thus the script provided for pouring cement includes:

- a cement trucks moves along to a construction site (2, 4)
- pours cement (7)
- cement hardens and dries (10, 12)
- cement truck navigates around other machines in the site (16–17).

While Will has some success in generating this script through co-construction, he also appears inflexible or limited in his script knowledge. When asked *what does it make* he responds by continuing to talk about the truck's activities (*Um # and it turns that way instead of coming this way* (16)), even elaborating with an explanation for these actions (*that's because they are many machines in the construction site* (17)). He stays with the script he knows in response to what may for him be a difficult or confusing question. There may be any number of responses to 'what does it make' in this context, but it is possible he doesn't know what it will make. Alternatively, this may not be what he is interested in.

8.5.1   Scenario and frame

Will's scenario for AT THE CONSTRUCTION SITE includes a specification of the setting (*the construction site* (4)) which he repeats fully (17) and generic elements of that setting: many machines in the construction site, cement, danger. He also performs a generic warning one might hear at a construction site: *Be careful. There might be danger* (20–21). Interestingly, as matters of frame and scenario models, the participants mentioned are all mechanical. The cement truck moves along, but no driver or other animate agent is included in the event frame. However, the performance of the generic warning and his subsequent *okay bye bye* suggest that while he has not directly mentioned any people as participants on the site, he does know that there would be drivers and/or other workers there and that they might interact in these ways. So, we might infer from his imaginative digression that his situational model includes people.

Though these generic elements are presented in such a way that they create a fairly vivid picture, they are not always linked together in predictable ways. Will's perspective shift to being in the site with the cautionary warning *Be careful. There might be danger. okay bye bye* (20–23) comes without a signal that would contextualize it. Similarly, his evaluation of his imaginative digression *That was great!* (24) apparently refers to his internal experience rather than being addressed to the interviewer. In these digressions the absence of contextualization cues may mean he either doesn't recognize the need to give the contextual details or the need to stay with the interaction. His conversational schema might actually not include either of these requirements.

Will has resources for expressing affect. For example, he uses increased intensity to indicate his enthusiasm for an event (*then it dries!* (12)), and in saying *bye bye*. He also positively evaluates in *that was great*. But he appears to use these resources without real reference to his addressee. We don't really know why he expresses enthusiasm for drying cement or what was great. Again, it may be that his conversational schema isn't weighted to use affect to align with addressees.

9   Modelling information across domains

9.1   Introduction

As we outlined in Chapter 5, the term context may be used to refer to a variety of apparently rather different constructs including the physical and social environments in which communication takes place, common patterns of interaction that might occur in those settings, as well as meanings made relevant by ongoing events and discourse. Our use of the term context includes these senses, but interprets them specifically as information available to speakers. This information is acquired, some of it actively 'learned', in interactions which individuals participate in and is represented in episodic, semantic, linguistic and other repertoires. Speakers use this acquired and learned information to interpret what is happening, to shape responses to new, incoming, information and to communicate. We use *context of culture, context of situation* and *phase* to describe information relevant for interpretation of particular texts or discourses. Respectively, these reflect broad patterns of culture associated with language and dialect variation, situation types which constitute patterns of culture, and the specific discourses which instantiate culture and situation. We are interested in instances of discourse because new information is acquired 'live', moment by moment in situations and because examining instances allows us to observe discourse behaviour which may be clinically relevant and from which generalizations may be abstracted and related to other evidences of neurocognitive integrity and function.

In the first part of this chapter we present detailed phasal analyses of discourse from conversations of people with autism spectrum disorders, and interviews with caregivers and people with Alzheimer's disease and relate these to contextual models. For the first two texts we also provide feature analyses that characterize some of the conceptual information and morphosyntactic information that informs the phasal analysis. These detailed analyses are intended for people likely to be directly involved in analysing clinical discourse. We also generalize and relate these analyses to the top-down models discussed in Chapter 8. We discuss some of the ways in which cultural and situational patterns relate to neurocognitive function. Finally we consider future directions for cross-cultural applications.

9.2   Phasal analysis A: The magic of the universe

In the first phasal analysis we return to *The Magic of the Universe*, introduced in Chapter 1. In the *Magic* text, a 15-year-old boy, James, with Asperger syndrome has a conversation with a research technician about his favourite videogame, Endorfun. Recall that primary phases are distinguished from each other by major shifts in one or more of the ideational, interactional or organizational functional relationships. Insofar as such shifts change the function of the situation, they change the situation type. This text has 2 primary phases, a dialogic phase (lines 1–2 and 11–15), in which James is asked about his favourite game, and a monologic phase on the topic of the game.

Text 9.1 The magic of the universe

(1) SPI: what's my favourite what?
(2) RES: your favourite game on the computer.
(3) SPI: well there's ex # well there's uh # eh # there's the there's this strange unusual game.
(4) SPI: uh well # there's a la a computer called an IBM Aptiva comes with games.
(5) SPI: uh # like my favourite is the # is from I is from a: place where there's a k.
(6) SPI: it's the game's about # it's a it's about a light bodied cube # k running getting the opposite colour on another light force called endorfun which is spelled e n d o r f u n.
(7) RES: umhum?
(8) SPI: and uh uh: light bodied cubes flying everywhere.
(9) SPI: and I have the power:
(10) SPI: I feel the magic of the universe.
(11) SPI: And et cetera et cetera et cetera.
(12) RES: is this a game you play by yourself James?
(13) RES: or with a partner?
(14) SPI: just myself.
(15) RES: hm.
(16) SPI: I am really completely good at it.

Each primary phase has two sub-phases. In Phase 1a, there is a clarifying (echo) question (*What's my favourite what?* (1)) and James is asked to identify a favourite computer game ({*what's*} *your favourite game on the computer* (2)). In Phase 1b, he is asked about the circumstances in which he plays the game (*is this a game you play by yourself or with a partner?* (12–13)) and he replies that he plays it alone (14). The second primary phase is distinguished from the first interactionally by the monologic pattern of turn-taking (all continuing turns by James), with a positive minimal response by the researcher (*umhum?*). Ideationally, phase 2 has a description of details and features of the game in its first sub-phase (Phase 2a: 3–8), and the perspective is third person. Phase 2a is also characterized organizationally by hesitations (4 occurrences of *uh*) and false starts (*a la, is the, is from, i, it's, the game's about, it's a, k, running*). In contrast, Phase 2b (9–11) has no hesitation fillers or false starts but is characterized by a perspective switch to first person (*I have the power* (9)) where James describes what he experiences when he plays the game, and by generic situation specific lexis associated with the game (*I feel the magic of the universe* (10)) and lexical repetition of *et cetera* (11).

In addition, there is a transition (16) which blends elements from both the first and the second phase (*I am really completely good at it*). Here the speaker's intonation indicates information structure for repeated elements as in *really completely good* where *really* and *completely* modify *good* rather than *really* being an adjunct of *completely.* Intonation also disambiguates *strange unusual game* in that *strange unusual* are coordinate (redundant) rather than contrastive attributes of *game*.

Phase helps to identify selections that realize generic schemas and scripts specific to the contexts of culture and situation of the participants. The situational and cultural parameters for each text are summarized below. However, phase also presupposes feature analyses since our interpretations of even the most mundane bits of discourse depend on our being able to relate semantic features to morphosyntactic and phonological features. In processing discourse online, we use knowledge of top-down models and features to construct (from the bottom up) relevant meanings that we associate with semantic information about situations. In order to illustrate these relationships we present a feature analysis for this text in Figure 9.1 and discuss the relations between contexts of culture and situation, top-down models, features and phase.

In Text 9.1, and indeed in all these texts, the temporal and geographical provenances of the context of culture are 1990s Canadian. Social and individual provenances vary. In this text, the researcher is an adult woman with tertiary eduction, whereas the research participant is a teenage boy with Asperger syndrome. Attributes such as age, gender, social class, education and ability as well as role relationships within a context of situation affect power and social distance relations between participants. Here, at least by virtue of her age (adult) and education, the researcher is the more powerful speaker relative to the research participant and, given their contextual roles, the default value for social distance is 'far'.[1] However, speakers may do things to shift default values, either deliberately because of their communicative goals or they may in some cases be unaware of the default parameters for social distance and power. The context of situation involves a characteristic type of research activity with this group which is for researchers to engage in and record conversational interactions with participants. So the mode of communication is face-to-face talk and the topic, 'favourite game', has potential since it refers to an experience that James knows well. James' understanding of the researcher's goal is not known.

Interactionally, the role relationships between researchers and study participants are relevant in terms of social power and distance. We noted that within the context of culture, the researcher's social provenance gives her greater power relative to James and the default social distance is far. The generic function of the researcher as interviewer interacts with and compounds features of provenance insofar as it is expected that the researcher will ask questions to guide the talk and the research participant will try to respond to them. However, since another explicit goal of the interaction is to gather information about the conversational skills of participants in unstructured settings, the researcher may try to minimize her position and role. She lets James develop his topic and offers a minimal response as supportive feedback. She also asks a question designed to allow him to keep talking about the game. That is, in conversation analysis terms, she lets him dominate the talk.

The scenario of medical (psychiatric) research interviews is underspecified, but generic features include:

- locations such as schools and clinics, as well as home visits
- there will be some sort of recording strategy used (audio, audio-video, other)
- there may be prompts, task materials, games or toys
- there is usually some attempt to ensure the comfort of the research participant in the interview setting by providing seating, tables and so on.

This part of this interview takes place on a break at school and is audio-recorded.

In Text 9.1, the two primary phases might be thought of in terms of the framing relevant to the overall generic situation. That is, the talk takes place in the context of a research interview so the researcher asks a question likely to elicit conversation and James responds with an extended monologue. James clearly has a frame for playing computer games. Games have themes, names, participants, action, one or more players and different skill levels. He offers information about all of these including his evaluation of his own abilities. The sub-phases within this second phase reflect James' knowledge of the computer game and his script for participating in the game.

9.2.1   Schemas

As suggested above, the researcher's understanding of her role in the generic situation presumably motivates her questions and the topic. James' responses show no overt awareness of the researcher's goals, but he does effectively respond to the immediate demands of the interaction. The primary phase boundaries correspond with these schemas. Schematic knowledge may also be involved in his negotiation of the perspective shift in the secondary phases of his monologue. While his presentation of his role in the game is relevant for the description, the absence of a transition between the game and his role might be surprising to an addressee. It may be that he does not have a schema for signalling perspective shift before performing it.

9.2.2   Script

The phasal analysis also reflects script knowledge at work in this text. The researcher clearly has a script for 'getting the research participant to talk' and James has good frame and script knowledge for responding to the particular question. He gives a detailed, organized and accurate description of the game showing that he knows it, and knows how to describe it.

The phasal analysis helps to identify patterns of functional selections that correspond with top-down models such as the scripts and schemas which are generically associated with the context of situation. However, as noted, these analyses presuppose feature analyses. The feature analysis for this text appears in Figure 9.1.

The feature array shows that the broad interactional patterns distinguishing the primary phases are instantiated not just by turn-taking sequences (where dialogue involves regular exchange of speakers, in contrast with monologue where one speaker 'holds the floor'), but also by morphosyntactic features such as the order of elements distinguishing statements (subject before tensed verb), from questions (subject following tensed verb), and question types from each other (+/– WH = WH/polar question). Dialogic turn-taking patterns include options for question/response pairs that we see in the first primary phase. The speakers (and we as observers) 'know what's going on' here and how to respond because morphosyntactic features correspond with properties of models for speech functions that characterize the interactional dimension of the situation. Similarly, the ideational domain reflects a particular context of culture: computer games are temporally, socially and geographically situated. The density of information and orderliness of presentation in James' description of the game can be shown if one extracts from the feature array the salient information about the game. Figure 9.2 is an attempt to give a visual representation of the density and links in his description.

In the line above each text box in Figure 9.1, the text is given with all false starts, hesitations and so on, included and coded. There is also some mark-up for syntactic structure and an indication of <u>focus</u> (underlined) and **prominence**

1.SPKR 1: [what^j ['s^i [my [favourite] **what**^j] [t^i [t^j]]]?

what	's	my	favourite	**what**	[t^i	[t^j]]]
[WH^j]	[V^i]	[DET]	[A]	WH^j]		
	PRESENT 3RD PERSON SINGULAR	PERSONAL 1ST PERSON SINGULAR POSSESSIVE	GRADE ATTRIBUTE			
THING/EVENT			POSITIVE PREFERENCE SUPERLATIVE	THING/EVENT		
		IDENTIFIED				IDENTIFIER
RESPONDING QUESTION						

2. RES: [your [favourite] [**game** [on [the [computer]]]]]

your	favourite	**game**	on	the	computer
[DET]	[A]	[N	[P	[DET	N]]]]
PERSONAL 2ND PERSON POSSESSIVE	GRADE ATTRIBUTE	COMMON COUNT SINGULAR	LOCATION	DEFINITE	COMMON COUNT SINGULAR
	POSITIVE PREFERENCE SUPERLATIVE	ACTIVITY ENTERTAINMENT +AGENT +RULES +WINNERS/LOSERS	LOCATOR		THING MACHINE
LOCATED:					
RESPONDING MINOR (ELLIPTICAL)					

Figure 9.1 Feature analysis for *The magic of the universe*

3. SPKR 1: [there's]$_{FS}$ [the]$_{FS}$ [there ['s [this [strange] [unusual] **game**]]]

there	's	this	strange	unusual	game
[[N]]	[V	[DET	[A]	[A]	N]]]
PRO EXISTENTIAL	PRESENT 3RD PERSON SING	DEMONSTRATIVE SINGULAR	GRADE ATTRIBUTE	GRADE ATTRIBUTE	COMMON COUNT SING
		NEAR	NOT ORDINARY NEUTRAL	NOT ORDINARY NEUTRAL	ACTIVITY ENTERTAINMENT +AGENT(S) +RULES +WINNERS/LOSERS
EXISTENT					

RESPONDING STATEMENT

4.SPKR 1: [there ['s [a]$_{FS}$ [[a]$_{FS}$ [a **computer**^{2} [t^2 called [an **IBM Aptiva**^{2} [t^2 comes with **games**]]]]]]]

there	's	a	computer	t²	called	an	IBM	Aptiva	t²	comes	with	games
[[N]]	[V	[DET	N²	[t²	[V	[DET	N	N	[t²	[V	[P	N]]]]]]
PRO EXISTENTIAL	PRESENT 3RD PERSON SING	INDEFINITE SING	COMMON COUNT SING		EN	INDEFINITE SING	PROPER	PROPER		PRESENT 3RD SING		COMMON COUNT SING
			THING MACHINE		ACTION: RESULTATIVE		NAME COMPANY	NAME BRAND		ACTION: MOTION	ACCOMPANI-MENT	ACTIVITY ENTERTAINMENT +AGENT(S) +RULES +WINNERS/LOSERS
EXISTENT												
			TH: PATIENT	EVENT			TH:RESULTANT			TH: TRANSFERENT	EVENT	CIRC: MANNER

CONTINUING STATEMENT

Figure 9.1 (continued)

5. SPKR 1: [uh]_H # [like] [[my favourite t²] [is]_FS [the]_FS # [is [from [a: **place** [where there's a]]]] [k]_FS INC

my	favourite	t²	is	from	a	place	where	a	there	's	a
[[DET	[A]	[t²]	[V	[P	[DET	N³	[WH³	[DET	PRO	V	DET 0]]]]
1ST PERSON POSSESSIVE SING	GRADE ATTRIBUTE		PRES 3RD PERSON SING		INDEFINITE SING	COMMON COUNT SING		INDEFINITE SING	EXISTENTIAL	PRES 3RD PERSON SING	INDEFINITE SING
	PREFERENCE POSITIVE SUPERLATIVE	[GAME]									
				LOC	LOCATION		LOCATION				
				SOURCE		LOCATED	LOCATOR				

LOCATED

CONTINUING STATEMENT (INCOMPLETE) EXISTENT: 0

6. SPKR 1: [it's]_FS [the game's about]_FS # [it's] [it's a]_FS [it] ['s [about [a light bodied **cube** # k [running][getting [the opposite colour [on another light force [called [endorfun [which is spelled e n d o r f u n]]]]]]]]]]]]

it	's	about	a	light bodied	cube	#	it	's	a	it	's	about	a	light bodied	cube	# k	running	getting	the	opposite	colour	on another	light	force		called	endorfun	which	is	spelled	endorfun
[[N²]	[V	[P	[DET	A	N⁴		[[t⁴_f]	t	RELTENSE	[[t⁴_f]	t	RELTENSE	ING	[DET	A	N⁴	V]	V]	[DET [A]	?GRADE? ATTRIBUTE	N_j⁵	[P [DET [A]	N	N⁶	[[t⁵_f]	t	RELTENSE	PRO	[WH¹²]	N¹²	EN	V	EN	PRO RELATIVE	PRES 3RD PERS SING PASSIVE	EN	V N]]]]]]]
PRO IMPERS 3RD SING NEUTER NOM	PRES 3RD PERS SING	INDEF SING	INDEF SING	GRADE ATTRIBUTE	COMMON COUNT SING		REL TENSE ASPECT		ING ASPECT CONTINUOUS	REL TENSE ASPECT		ING ASPECT CONTINUOUS	DEF	INDEF SING	COMMON COUNT SING	INDEF	COMMON	DEF	ALTER-NATIVE ?	PROPERTY	COMMON COUNT SING	PROPERTY	THING ABSTRACT +POWER	REL TENSE PRO PASSIVE		PROPER	NAME BRAND				COMMON COUNT NOUNS
ACTIVITY ETC.				SMALL WEIGHT BODY MADE OF LIGHT	THING SHAPE GEO-METRIC				ACTION MOTION ON FOOT FAST			ACTION TRANSFER							POLAR CONTRAST							ACTION RESULT ATIVE	NAME BRAND			ACTION VERBAL RESULT-ATIVE	THING LETTERS
ATTRIBUAND				ATTRIBUTE																											
										AGENT		EVENT					AGENT	EVENT		GOAL: LOCATION		TH: TRANSFERENT		TH: RESULT	EVENT	TH: RESULT			TH: PATIENT	EVENT	TH: RESULT

CONTINUING STATEMENT

Figure 9.1 (continued)

mmhm
RESPONDING

8. SPKR 1: [and [uh]$_H$ [uh:]$_H$ [[light bodied cubes] [t [flying **everywhere**]]]]]

and	light bodied	cubes	t	flying	everywhere
[C	[[A	NJ^4	[t	[V	[PRO]]]]
ADD	GRADE ATTRIBUTE	COMMON COUNT PLURAL	TENSE ASPECT	ING CONTINUOUS ASPECT	INDEFINITE LOCATION
	SMALL WEIGHT BODY MADE OF LIGHT	THING SHAPE GEOMETRIC		ACTION MOTION IN AIR/SPACE	INCLUSIVE
	AGENT/TH: TRANSFERENT			EVENT	CIRC: LOCATION
CONTINUING STATEMENT MINOR (ELLIPTICAL)					

9. SPKR 1: [and [I] [have [the **power**]]]]

and	I	have	the	power
[C	[[N]^7	[V	[DET	N^8]]]
ADD	PRO PERS 1ST PERSON SING NOMINATIVE	PRESENT	DEFINITE	COMMON COUNT SINGULAR
	DEF SPEAKER	POSSESSIVE RELATION		ABSTRACT FORCE POSITIVE
	POSSESSOR	STATE	POSSESSED	
CONTINUING STATEMENT				

Figure 9.1 (continued)

10. SPKR 1: [[I] [feel [the magic of the **universe**]]]

I	feel	the	magic	of	the	universe
[[N]^7	[V	[DET	N^9	P	DET	N]]]]
PRO PERS 1ST PERS SING NOMINATIVE	PRESENT	DEF	COMMON NON-COUNT		DEF	COMMON COUNT SINGULAR
DEF SPEAKER	MENTAL REACTION		ABSTRACT PROCESS POSITIVE			LOCATION INCLUSIVE
EXPERIENCER	STATE	PERCEPT				
CONTINUING STATEMENT						

11 SPKR 1: [and **[et cetera] [et cetera] [et cetera]**]

and	et	cetera	et	cetera	et	cetera
[C	[C	PRO]	[C	PRO]	[C	PRO]]
ADD	ADD	THE SAME EVENTS STATES REPEATED	ADD	THE SAME EVENTS STATES REPEATED	ADD	THE SAME EVENTS STATES REPEATED
CONTINUING NO SPEECH FUNCTION						

Figure 9.1 (continued)

12. RES: [[is^i [[this] [t^i [a game [[you] play [by yourself [James]? [or[with a partner?]]]]]]]]

is	this	a	game	you	play	by	yourself	James	or	with	a	partner
[V^i	[[N]^4	[DET	N^4	[[N]^7_j	[V	[P	N^7_j	[N^7_j	[C	[P	[DET	N^10_j]]]]]]]
PRES 3RD SING	PRO DEMONSTRATIVE SING	INDEFINITE SING	COMMON COUNT SING	PRO PERSONAL 2ND PERS NOM	PRES PLAIN		PRO REFLEXIVE 2ND PERS SINGULAR	PROPER			INDEF SING	COMMON COUNT SING
	NEAR		ACTIVITY ETC.	SINGULAR ADDRESSEE	ACTION ENTERTAIN			NAME PERSONAL FIRST MALE	ALT	ACCOMPANIMENT		HUMAN CO-PARTICIPANT EQUAL
	CLASSIFIED	CLASSIFIER		AGENT	EVENT	CIRC: MANNER				CIRC: MANNER		
RESPONDING QUESTION POLAR (ALTERNATIVE)												

13. SPKR 1: [just [[myself]]

just	myself
[A_v	[N^7_j]
DEGREE (SINGLE)	PRONOUN REFLEXIVE 1ST PERS SINGULAR
	SPEAKER
	MANNER
RESPONDING STATEMENT (MINOR)	

Figure 9.1 (continued)

14. SPKR 1: [[I] [am [[really] [completely] **good** [at it]]]]

	I	am	really	completely	good	at	it
	[[N^i]	[V	[[A$_V$]	[A$_V$]	A	[P	N^i]]]]
	PRO 1ST PERS SING NOMINATIVE	PRES 1ST PERSON SINGULAR	DEGREE	DEGREE	GRADE ATTRIBUTE		PRO 3RD PERS SING ACCUSATIVE NEUTER
	SPEAKER		REAL	INCLUSIVE	VALUE POSITIVE		THING OTHER
	ATTRIBUAND		ATTRIBUTE				
	CONTINUING STATEMENT						

Key for abbreviations and codes

A = adjective, ACC = accusative case, ADD = additive relation, ALT = alternative relation, A$_V$ = adverb, C = conjunction, CIRC = circumstance, DEF = definite, DET = determiner, EN = past participle, FS = false start, H = hesitation, INC = incomplete, INDEF = indefinite, ING = present participle form, LOC = locational relation, NOM = nominative case, P = Preposition, PERS = Personal (after PRO), PERS = person after 1st/2nd/3rd, PRO = pronoun, RES = Researcher, SING = singular, SPKR = speaker 1, t = trace, V = verb, WH = interrogative/relative pronoun, # = pause, [:] = lengthening of the immediately preceding sound, 0 = potential but unrealized argument roles/predicates, superscript indices are for coreference.

Figure 9.1 (continued)

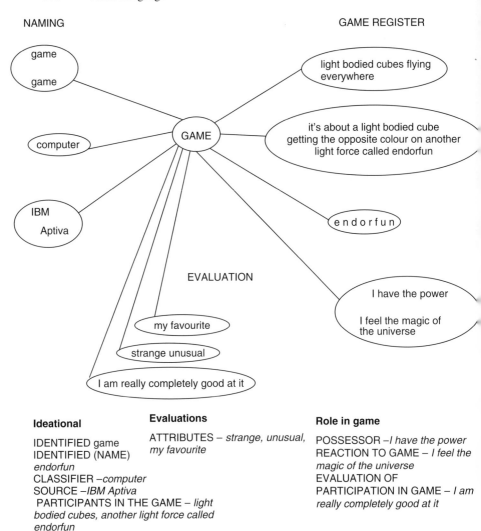

NAMING

GAME REGISTER

game

game

computer

IBM
Aptiva

GAME

light bodied cubes flying
everywhere

it's about a light bodied cube
getting the opposite colour on another
light force called endorfun

e n d o r f u n

EVALUATION

my favourite

strange unusual

I am really completely good at it

I have the power

I feel the magic of
the universe

Ideational

IDENTIFIED game
IDENTIFIED (NAME)
endorfun
CLASSIFIER –*computer*
SOURCE –*IBM Aptiva*
 PARTICIPANTS IN THE GAME – *light
bodied cubes, another light force called
endorfun*
WHAT THE PARTICIPANTS DO –
flying everywhere
GOAL OF GAME –*it's about a light
bodied cube getting the opposite colour
on another light force called endorfun*

Evaluations

ATTRIBUTES – *strange, unusual,
my favourite*

Role in game

POSSESSOR –*I have the power*
REACTION TO GAME – *I feel the
magic of the universe*
EVALUATION OF
PARTICIPATION IN GAME – *I am
really completely good at it*

Figure 9.2 Visual representation of *The magic of the universe* logic

(bold face). In the first line of each text box the text is repeated without fluency features, but with focus and prominence marking. The second line gives a syntactic parse, the third line gives subcategory information about lexical items while the fourth glosses semantic features (in lexical 'shorthand') for the same items. The next lines provide argument role analyses. The final line in each text box provides information about speaker turn, speech function, and clause status (where this is not major and full).

Trying to imagine the demands of this discourse in functional and neurocognitive terms offers some additional insight with respect to James' performance. His response requires that he decide what he wants to say. Leaving out the decision itself, this presumably involves not simply semantic and episodic search and retrieval, engaging (at least) prefrontal (minimally left inferior frontal gyrus) and left temporal lobes and hippocampus (Petrides *et al.* 1995; Fletcher *et al.* 2000), but also that, once retrieved, he maintains the information online (also hypothetically, left inferior frontal gyrus (Stowe *et al.* 2005) and perhaps a dorsomedial-superior temporal sulcus loop (Vigneau *et al.* 2006)), while he organizes it into a coherently related series of sentences. This organization is likely to engage several additional regions in the prefrontal cortex as well as anterior, medial and posterior temporo-parietal areas associated with language and discourse processing. (See Vigneau *et al.* 2006 for a meta-analysis and review of left hemisphere language processes.) Some of these activations, such as the anterior temporal poles, would typically be bilateral, minimally adding processing power given the complexity of the recall required for the response. (See e.g. Ferstl *et al.* 2008 and Mason and Just 2007 for discourse networks and Frith and Frith 2003 and Gallagher and Frith 2003 for theory of mind networks. See Ferstl and von Cramon 2002 for comparison.)

These networks, or something like them, are needed not only to gather the ideational information and organize its linguistic representation but additionally, in order for the discourse to be judged 'successful', James also needs to imagine what his addressee already knows and what she will need to be told in order to interpret his response and then he has to organize what he says with those needs in mind. That is, there are layers of processing requiring imagination, planning, maintenance and manipulation of message that must be co-ordinated with the linguistic information to produce something that works in its context.

Thought about in these terms, James' initially dysfluent speech must first be interpreted in relation to the complexity of the ideational representation that he attempts – the detail and logical order of the first phase of his response are cognitively quite demanding. That he manages as well as he does suggests that he has significant cognitive resources available, and perhaps that his dysfluencies are a result of online processing limitations relative to cognitive load. We do not know if this is so of course. The dysfluencies could reflect a restricted area such as retrieval or planning. But these questions can be investigated.

Perhaps of more obvious interest though is his failure to provide a transition for his shift to first person performance of his role in and experience of the game. This sort of unexpected shift is not uncommon in the discourse of people with autism spectrum disorders (de Villiers *et al.* 2007) and may reflect, as we suggested, problems with schemas for transitions. Again, this is quite open to investigation. One possibility is that speakers know the schemas but find the demands of taking the addressee into account in monitoring and manipulation of information beyond their online processing capacities (so establishing what those capacities are is of interest). Alternatively, monitoring and manipulating behaviour in relation to the needs of an addressee might be specifically difficult for speakers with ASDs with the result that they either do not acquire schemas for transition or that they do not use them. Current models for discourse comprehension and theory of mind suggest that there is a central role for subregions of the medial prefrontal cortex in discourse monitoring and in emotion processing and self-awareness. A number of recent studies suggest that these same regions are functionally and structurally different in people with autism spectrum disorders (e.g. Fletcher *et al.* 1995; Gilbert *et al.* 2008; McAlonan *et al.* 2005; Thakkar *et al.* 2008). Finding out whether the absence of transitions in ASD discourse is an effect of such functional and structural differences would help to explicate relations between neurocognitive function and behaviour in ASDs.

9.3   Phasal analysis B: My Mom

Text 9.2 is from a medical research interview involving two caregivers, a researcher and a patient with AD, Cleo, who we introduced in Chapter 1. They have been discussing the possibility of Cleo coming to harm without people to help her.

Text 9.2 My Mom

(1) CG1: It's a concern to us when you go for a shower or to me when you go for a shower and turn the hot water on and jump in without cooling it off and the same thing you go for a drink sometime and you turn the hot water on instead of cold water well that is a concern.

(2) P: I still say that that's not something that's that a normal person wouldn't do.

(3) CG1: Well you could get scalded.

(4) CG: No no hell no

(5) CG: I'm normal

(6) CG: I would never do that.

(7) P: No no ((laughter))

(8) CG: I'm normal <xxx> [>].

(9) CG2: <xxx fingers> [<].

(10) P: My Mom my Mom used to have a: people used to say she doesn't even put her you know [if] she doesn't even bother to put the this here and that there

(11) P: I don't know

(12) P: she is always taking care of herself

(13) P: she's always you know

(14) P: and then she'd turn right around and disconnect what I had been talking about

(15) P: and I mean she's everybody used to think you know I I'll be lucky if I'm doing that or I'll be lucky

(16) P: if I **you're not lucky girl you've had it**.

(17) P: And ah # I don't know #

(18) P: what have we got to now?

(19) CG1: Scalding scalding in the hot water

(20) P: No no

The passage of dialogue here is part of a primary phase (1–9) in which one of Cleo's caregivers articulates the possibility of harm (scalding). Cleo suggests that this could happen to a 'normal person' (2). The caregiver responds by claiming normality for himself and denying that he could make such a mistake (3–8). Cleo appears to agree and after brief incomplete exchanges, she shifts topic and begins the second primary phase (10–18) as a monologue. It may be that the topic here is related to scalding if she is trying to link and contrast herself with her mother's self-sufficiency (*she was always taking care of herself*) and competence. One possible interpretation of her statements *I mean she's everybody used to think you know I I'll be lucky if I'm doing that or I'll be lucky* is that people used to think that they would be lucky if they were like her mother. However, Cleo makes other statements that appear to contradict this inference. For instance, one could infer that Cleo is suggesting her mother was disorganized and incoherent from the statements *people used to say she doesn't even put her you know [if] she doesn't even bother to put the this here and that there* and *and then she'd turn right around and disconnect what I had been talking about*. If this is so, then the *if you're not lucky girl you've had it* could refer to the possibility that if Cleo is not lucky she will be disorganized and incoherent like her mother. Figure 9.3 graphically presents these contrasts.

We cannot really resolve the contradictions that appear here because the frequency of incomplete utterances, false starts, indefinite reference and reference without antecedent, together with limited lexicalization and marked modalization are features which make it difficult to identify topic or even a coherent relationship between the predications that are actually complete. It is also uncertain how her monologue is related to the preceding topic and this is in fact apparent both in her final question (*what have we got to now?* (18)) and in her caregiver's reintroduction of the topic of scalding.

If we were to describe this exchange in terms of contextual features and top down models, we might note that the social provenance differs from Text 9.1 in that all the speakers here are adults, and so are peers in that respect. However, since one of the participants is being treated for AD, her competence to independently and safely carry out every day tasks is being discussed. The social

Figure 9.3 Visual representation of propositions in *My Mom*

distance between speakers is also affected by individual provenance insofar
as the caregivers are Cleo's family members and so they may be described
as being socially 'near' with respect to each other, while all of them are distant from the researcher. (We omit details of family relations although these
of course will affect power and social distance and, in more ethnographically
detailed descriptions, would help to inform the analyses.)

Within the context of situation, the function of the interview as a whole is to
gather information that will aid in the assessment of the patient's response to
treatment with a cholinesterase inhibitor and to set goals for treatment evaluation
(Rockwood *et al.* 2002). Input from the patient and caregivers are thus highly val-
ued, and so although the usual minimal scenario supports for research interview
are in place (here, a tape recorder and a set of objectives which the researcher has
explained to the participants), the interview occurs as a home visit and the interviewer does not closely follow a script. The interactions are thus fairly spontaneous. We see this insofar as the researcher does not intervene in the monologue
and allows the caregivers to respond to Cleo's request for discourse monitoring
support (*what have we got to now*). Nevertheless, the ideational direction is guided
by the presence and interventions of the researcher as she has asked the family
about any concerns they may have with respect to Cleo's ability to carry out every
day activities. The first primary phase (scalding) overtly reflects this.

This phase also suggests the participants have conflicting schemas and frames. Caregiver's explicit expression of concern about harm reflects an experiential frame:

- Cleo's ability to manipulate every day objects is impaired,
- so she could get hurt,
- the cause of her inability is Alzheimer's disease.

Cleo's statement (2) that 'normal' people might also be at risk of scalding makes explicit a schematic contrast between 'normal people' and people with AD that is at work in the discourse. Her attempt to include 'normal people' as at risk may be a rejection of the schema. Her caregiver's subsequent insistence on his own ability and normality (*hell no # no # no # I'm normal. I would never do that...I'm normal* (4–8)), leave Cleo with little room (or dignity). She is by implication both not competent and not normal. It is in this context that she shifts the topic to her mother and attempts a comparison.

The second primary phase (10–16), her monologue about her mother, incoherent though it is, can be read as motivated by a desire to resist the schema that has been operationalized. She does not manage the new topic well, but the strategy of shifting topic when you do not like what is being said and you have not succeeded in arguing for another view does reflect schematic knowledge of options within turn-taking models for conversation (Garcia and Joanette 1997).

The details of her difficulty in coherently developing the new topic can be made explicit through a feature analysis. We present one for the second primary phase in Figure 9.4. As with Figure 9.1, the line above each text box in Figure 9.4 gives the text with fluency features included and coded, some mark-up for syntactic structure and an indication of <u>focus</u> (underlined) and **prominence** (bold face). In the first line of each text box the text is repeated without fluency features, but with focus and prominence marking. The second line gives a syntactic parse, the third line gives subcategory information about lexical items while the fourth glosses semantic features for the same items. The next lines provide argument role analyses. The final line in each text box provides information about speaker turn, speech function and clause status (where this is not major and full). The feature analysis for Text 9.2 shows that Cleo has low levels of basic and subordinate level features as a proportion of her talk (Nicholas *et al.* 1985; Smith *et al.* 2001). There are, for example, thirty NP positions in her ninety-nine word monologue referring to seven different object concepts shown in Figure 9.4. Only three of these concepts are lexically represented. There are the two basic level items, *mom* and *girl,* and the superordinate *people,* each of which is repeated once. The only other object references occur pronominally and include the speaker (pronominal *I*), the addressee (pronominal *you*), and unspecified transferred objects (*this* and

10. [**My Mom**]_FSTOP [my Mom used to have]_FS [a:]_HES [people used to say [she doesn't even put her]_FS [you know]CHECK [if]_FS [she doesn't even bother to put the_FS **this here** and **that there**]]]

people	used	to say	she	doesn't	even	bother	[t¹]	to put	this	here	and	that	there
[[N]²	[V	[V	[[N]¹	[V	Av	V		V	N	PRO_LC	+	N	PRO_LC]]]]
INDEF COMMON PLURAL	PAST ASPECT	INF	PERS PRO 3RD PER SINGULAR FEMININE NOMINATIVE	PRES NEG	DEG	BASE		INF	PRO DEM SING			PRO DEM	
THING² HUMAN	HABIT	ACTION VERBAL		NOT		AFFECT MENTAL REACTION	t¹	ACTION TRANSFER	NEAR	NEAR		FAR	FAR
AGENT		EVENT	MESSAGE			STATE	PERCEPT						
			EXPERIENCER¹				AGENT¹	EVENT	THEME	GOAL:LOC	+	THEME	GOAL:LOC
RESPONDING STATEMENT													

11. [[I] [don't **know**]]]

I	don't	know
[[N]³	[V PRESENT NEG	V]]
PRO PERSONAL 1ST SING NOMINATIVE		BASE
DEF SPEAKER	NOT	MENTAL COGNITION
EXPERIENCER		STATE
		PERCEPT: 0
CONTINUING STATEMENT		

Figure 9.4 Feature analysis for *My Mom*

12. [[she] [is always [taking **care of herself**]]]

She	is	always	taking	care	of	herself
[[N]	[V	A_V	[V	[N	[P	N]]]]]
PRO¹ PERSONAL 3RD SING FEMININE NOMINATIVE	PRESENT 3RD SING CONTINUOUS ASPECT	ASPECT	ING CONTINUOUS ASPECT	COMMON NON-COUNT		PRO1 REFLEXIVE 3RD SING FEMININE
DEF OTHER		FREQUENCY	ACTION	ACTION/STATE		?DEF OTHER?
AGENT		CIRC: TIME	EVENT	EVENT		TH: PATIENT
CONTINUING STATEMENT						

13. [[she]['s always]∥υ [[you] [know]]CHECK

She	's	always	you	know
[[N¹]	[V	[A_V]]]	[[N]	[V]]
PRO PERSONAL 3RD SING FEMININE NOMINATIVE	PRES 3RD SING	ASPECT	PRO PERSONAL 2ND NOMINATIVE	PRES PLAIN
DEF OTHER		FREQUENCY	EXPERIENCER	MENTAL COGNITION
NO ARGUMENT ROLE		CIRC:TIME		STATE
CONTINUING NO SPEECH FUNCTION				PERCEPT : 0

Figure 9.4 (continued)

14. and (then [[[she] ['d turn right around] and [disconnect [what I had been talking about]]]])

and	then	she	'd	turn	right	around	and	t³	disconnect	what	I	had	been	talking	about	
C	{C	[[[[N]¹	[V	V	Av	P]]	C	[[t³]	[V	[N⁴	N³	V	V	V	V	P	t¹]]]]]
		PRO PER 3RD SING FEMININE NOM	MODAL PAST ASPECT	BASE	DEG				BASE	WH	PRO PER 1ST SING NOM	PAST PERF ASPECT	EN CONT ASPECT	ING		
	ADDITIVE SEQUENCE	DEF OTHER	HABIT	ACTION	FULL CIRCLE		ADD	DEF OTHER	ACTION	MESSAGE	DEF SPEAKER			ACTION		
		AGENT		EVENT		GOAL: LOCATION		AGENT		THEME: TRANSFERENT						
									AGENT EVENT						EVENT	RANGE
																SOURCE 0
																RECIP 0

CONTINUING STATEMENT

---

15. and [I mean] [she's]_IFS [everybody [used to think [you know]_CHECK [I]_FS [[I ['ll be lucky [if I'm doing that]]]] or [I'll be lucky]]]]]] (??IU)

(embedded clause: [I]_FS [[I ['ll be lucky [if I'm doing that]]]] or [I'll be lucky]]]]]] (??IU))

I⁵/³	I	'll	be	lucky	if	I'm	doing	that	or	I	'll	be	lucky
[N	[N⁵/³	[V	V	A]	[C	V	V	N²]]	[C	[N⁵/³	[V	v	A]]]
PRO PER 1ST SING NOM	PRO PER 1ST SING NOM	MOD AL	BASE	GRADE	COND	PRES 1ST SING CONT ASPECT	ING CONT ASPECT	PRO DEM SING	ALTERNATIVE	PRO PER 1ST SING NOM	MOD AL	BASE	GRADE
		FUT		POSITIVE CHANCE	COND		ACTION	?			FUT		POSITIVE CHANCE
DEF? SPEAKER?	DEF? SPEAKER			STATE	CIRC: CONDITION				OR	DEF? SPEAKER			STATE
ATTRIBUAND						AGENT				ALTERNATIVE			
								EVENT RANGE					

Sentence 15 (main):

and	I	mean	everybody	used	to think	you know	I⁵/³	'll	be	lucky	if	'm	doing	that	or	I	'll	be	lucky
	[[N³	V]	[[N⁵	[V	V		[[N	[V	V	A]	[C	V	V	N²]]	[C	[N⁵/³	[V	v	A]]]
	PRO PER 1ST SING NOM	PRESENT PLAIN	PRO INDEF	PAST	INF		PRO PER 1ST SING NOM	MOD BASE		GRADE	COND	PRES 1ST SING CONT ASPECT	ING CONT ASPECT	PRO DEM SING	ALTERNATIVE	PRO PER 1ST SING NOM	MOD AL	BASE	GRADE
ADD	DEF SPEAKER	MENTAL COGNITION	INCLUSIVE HUMAN		MENTAL COGNITION	MESSAGE (of an elliptical?)	DEF? SPEAKER?	FUT		POSITIVE CHANCE	COND		ACTION	?		DEF? SPEAKER			POSITIVE CHANCE
	AGENT	EVENT	EXPER		EVENT	PERCEPT	ATTRIBUAND			STATE	CIRC: CONDITION				OR	ATTRIBUAND			STATE
	AGENT	EVENT			EVENT						AGENT			EVENT RANGE					

CONTINUING STATEMENT

Figure 9.4 (continued)

16. {if [[you] ['re not **lucky**]] [girl] [[you] ['ve **had** it]]]

if	you	're	not	lucky	girl	you	've	had	it
{C	[[N]^{37}	[V	NEG	[A]]	[N^{37}]	[[N^{37}]	[V	V	N]]]]
	PRO PERSONAL 2ND SING NOM	PRES PLAIN		GRADE	COMMON COUNT SING	PRO PERSONAL 2ND SING NOM	PRES PERF ASPECT	EN	PRO PERSONAL 3RD SING ACCUSATIVE NEUTER
COND	ADDRESSEE? SPEAKER?		NOT	CHANCE POSITIVE	HUMAN FEMALE YOUNG ADDRESSEE	ADDRESSEE? SPEAKER?		FINISH	
CIRC: CONDITION	ATTRIBUAND		NOT	STATE		POSSESSOR		STATE	POSSESSED
CONTINUING STATEMENT									

17. and uh$_H$: (pause) [[I] [don't **know**]]

	don't	know
[[N]^3	[V	V]]]
[N^3	[V	V]
PRO PERSONAL 1ST PERSON SING NOM	PRES NEG	BASE
DEF SPEAKER	NOT	MENTAL COGNITION
EXPERIENCER		PERCEPT: 0
		STATE
CONTINUING STATEMENT		

Figure 9.4 (continued)

18. [<u>what</u> [6] [have [i] [we [t[i] [got [to t[6]]] **now**]]]]?

what	have	we	t[i]	got	to	now
[WH[6]	[V[i]	[N		[V	[P	[t[6]]
	PRES PLAIN PERF ASPECT	PRO PER 1ST P NOM		EN		PRO-TIME]]]]
	COMPLETE	SPEAKER + ADDRESSEE		ACTION		DISCOURSE TOPIC	PRESENT
		AGENT/THEME		EVENT		GOAL[6]	CIRC: TIME

CONTINUING
STATEMENT (INFORMATION MONITORING)

Key for abbreviations and codes

A = adjective, ACC = accusative case, ADD = additive relation, ALT = alternative relation, A$_v$ = adverb, C = conjunction, CIRC = circumstance, DEF = definite, DEG = degree, DET = determiner, EN = past participle, EXPER = experiencer, FS = false start, H = hesitation, INC = incomplete, INDEF = indefinite, ING = present participle form, LOC = locational relation, NEG = negative element, NOM = nominative case, P = Preposition, PERS = Personal (after PRO), PERS = person after 1st/2nd/3rd, PRO = pronoun, SING = singular, t = trace, TOP = topic element, V = verb, WH = interrogative/relative pronoun, # = pause, [:] = lengthening of the immediately preceding sound, 0 = potential but unrealized argument roles/predicates, superscript indices are for co-reference.

Figure 9.4 (continued)

that). There is additionally, an expletive (empty) *it*, relative and interrogative uses of *what*, and personal pronouns referring to the participants although often ambiguously as can be seen from the reference chains in the feature analysis. For instance, three of the four uses of first person singular *I* in (15) could refer either to the indefinite *everybody* of the main clause or to Cleo and, similarly, the second person *you* in (16) could refer to Cleo, to an unspecified addressee, or to a generic, narrative 'you'. *Girl,* used here in second person address, shares the same ambiguity. These unresolved ambiguities together with the lack of antecedents for definite referring expressions contribute to the incoherence of Cleo's monologue.

The effects of under-lexicalization, referential incompleteness and ambiguity are compounded in Cleo's discourse by other features. For example, there are eight false starts, two hesitations, and at least one incomplete predication (13) in her brief monologue. (The second instance of *I'll be lucky* in (15) is grammatically complete but *lucky* can take a complement and in context it seems to be lacking one so it is coded as (IU) – incomplete utterance.) Her discourse is also modalized with three instances of *you know,* a monitoring question in (18) (*what have we got to now*), two negative mental cognition predications and an *I mean.* Most of the fluency features occur at the beginning of her monologue suggesting she has an initial problem with planning what she has to say. However, the ambiguities and incomplete utterances, modalization, under-lexicalization, and references without antecedent are persistent, which suggests that she has ongoing ideational and executive difficulties. Generously construed, her *If you're not lucky girl you've had it* may be an attempt to comment on her own (or someone else's) situation as we noted earlier. However, the absence of clear referents together with the fact that she repeats *lucky* (*I'll be lucky if...I'll be lucky*) and speaks markedly loudly raises the possibility that Cleo is motivated here simply by the words just spoken – that she has moved into stereotypic utterance or is just echoing her own talk.

Cleo's limited lexicalization together with the other features described result in a monologue that is genuinely incoherent. We know she is talking about her mother and that she begins by trying to make some sort of comparison, but beyond that it is really not possible to sort out what she is saying. Indeed, by the end of the monologue it seems that she herself has lost the thread of her discourse – she is not just at a loss for words, she has lost her idea. Because of this, she fails even in the underspecified goal of changing the topic since the response to her *where have we got to now* is a reinitiation of the topic (and schema) of *scalding* and her competence.

Cleo's difficulties at word and clause level reflect not only problems of lexical access (*the this here and that there*) and local planning (*My Mom my Mom used to have a: people used to say she doesn't even put her you know [if] she doesn't even bother to put the this here and that there* (10)), but also executive difficulties in selecting, inhibiting and monitoring her discourse for coherence so that the problems we see in detail at word and clause level redound through the discourse. Cleo has a schema for getting out of a sticky conversational spot, and her syntax seems adequate, but she cannot here marshal the executive and conceptual resources needed to communicate successfully.

Again, thinking about these difficulties in relation to typical functional impairments in AD can shed light on the possible causes of the difficulties Cleo has. For example, glucose metabolism (a measure of functional integrity) is reduced in early AD in posterior cingulate, temporo-parietal and prefrontal association cortices (Herholz *et al.* 2002). The prefrontal deficits include bilateral ventrolateral and ventromedial regions (Herholz *et al.* 2002) associated with language and emotion processing. Moreover, women are more likely to have reduced prefrontal metabolism (Herholz *et al.* 2002).[2] It seems quite likely then that the difficulties we see in Cleo's monologue are not just effects of a memory deficit or restricted lexical access, but actually correspond to dysfunction in prefrontal cortex associated with executive functions such as selection and planning and sub-components of verbal working memory systems (Baddeley *et al.* 2001; Baddeley 2003; Baudie *et al.* 2006). Unravelling the relations between cause and effect could help us better understand and monitor change in AD.

9.4   Phasal analysis C: Cow parts

Text 9.3, Cow parts, is a semi-structured conversation between a research technician and a fifteen-year-old boy, Warren, with Asperger syndrome. Thus it shares social provenance with Text A, the *Magic of the Universe,* in that the researcher's position is +power and the default social distance is far because she is an educated adult woman talking to a teenage boy with an ASD. The generic functions of the situation are also similar. This is a medical research interview in which the researcher's primary goal is to engage Warren in casual conversation so his conversational skills may be observed. The interaction takes place in a setting familiar to Warren and is audio recorded. This text has three phases, one about edible cow parts, one about summer vacation, and a short transitional phase (18–21) which blends these experiences.

Text 9.3 Cow parts

   (1) SPI: <and> [<] uh I don't think we're gonna eat the liver.
   (2) RES: ((coughs))
   (3) SPI: I don I don't think we're gonna eat the kidneys either # I don't think.
   (4) SPI: but we could eat the stomach.
   (5) SPI: put them in water.
   (6) SPI: and then put different meats and stuff in.

(7) SPI: vegetables.
(8) SPI: cook it up.
(9) SPI: they used to we might be able to y eat the brains.
(10) RES: did you take a holiday this summer?
(11) SPI: this summer?
(12) RES: umhum.
(13) SPI: nope.
(14) RES: no?
(15) RES: two summers ago you went to Europe didn't you?
(16) SPI: yeah.
(17) RES: that was a nice long holiday.
(18) SPI: once um I saw this show that <this> [>] these two girls went to England.
(19) RES: <umhum> [<]?
(20) SPI: and then they chose out something.
(21) SPI: and it turns out to be cow's brain.
(22) RES: mm: .
(23) SPI: have you ever tried those before?
(24) RES: no.
(25) RES: I haven't.
(26) SPI: well I want to.
(27) SPI: I might want to try a brain soup.
(28) SPI: ((laughs)).

In Phase 1 (1–9, 22–28), Warren is describing parts of a cow that might be eaten. He displays reasonable frame knowledge of internal organs, but has less information about what is actually edible. His speech is both coherent and interactive. He maintains and develops topic (1–9) and asks the researcher about her own experiences with his topic *have you ever tried those before?* (23). His questioning of the researcher is consistent with a schematic model for a casual conversation between peers. In (28) he laughs which suggests that he may be comfortable in the interactive situation.

In Phase 2 (10–17), the researcher takes five of eight turns, and Warren's turns consist of two polar responses without elaboration and an echo question *this summer?* (11) seeking clarification. In this phase, the researcher introduces a new topic which Warren does not take up. First, she asks him if he took a holiday the previous summer (10). Her attempted transition to *holiday* fails perhaps because Warren did not take a holiday. She then moves on to the topic of a particular summer vacation she is aware of (*two summers ago you went to Europe didn't you?* (15)), and begins to develop this topic (*that was a nice long holiday* (17)). In short, we see her functioning in her role as researcher, attempting to shift the topic from edible cow parts to the more socially neutral 'summer holidays'. Warren's response (lines 18–21) is interesting in that it blends elements from Phases 1 and 2, (*went to England* and *cow's brain*), creating a transition back to the topic of edible cow parts. He reinitiates Phase 1 with a shift in speech function (*Have you ever tried those before?*). This may suggest that Warren does not recognize the background generic scheme of the research interview, nor the provenance differences but is responding to the researcher as a genuine peer. Additionally, he may not be aware (or concerned) that his topic might be distasteful for her. Nevertheless, in combining travel with brain soup to get his own topic back on the floor, Warren shows conversational skill.

Warren's renewal of Phase 1 may be a discourse sign of 'special interests', a characteristic pattern of the discourse of people with ASDs. Such shifts to previous topics are often perseverative, particularly after others' unsuccessful attempts at topic changes. For researchers, tracking such shifts may be a way of identifying and monitoring ideational perseveration in discourse. Its relationship to, for instance, anterior cingulate function could then be investigated (Thakkar *et al.* 2008).

9.5   Phasal analysis D: Squirrels

The final phasal analysis is of a conversation in which a woman being treated for AD, Doris, has been asked about a visit to friends in Montreal. This is another medical research interview which occurred as a home visit: it thus has many of the provenance and situational features we saw in Text 9.2. Here, all participants are adult women and so are equal at least in these respects. Doris and her caregiver are family and so are socially near. Their social relationship to the researcher is far (because of her professional role in the situation) but this is the fourth home visit so they are familiar with each other. However, Doris is elderly and is being treated for AD, so it is possible that she will be treated and/or will act as a less powerful participant. The role of the researcher is similar to that of the researcher in Text 9.2. Treatment goals were set on the first visit and she is now helping Doris and her caregiver assess whether Doris is better, worse or stable on those goals. Text 9.4 arose as part of a response to questions about Doris's mood. The caregiver has said that Doris was really happy about a visit the family made to some friends in Montreal. Here she is recalling an earlier visit to the same friends.

Text 9.4 Squirrels

(1) P: I know you see I know what nice people they are because I
(2) CG: they sure are
(3) P: stayed with them for a I guess it was a week in Montreal
(4) CG: a whole week yes
(5) P: but not # may not have been a whole week but I almost believe it was # Mary and I
(6) CG: yes yes that's right
(7) P: yes

(8) CG: yes # and you knew them anyway from xxx.

(9) P: I knew them anyways I went and stayed there with them

(10) CG: yes

(11) P: and I can see myself swinging on the swing.

(12) CG: is that right

(13) P: ((laughter))

(14) CG: in their backyard

(15) P: in their backyard

(16) CG: yes

(17) P: and uh the the thing that makes me remember it I guess is because uh # a a squirrel came out along the fence while I was swinging and I never saw that type of squirrel before. They're very large to what our squirrels are and they're much darker in colour

(18) CG: yes # they have very large black squirrels there

(19) P: mmm

(20) IV: umhum

(21) CG: and if you haven't seen them before it does seem unusual

(22) P: yes it did to me ((laughing))

(23) CG: and very large grey squirrels as well dear # I didn't tell you # we didn't see any black ones this time but we saw a couple of grey ones.

(24) P: yes # I don't remember seeing any grey ones but I saw the black ones

(25) CG: the black ones

(26) P: yes

(27) CG: and they go in there and they eat up Myrtle's garden

(28) P: umhum # yes that's what she said when I went in complaining to her about the squirrel ((laughing))

(29) CG: yes

(30) P: and uh she said well dear they won't hurt you but ((laughter)) they'll hurt my garden

(31) CG: yes

(32) P: chase them away she said they'll tear hurt my garden

(33) IV: How long ago was this visit # approximately?

(34) P: oh I don't know three or four years

(35) CG: oh I # longer than that

(36) P: longer than that

(37) CG: oh yes # gosh

(38) P: ((giggle))

(39) CG: a good ten

(40) P: ((laughter)) yes I guess it was

(41) CG: a good ten or more

(42) IV: ok

(43) P: I I went uh # I went there to the what was it? I forget ((chuckles))

(44) CG: Rotary Club meetings

(45) P: yes #

(46) CG: or was it the world # Rotary Club

(47) P: Rotary Club meetings yeah um hum

(48) CG: there in Montreal

(49) P: in Montreal # and uh # we went and and stayed uh at uh # uh # Prof and Mrs Smith's
in oh ah they they lived in # live in Granby # just outside of Montreal. Everyday we
went in to Montreal to the meetings and uh it was wonderful uh # uh Gwen uh the girl
that I went with # and I stayed there and went in and we always went early and got uh
uh seat way up ((laughing))

(50) CG: on the top of the Olympic Stadium I think it was

(51) P: Olympic Stadium yes # it was Olympic Stadium uh we had a wonderful time #
there were people there from everywhere # Rotary Club # I guess ((laughing)) oh
we had a wonderful time # but uh that's where I first saw those black squirrels

(52) CG: umhum

(53) P: I thought all squirrels were little brown ones

(54) CG: I know # the tiny little things we have here # yes

(55) P: they're big ((laughing)).

Text 9.4 has two primary phases, both dialogic, but differing ideationally
according to the details being recalled. In Phase 1, (1–10, 33–51), the topic is
the visit, when it occurred and the reason for it. Phase 2 (11–32, 51–55) elaborates on a particular memory of a backyard and squirrels. Overall, Doris is
able to offer good accounts of these events though her caregiver supplies some
details and actively supports her recall. Ideationally, both phases are characterized by mental processes associated with memory and proper names, consistent with the generic situation of trying to recall details of events and their
participants. The discourse has informal features such as laughing and terms
of endearment (*dear* (23, 30)) though, noticeably, all instances of laughing are
Doris' (13, 22, 28, 30, 38, 40, 49, 51, 55).

In Phase 1, Doris reports her experience of the visit – its general location and
duration and the people she stayed with. Proper names for people, times and
places appear in syntactically prominent positions reflecting this topic. There is
also positive evaluation, as it was a visit she enjoyed: the people were *nice* (1),
and the visit was *wonderful* (49, 51). These features all reflect good schematic
knowledge for reporting a trip and visit.

In Phase 2, Doris reports with vivid clarity a personal experience of swinging
(*I can see myself swinging on the swing*) and discovering a large black squirrel.
A discussion of squirrels, their attributes and behaviours follows, including
reported events (and reported speech) concerning squirrels in Myrtle's garden.
This discussion is interrupted when the interviewer asks about the time of the
visit, resuming Phase 1's topic, but is renewed in (51), when Doris again recalls
her first encounter with 'those black squirrels': (*P: we had a wonderful time,
but uh that's where I first saw those black squirrels*).

In the reconstruction of these experiences, we see a pattern of echoing lexical
words and phrases between the caregiver and Doris which continues throughout
the discourse (CG: *you knew them anyway.* P: *I knew them anyways.* (8–9) //
CG: *in their backyard.* P: *in their backyard (14–15) //* P: *I thought all squirrels*

were little brown ones. CG: *I know # the* **tiny little** *things we have here # yes* (53–54)). Interactionally, the participants positively align themselves to each other when they do this, particularly when there is no possible doubt about what is repeated as in (53–54). The pattern of repetition also appears recipro-cal as does their habit of giving positive feedback. This reciprocity allows the caregiver to unobtrusively supply details and development for Doris, and to confirm details Doris offers on her own. For example in lines (3–4) the caregiver confirms the duration of Doris' visit by repeating it:

(3) P: I guess it was a week in Montreal.
(4) CG: a whole week yes.

Indeed, the caregiver confirms almost every detail Doris offers, and when she does not confirm she supplies information as in (43–49), where she supplies both the name of the event and the place, which Doris confirms and repeats.

(43) P: I I went uh # I went there to the what was it? I forget ((chuckles))
(44) CG: Rotary Club meetings
(45) P: yes #
(46) CG: or was it the world # Rotary Club
(47) P: Rotary Club meetings yeah um hum
(48) CG: there in Montreal
(49) P: in Montreal # and uh # we went and and stayed uh at uh # uh # Prof and Mrs Smith's
in oh ah they they lived in # live in Granby # just outside of Montreal.

Nevertheless, Doris' account is good. She recalls proper names of people (e.g. *Annie, Prof and Mrs Smith*), names the place she stayed in (*Granby*) and provides substantial information in Phase 2 about the squirrel she saw, the yard and her friend's reaction to squirrels, including reported speech (*she said well dear they won't hurt you but they'll hurt my garden* (30)). It is only with the renewal of Phase 1 in line (33) by the interviewer (*How long ago was this visit # approximately?*) that Doris shows difficulty with recalling details of time or names:

(33) IV: How long ago was this visit # approximately?
(34) P: oh I don't know three or four years
(35) CG: oh I # longer than that
(36) P: longer than that
(37) CG: oh yes # gosh
(38) P: ((giggle))
(39) CG: a good ten
(40) P: ((laughter)) yes I guess it was
(41) CG: a good ten or more
(42) IV: ok

Here she has misjudged the time elapsed but accepts and confirms her caregiver's correction and goes on to offer the reason for her visit, and then reiterate what was for her the episodically salient part of the experience, big black squirrels.

Doris manages not only to describe her visit, but also to say why she went, and why she recalls it so vividly. This is a kind of discourse that people with mild/moderate AD often can manage quite well, relying as it does on some very general discourse schemas and recall of personal experiences from a relatively distant past (more than ten years ago). Her report makes few demands on her ability to recall more recent experiences, nor to reference or relate information from an encyclopedic inventory. Moreover, her caregiver provides continuous support, offering names and times, confirming her statements and positively aligning with her value judgements. The result is a coherently co-constructed account of why she was so pleased about the more recent family visit. This co-construction, supportive as it is, does limit our ability to evaluate Doris' performance since she does not have to rely exclusively on her own abilities for lexicalization. Note however, that when she is asked to estimate the time of the visit she is dramatically wrong. This sort of temporal conflation is very common in AD, although whether it is linked to the clinically recognized symptom of temporal disorientation and its associated neural substrate is another question to be answered (Hirono *et al.* 1998a).

9.6   Summary discussion

We have presented phasal analyses of four texts involving two high functioning youths with ASDs and two women in different stages of AD. The phasal analysis lets us relate local variation in functional selections in instances of discourse to individual and generic information patterns. These individual and generic information patterns may then be abstracted as characteristic of the speaker and his or her negotiation of the situation. The features in Figures 9.1 and 9.4 provide more explicit representations of the information that is used to do phasal analysis. When a discourse analyst says, for instance, 'the interaction relationship has shifted', that is based on a deconstruction of some set of features signifying turn, speech function, addressee relationships and so on. Similarly, a shift in ideational relationship will be realized by some change in the predications, lexical selections, tense and/or aspect choices which the feature analysis makes explicit. Obviously, we do not expect doctors, nurses and families to conduct research on discourse phase. What we have suggested is that phasal analysis is a tool that will be of use to researchers and /or discourse analysts for descriptions that relate functional selections made within grammatical structures to generic models of situation and contexts of culture.

Contexts of culture and situation provide parameters for describing and interpreting contextual variations relevant to discourse phase. At times, spelling out the generic properties of models results in information that appears banal – as 'normal process' generic features often are. But precisely because they are the unnoticed and unexamined fabric of our everyday experience, they inform and shape it and our ability to recognize difference.[3] Another way of looking at cultural and situational norms is through the lenses of conversation analysis and relevance theory as discussed in previous chapters. Conversation analysis highlights conventions around interaction and ideation by focusing on exchange structures and topic. Relevance theory draws attention to (schematic) default assumptions for the goals of communication and some of the processes that contribute to the construction of relevance in discourse. We can use the information from the phasal analyses to relate discourses to such norms and to provide explicit bases for judgements about normativity and for new generalizations. For example, as outlined in Chapter 3, the model for conversation between peers assumes there will be a relatively equal distribution of talk and topic. Who 'counts' as a peer depends on both contexts of culture and situation of participants. Where the context of culture and situation are shared among speakers, recognition and performance of role relationships relative to talk and topic may be automatic and unproblematic. Speakers will not only take turns at talk and share responsibility for topic development, they will shape their discourse in terms of what they believe the other speaker(s) know and/or need to know, and in terms of the goals of the interaction.

Conversations and interviews which occur in medical and research contexts share many of the properties of conversation but also differ. In the present chapter, Texts 9.2 and 9.4 are extracts from semi-structured interviews involving patients with Alzheimer's disease. Part of the role of the researcher here is to elicit specific information about a patient's cognitive status and ability to perform activities of daily living (ADLs), but also to allow participants to expand freely on these topics and to introduce their own concerns. The role of caregivers and patients is to supply this information. Topic initiation, sharing and relevance construction are shaped by these goals. Texts 9.1 and 9.3 are extracts from research interactions designed to investigate the informal conversational skills of speakers with autism spectrum disorders. While the research participants in each of the texts conform to expectations in many ways, in all of the texts, one or more elements of interaction, topic and/or relevance construction do not conform to expected norms. These normative patterns and differences for research participants are summarized in Table 9.1.

People with particular disorders may habitually employ different discourse features to negotiate generic situations, creating new patterns within familiar contexts of situation. We have illustrated some of these types of differences for individual speakers with AD and ASDs. For example, people with mild or moderate AD tend to be good interactionally, usually respecting turn and trying to participate, but they may also show a level of dependence which is atypical for adults in an interview situation when they are being asked about

Table 9.1. *Normative patterns for conversation and relevance construction*

	Text 9.1: Magic of the universe	Text 9.2: My Mom	Text 9.3: Cow parts	Text 9.4: Squirrels
Role				
Be responsive	✓	✓	✓	✓
Contribute	✓	✓	✓	✓
Relevant	✓	X	✓	✓
Develop topic	✓	X	✓	✓(?)
Develop mutual topics	na	X	X	✓
Topic				
Start	✓	✓	✓	✓
Develop coherently	✓	X	✓	✓(?)
Complete	✓	X	✓	✓
Quantity				
Provide enough information	✓	X	✓	✓(?)
Don't provide too much information	X	na	✓	✓(?)
Manner				
Signal shifts in perspective	X	X	✓	na
Give sufficiently lexicalized reference for coherence	✓(?)	X	✓	✓(?)
Quality				
Truthful	✓	✓	✓	✓

themselves. The interactional dependence is most likely created by ideational and organizational difficulties – limited (access to) episodic information, difficulties with lexical retrieval and reduced executive function resources can force one to rely on caregivers or other conversational participants for personal information, discourse monitoring information, and even the words needed to articulate an experience or desire. This shows up in discourse in features such as those we have discussed – high proportions of modalization, discourse and episodic monitoring questions, comparatively low lexical density, ideational perseveration, difficulties with fluency and coherence, and in some patients confabulation and other more severe manifestations of cognitive dysfunction. Notably too, when we see successful discourse of speakers with AD, it may be the case that caregivers or other speakers are supporting their conversational participation in precisely these areas. The extent to which such patterns co-vary with disease phase and treatment is another matter of ongoing research, as is the matter of their relationships to neural structure and function. In the next section we sketch, very provisionally, the sort of architecture and neural components implied by the schemata we have used.

9.7   Discourse and neurocognitive function

Neurological function and dysfunction affect the information available to speakers, their abilities to relate information from different domains and consequently the ways in which they use language to negotiate contexts. Increasingly, these different domains are described in terms of large-scale functional neural networks. The emphasis on such networks has been partly created by developments in neuroimaging – as investigations into particular processes, structures or disorders reveal simultaneous, or at least co-ordinated, activations in different brain regions (Guye *et al.* 2008 for review). Moreover, diffusion tensor imaging is enabling the mapping of long distance fibre tracts which support such distributed networks (e.g. Catani *et al.* 2005; Catani and Mesulam 2008; Catani and Thiebaut de Schotten 2008). However, the idea of large-scale neural networks has been around for much longer than the technologies supporting visualization of activation patterns and structural connections. In the ongoing interactions between biological sciences and developments in AI, the use of large-scale neural networks as ways of thinking about (and/or formally modelling) complex dynamic systems has contributed to models of language (e.g. Hudson 1984; 2007) and neural organization (e.g. Mesulam 1998).

Mesulam (1998) proposed a model in which large-scale functional networks are linked by transmodal communication centres. These centres or hubs enable complex multi-modal representations which we think of as 'cognition', 'memory' and 'emotion', which we refer to when we talk, and which constitute the content and texture of consciousness. Among the large-scale networks are those dedicated to memory, emotion, executive functions and processing capacities (working memory), and language. Sensory modes are also served by networks as are attention and awareness, and motion processes. Memory processes are supported through a network centred in the hippocampal–entorhinal complex. There are links to unimodal and heteromodal association areas as well as to prefrontal cortex which are differentially activated depending on what is being encoded or recalled. Top-down processes of reasoning, planning, inferencing and so on are mediated by centres in prefrontal cortex as are working memory, selection, inhibition and monitoring processes. There are bidirectional links to limbic and other systems including those centred in the amygdaloid complex associated with emotion processing. Systems associated with attention and awareness which modulate all other processes are distributed through the hypothalamus, amygdala and basal forebrain. In this framework, language was conceptualized as supported through networks with centres in the temporal lobe (Wernicke's area) and (typically) left inferior frontal gyrus in prefrontal cortex (Broca's area). Revisions to the language component of the model have been proposed in the light of recent imaging findings supporting a more extended language network with three pathways in fibre tracts linking prefrontal, temporal and parietal lobes (e.g. Cantini and Mesulam 2008). Exactly how recent findings will affect our understanding of the role of regions such as 'Broca's area' is not clear, but interpretations of the imaging data suggest that subregions contribute different functions to language processing, potentially including a phonological working memory component and one or more subregions associated with semantic processes such as retrieval and categorization. It is also not clear yet whether any specific syntactic processing occurs in this region – a number of studies suggest that activation patterns are equally consistent with working memory demands (e.g. Stowe *et al.* 2005; Wartenburger *et al.* 2004; Fiebach *et al.* 2005; Vigneau *et al.* 2006). Similarly, the exact roles of the parietal area and extended temporal involvement are still being worked out. However, it seems clear that subregions of the temporal lobe are extensively involved not only in semantic but also syntactic and phonological processing, and that parietal areas are involved in processing complex sentences and inferential relations in discourse (Vigneau *et al.* 2006).

What is most salient for our present purpose, however, is the architecture in a model such as that proposed by Mesulam. There are no 'stores' or 'word-hoards' for lexemes, concepts, frames or schemas, but directories linking different kinds of information in unimodal, heteromodal and transmodal association areas. Thus, beginning a long and auspicious line stretching, at least, from de Saussure and Hjelmslev at the beginning of the twentieth century to Lamb (1966; 1998) and Jackendoff (e.g. 2002), in current work a word is regarded as a set of relations between meanings and auditory, visual or tactile signs. Similarly concepts do not 'exist' in particular neural regions but are distributed across unimodal and heteromodal areas according to how they are acquired or learned and their subsequent associations formed through transmodal interactions.[4] Accessing a concept or a word is thus a matter of linking its meaning, value and representation through transmodal gateways such as those proposed for Wernicke's area (Mesulam 1998).

We would like to summarize some of the systems and networks we have discussed so we offer Table 9.2. However we do so very tentatively. The complexity of the systems involved in discourse processing means that only the most obvious neural systems can be included. Also, the transitional state of knowledge with respect to the details of the neural networks associated with language and discourse processing argue for extreme caution. Until the publication of Catani *et al.* (2005), linguists and neurologists simply did not know about the linguistic role of the secondary fibre tracts in the arcuate

Table 9.2. *Types of information and related systems*

	Normal potential	Neurocognitive systems	Neural network centres	Discourse effects
Context of culture (contexts of user)	Languages and dialects (Temporal, geographical, social and individual variations)	Semantic memory Linguistic systems	Medial temporal lobes (MTL) (temporal-parietal lobes)	Localization Dialects (semantic, morphosyntactic, and phonological feature patterns)
Context of situation (contexts of use)	Functional varieties (ideation, interaction, medium combination options)	Semantically and episodically encoded scripts, schemas, scenarios, frames	MTL and parahippocampal formation, Amygdala, temporo-parietal lobes	Functional variation in linguistic feature patterns: Event sequences; discourse structures; contextualization features; affect and interactional features
Phase	Discourse instances	Semantic recall Episodic encoding Episodic recall	R/L VLPFC, Temporal-parietal lobes and HC (episodic recall more likely than encoding to engage the right hemisphere)	Predication Lexical selection
		Maintaining	D/VLPFC	information processing effects associated with message organization, interaction and affect
		Monitoring Planning	D/VLPFC, VMPFC, ACC, OFC	
		Attention	Thalamus	modulates everything
		Inferencing Integration	Extended language network: D/VMPFC anterior temporal poles, posterior temporal-parietal regions	Coherence Semantic complexity Spatial imaging

ACC = anterior cingulate cortex; D = dorso; DL = dorsolateral; HC = hippocampal complex; L = left; M = medial; MTL = medial temporal lobe; OFC = orbito-frontal cortex; R = right; VL = ventrolateral; PFC = prefrontal cortex

fasciculus. Moreover, up until about the same time, most linguists and neurologists would have confidently assured anyone who was interested that syntax is processed in Broca's area – we do not know this with such certainty anymore. So Table 9.2 must be read as merely a partial summary of our discussion, intended to be suggestive rather than definitive – and likely to need revision as new technologies and means to interpret their results change what we think we know.

Only the final row in Table 9.2 is intended to refer to anything that might be considered a process and the items listed in the column 'Neural network centre' are not intended to suggest traditional localizations. We do not mean for instance that 'semantic memory is in the medial temporal lobe' or that 'inferencing happens in dorsal/ventromedial prefrontal cortex'. Rather, we are simply labelling the neural areas that we have discussed as possible network centres for the processes to the left of them. The items in the column labelled 'Discourse effects' are, similarly, not 'outputs' of the named neural centres. They are discourse phenomena that might be affected by activity centred in these regions.

Much more confidently we offer the summary of discourse and contextual features given in Table 9.3. This summarizes the major areas of investigation in clinical discourse analysis that we have discussed and suggests some interactions. **Context of culture** and **Context of situation** identify parameters for what speakers know. This variation is semiotic: it is relevant to speakers' semantic and episodic memory, and includes the languages and varieties they know. **Language** refers specifically to linguistic structures, features and functions as resources for instantiating semiotic potential. **Discourse processes** is self-explanatory. Some of these processes are cognitive, such as inferencing, metaphor and topic shift. Others are or may be signs of cognitive function, such as confabulation, hesitation phenomena and modalization. Still others, such as turn-taking and evaluation, are discourse behaviours which may reflect cognitive and affective processes and functions. Finally, the **Research areas** column indicates some topics we have discussed related to discourse processes, language and context.

9.8   Intra- and intercultural relevance

We have found the approaches we have presented helpful in the struggle to understand how discourse may be interpreted in relation to people's neurocognitive functioning. In closing we would like to suggest that the model, which was originally developed for ethnographically grounded discourse analysis, may also be useful as an aid for achieving intra- and intercultural relevance. There are two ways to go about this. One is to attempt to design tools which are sufficiently context independent so as to overcome differences in, for instance,

Table 9.3. *Summary of discourse and contextual features*

Context of culture	Context of situation	Language	Discourse processes	Research areas
Provenances Individual participant demographics as relevant in terms of age, geographical provenance, and social provenance (class, gender, education, other)	Medium Spoken (spontaneous, prepared, read aloud) Written (spontaneous, edited)	Phonetic and phonological features Prosodic features (e.g. intonation tonicity) Syntactic markedness options Cohesive options Discourse schemas	Hearing/articulation Parsing/producing Discourse intonation Inferencing (reference presupposition, implicatures) Information processing indices (e.g. hesitation, pause, false start, repairs, incomplete utterances)	Processing abilities Relevance construction Syntactic complexity Lexical density and richness Executive functions
	Interaction Roles +/- power +/- social distance Affect (evaluation, attitude) Emotion	Speech functions Modalization options Lexis	Negotiation of speaker roles and alignment (selection of speech acts, modality, turn, overlap, evaluative lexis)	Social skills Conversational schema Theory of mind
	Ideation Concepts Frames Schemas Scripts Scenarios	Lexis Argument and circumstantial roles Morphosyntactic structures	Lexical selection, Predication, Metaphor, Metonymy, Irony, Humour, Confabulation, Gist/recall, Topic (initiation, development, shift)	Relevance Conceptual structure organization Semantic and episodic memory Executive functions

levels of literacy, types of experience relationship available, differences in writing systems and so on. Another approach is to develop culturally specific neuropsychological tests. Both approaches presuppose articulated descriptions of the relevant languages, discourse patterns and contexts of situations within particular contexts of culture. These approaches are not mutually exclusive, and both are likely to provide somewhat different kinds of information about clinical populations. For instance, from an epidemiological perspective having neuropsychological inventories and rating scales with universal applicability and relevance allows commutability of information across cultural boundaries. This is important in understanding epidemiological patterns and disease processes. However, neuropsychological inventories and rating scales which are intended to operate interculterally may be limited in the amount of detail they provide precisely because they are universal. (As the level of abstraction increases, the amount of specific information decreases.) The second approach, of designing culturally specific neuropsychological inventories and scales avoids this but presents problems of commutability of information. An alternative, third way is to develop both kinds of tool so that there is commutability at the level of generalization and sensitivity to culturally specific variations.

Clinical discourse analysis is a novel approach to enduring questions about relationships between brain and behaviour. The challenges involved in mapping information from different kinds of study such as neuroimaging, neuropsychology, cognitive neurology, medicine and discourse analysis are many. However, the opportunities for achieving new understanding of disorders and diseases in terms of how they alter everyday behaviour are also many and, if pursued, may help some people live the best lives they are capable of.

Closing remarks

We wrote this book because we thought a description of the work we do could be helpful for people who want to investigate and understand discourse in clinical contexts. In modelling comprehensive discourse analyses and showing how such analyses may be systematically related to aspects of neurocognition, we hope to have illustrated the usefulness of taking a unifying approach to investigating natural language behaviour, and particularly extended discourse, in relation to neurocognition. Our practice of hybridizing techniques from functional and formal linguistic models, from conversational analysis, ethnomethodology, situational linguistics and pragmatics, as well as from structuralist and semiotic discourse models, artificial intelligence and neuropsychology and bundling them together in order to account for all the different aspects of language that potentially contribute to discourse patterns is driven by the need for comprehensive accounts that are beyond the scope of individual frameworks or discourse models (that we know). We have suggested ways in which the resultant hybrid methodology for clinical discourse analysis can be combined with neuropsychological and neuroimaging techniques and adapted to different situations and cultures. While we have been most concerned to address the need for comprehensive analyses, we have also shown that the amount of detail included in analyses can be adjusted according to the scope and purposes of particular investigations.

We have further suggested that clinical discourse analysis has at least the following potential applications. Most broadly, clinical discourse analyses can be used to identify linguistic and discourse patterns associated with affect and neurocognitive function generally and so may be useful in researching a wide range of brain–behaviour relationships. In the context of affective or neurological disorder, clinical discourse analyses can be used

- to make explicit the linguistic and discourse patterns that inform clinicians' intuitive diagnostic judgements;
- to refine and develop diagnostic criteria for particular disorders;
- to develop tools for monitoring and assessing endogenous or therapy-induced changes in affect and neurocognitive function;
- to inform the development of cognitive and/or behavioural therapies.

These broadly stated applications suggest that there is extraordinary potential for clinical discourse analyses to aid and inform research and clinical practice in affective and neurocognitive disorders. However, we have also been at pains to point to limitations. Clinical discourse analysis provides another set of tools for informing clinical judgements and research – but the value of analyses will be determined by its relation to data from other sources such as neuropsychological evaluation and neuroimaging. Clinical discourse analysis is thus by definition work that is most relevantly pursued collaboratively with multi-disciplinary teams in hospital or research labs. Discourse analysts are not typically also neurologists or psychologists and discourse analyses may inform, but are unlikely to replace, other diagnostic practices.

We have not tried in this book to do more than point to the existence and utility of technologies for text collection, analysis and comparison. There are many such tools and they improve annually so that it is now quite practical for instance to work with parsing programmes in big projects instead of manually analysing syntactic data. However, from our perspective there is real value in training discourse analysts to be able to do analyses manually in the first instance so they know intimately the structures, patterns and meanings emerging from analyses independently of computer mediation. Similarly, when beginning to work with the discourse of any clinical group, taking time initially to perform detailed manual analyses can be invaluable. In both cases, analysts will be better prepared to design and interpret computationally mediated analyses or searches because they will have the experiential base for understanding the discourse patterns they encounter. What we have tried to do is provide enough information and models for (future) discourse analysts to develop that experiential base, and to show relevance and potential of such activity for clinicians and other caregivers.

Finally, given that we have pointed regularly to the importance of neuropsychological evaluation and neuroimaging in research, diagnosis and monitoring, one may wonder whether we are not proposing elaborate training and research that is or will soon be made redundant by these practices and technologies. To this we respond with three observations.

First, we have tried to show that detailed descriptions even of very aberrant discourse of individuals can be informative about their cognitive and/or affective states and so may have independent clinical and research value. The sort of information generated from such analyses may complement, for instance, information about blood flow or glucose metabolism from imaging studies or executive function reflected in ability to count backwards by sevens or draw clocks, but it is clearly qualitatively different and potentially more informative about how, for instance, regional metabolism and executive functions may be reflected in everyday talk and behaviour.

Second, the sort of comprehensive detailed descriptions of discourse patterns for particular neurological disorders has, for the most part, not yet been undertaken (or published) so the extent to which such analysis may be of value in areas other than those we examine is simply not known.[1] This is an odd state of affairs given the centrality of discourse to human sociocognitive behaviour. One cause has perhaps been the overwhelming complexity of the task, combined with what appeared to be limited rewards for the work involved. However, as we suggested in the introduction, the new technologies for developing and analysing corpora are in fact making such projects much less daunting and potentially more rewarding. Also, another possible cause for the lack of detailed published discourse descriptions of neurological and affective disorders is a tendency to search for deficits in discourse behaviours rather than to begin with comprehensive characterizations of patterns. The search for markers and deficits is quite understandable but, when it doesn't yield results, it is possible to conclude that discourse analysis is not useful. Against this, we have argued that comprehensive analysis and identification of patterns as illustrated in the preceding chapters are more likely to be rewarding, at least as a point of departure for investigations.

Third, there are extremely active searches for reliable neuroimaging correlates of Alzheimer's, autism and a host of other neurological disorders and diseases, and some well-established neuropsychological diagnostic tests. Some of these searches have already produced results and no doubt others will – so aren't clinical discourse analyses likely to become almost immediately redundant? To this we point to the social realities surrounding the diagnosis and management of neurological disorders. Alzheimer's may serve as an example. Most people who get Alzheimer's will never visit a memory clinic, see a neurologist or have even a CT scan. At best, they will be seen and treated by a family physician or other primary caregiver who may not have (or request) access to neuroimaging or expert neuropsychological advice. This is the case even in the wealthiest countries where extensive resources are dedicated to developing the technologies and there is wide access to health care. Given that the number of people with dementia is expected to triple or quadruple by 2050, it seems unlikely that access will change dramatically, even if imaging becomes less costly and more people are trained as neurologists and neuropsychologists. Thus, while we are excited about the opportunities provided by new technologies, we see these as research and diagnostic tools that are likely to remain primarily in teaching hospitals and research institutes. Primary care providers will continue to need tools that effectively allow on-the-spot evaluation for diagnosis and monitoring. We hope clinical discourse analysts will help to develop such tools to support and improve on clinical practice in at least some of the ways we have discussed in this book.

Finally, as we pointed out in Chapter 9, imaging technologies are unsettling even some of the most well-founded assumptions about the neural instantiation of language and offering new information and new sources of information about what happens in our heads when we talk. But interpreting what the new information means is another matter and requires neuropsychological and other expertise. We believe clinical discourse analysis of otherwise well-characterized neurological populations can contribute to the interpretive processes and to our understanding of language and discourse in neurocognitive terms. The project is ambitious and the challenges enormous – but the resources are available and the needs addressed are real so we hope people will accept the challenge.

Notes

NOTES ON CHAPTER 2

[1] The debate revolves around the salience given to executive function relative to memory disorder. Diagnostic criteria which treat AD as prototypical of dementia typically require memory impairment and impairment in another area such as executive function (e.g. DSM-IV). However, in dementia arising from causes other than AD, memory impairment may not be a prominent feature. For discussion, see for instance Bowler and Hachinski (2003: 7–8), Mesulam (2000) and Royall *et al.* (2005).

[2] Researchers have differed in their diagnostic and inclusion criteria in epidemiological studies of the dementias. The variance in prevalence estimates with the frontotemporal and other dementias is partly an artifact of such differences. Knapp *et al.* (2007) review the general difficulties.

[3] Dubois *et al.* (2007) have proposed a revision of diagnostic/research criteria to allow earlier diagnosis of AD and the elimination of the 'possible' NINDS-ARDRA category. They propose a combination of episodic memory impairment plus neuroimaging, spinal fluid evaluation, or proven AD mutation in the family. Their goal is to allow identification of AD before patients are actually demented.

[4] Semantic memory refers to stored information that is decontextualized. For example, speakers will normally know the names and some attributes of common plants and animals. However, it is unusual for speakers to remember the contexts in which they acquired such information – they simply 'know' that cats are called cats, that they meow, and so on. In contrast, episodic memory refers to contextualized memory – rememberers not only 'know' about something, but they remember some aspect or aspects of the context they learnt it in – episodic memories are at least bimodal. Episodic memory is often associated with personal or autobiographical memory. However, personal and autobiographical memories may over time become decontextualized parts of a semantic repertoire about one's life. See Tulving (e.g. 1972 for an early articulation, 2002) for a recent account. While some parts of the networks supporting semantic and episodic memory systems are matters of ongoing research, lesion studies, imaging and studies of neurodegenerative diseases all suggest that the hippocampal complex is central to episodic memory and that the left temporal cortex is central to semantic memory. (See Cabeza and Nyberg 2000 for an imaging review.) Neurodegenerative diseases differentially affect memory systems. For example, hippocampal involvement in AD impairs recent episodic memory while damage to the temporal lobe is a hallmark for semantic memory. (See e.g. Perry and Hodges 1996 for a review.)

NOTES ON CHAPTER 4

[1] The systems for speech functions are adapted from Asp 2001; Gregory 1988; 2009c.

[2] The conceptual/lexical relations are from Gregory, published in Watt (1990).

NOTES ON CHAPTER 6

[1] This material was presented in poster format as Asp, E., Fisk, J., Klages, J., Kydd, D., Song, X, and Rockwood, K. Language performance may distinguish mild AD and SIVD. VAS_COG 2005, Florence, Italy. Details are available from E. Asp.

NOTES ON CHAPTER 7

[1] Alternatively, or additionally, one can measure lexical richness using Brunet's Index or Honoré's Statistic (Brunet 1978; Honoré 1979). Brunet's index quantifies the amount of lexical variation in a text calculated over the text length. Honoré's Statistic gives a value for the number of words used only once (Holmes 1992; 1994). These measures are not sensitive to text length. Lexical richness measures give an idea of how varied that information is and how much a speaker is inclined to select alternative lexical items and thus they add valuable perspective to the standard measures of lexical pattern such as type token ratio or lexical density, particularly in clinical contexts (Holmes and Singh 1996; Singh and Bookless 1997).

[2] The *would* in this instance is not included in modalization because it is used in its aspectual sense to refer to habitual aspect rather than hypothesis.

NOTES ON CHAPTER 8

[1] Some authors include elements of setting and participants in scripts. However, since these can be handled by other constructs, we find it useful to limit script knowledge to ordered action sequences that characterize a situation. This is consonant with Schank and Abelson's (1977: 41) description of scripts as 'a predetermined stereotyped sequence of actions that defines a well known situation'.

[2] Chwilla and Kolk (2005) examine ERP responses to three-word lexical items around which conventional scripts might be constructed (e.g. director, bribe, dismissed) and find that activating script knowledge presents an N400 effect similar to the one that occurs for semantic relations. They conclude that script information is accessed and integrated immediately, that it constitutes a central aspect of word meaning, and that the patterns of activation (insofar as they are deducible) spread from Wernicke's area to more anterior sites in the left hemisphere and then to anterior temporal and orbital sites in the right hemisphere.

[3] Emotional liability is included as a clinical sign of AD (DSM-IV). It refers to a tendency to display uncontrolled and sometimes extreme or incongruous emotions.

NOTES ON CHAPTER 9

[1] Hypothetically, the gender difference might have contrapuntal effects – increasing social distance but decreasing the perceived social power of the researcher.

[2] Women also have more white matter disease which is linked to cognitive decline (van Dijk *et al.* 2008) and the development of dementia.

[3] In the present discourse analyses, the experiential fields the speakers are absorbed in are culturally specific, in temporal, geographic and social provenances. The research activities that include school, clinic or home visits, lengthy interviews and other data collection designed to investigate specific disorders and treatments are also likely to be culture specific and generate their own generic situations. Even the disorders themselves may be culture specific in several kinds of ways. One is that prevalence of particular disorders may vary, affecting everything from conceptual schemas and frames related to the disorder to public health policy and social supports. Another is that depending on factors such as socioeconomic status and attitudes, people may or may not seek treatment. This may be not only because the kinds of treatment and their cost to individuals vary (and so may be beyond the means of some sociocultural groups) but also because frames and schemas vary. If memory loss is regarded as normal in old age, for instance, people with AD may not be defined as ill until the symptoms are severe. And if drug treatments are only publicly funded for moderate or severe AD, then treatment of people with mild AD may be limited to people whose families can afford it.

[4] Such a model may shed light on the current debate about category specific deficits for object concepts. The discussion hinges around evidence that damage to neural tissue in different brain regions differentially affects (access to) concept categories such as animals and tools. For example, perceiving animals (and faces) appears to be associated with bilateral activation of the lateral fusiform gyrus in contrast with perception of tools which bilaterally activates the medial fusiform gyrus (Chao *et al.* 1999; Grill-Spector 2003). Current 'competing' explanatory hypotheses for these differences include 'sensory-functional', 'domain specific' and 'conceptual structure' approaches (reviewed in Tyler and Moss 2001; Caramazza and Mahon 2003; Thompson-Schill 2003).

The sensory-functional hypothesis prioritizes modality and use as organizing principles for categories. The overarching hypothesis is that concepts are represented as features at least partially distributed along the neural pathways associated with their acquisition. So, tool concepts might be partially represented in neural regions close to those activated by their use whereas animal concepts might be primarily represented in neural regions close to those associated with, for instance, their shapes (e.g. Warrington and Shallice 1984; Warrington and McCarthy 1987; Thompson-Schill 2003). The domain-specific hypothesis prioritizes taxonomic domains: animals, fruits and vegetables, conspecifics and tools are postulated as potentially phylogenetically motivated, conceptual domains (Caramazza and Shelton 1998; Caramaza and Mahon 2003). Under either of these hypotheses, damage in a region that affected one category need not affect concepts in another category because the categories are stored in different areas of the brain.

The conceptual structure approach also posits distributed features for concepts, but prioritizes their internal feature structure as the salient factor in category specific deficits. In this framework, domains such as animals and tools have different internal conceptual organizations. Animals have many shared features but few distinctive ones. Tools have a few highly salient distinctive features (they are designed usually for one purpose), but few shared features. The model predicts that the superordinate category of animals will be less vulnerable to damage because it will have multiple connections with other concepts within the same domain. However, basic level concepts such as CAT and COW will be more vulnerable because they have few distinctive features and those they have are not highly correlated with each other. Tool concepts may be resistant to damage (as compared with basic level animal concepts) because although they have fewer features in general, those features they do have are distinctive and correlated with each other. Under this view, conceptual structure is an emergent property of the connections between features, and category deficits are interpreted as damage to feature structure levels (Moss *et al.* 2007).

Mesulam's model is most obviously consistent with the sensory-functional hypothesis of Warrington and Shallice. However, it would not appear to rule out the other possibilities of domain specific and modality neutral concept organization. Rather, as suggested by Thompson-Schill (2003), domain specific organization (and apparent deficit) could occur as an emergent property of a distributed sensory-functional organization of semantic categories. That is, the two apparently clear categories which may be differentially impaired, tools and animals, are respectively associated with function and vision. Deficits for these categories might thus be evidence of deficit for functional or modal attributes rather than for the categories as such. Martin's (2007) review of functional neuroimaging studies of object concepts similarly suggests that modal-functional and domain-specific views of conceptual organization are not necessarily mutually exclusive: studies collectively suggest that distributed representation of features for object concepts according to modality or use may co-exist with dedicated domains for categorical learning.

NOTES ON CLOSING REMARKS

[1] An exception to this general state of affairs is work on schizophrenic discourse. See for example the early work of Rochester and Martin 1979.

Appendix A: Some basic grammatical terminology and relations

GRAMMATICAL TERMINOLOGY

CLAUSES AND UTTERANCES

In Chapter 3 we defined the terms Clause and Utterance (pp. 29–32). Here we include brief definitions for convenient reference. The reader is referred to Chapter 3 (pp. 29–32) for broader definitions and examples.

English **Clauses** can be defined syntactically as consisting of a verb, its arguments and adjuncts as in *Cosmo bit Piper yesterday.* Independent clauses can also be used alone to ask a question, make a statement or exclamation, or give a command. A simple Clause is also typically spoken as a single tone group.

Meaningful speech phenomena which do not meet the criteria for clause such as incomplete utterances, minimal responses, idiosyncratic vocalizations, and isolated hesitation fillers are labelled as **utterances**. **Utterance** refers to any unit which can be assigned a speech function, and/or has a distinct tone group, and/or is a linguistic signal of ideational, interactional, or organizational information about a speaker's message.

MORPHEMES

Morphemes are smallest contrastive units in the grammar. *Rabbit, dog, -s*, in *dogs, -ed* in *called, -ity* in *fatality, un-* in *unhappy, brush* in *toothbrush* are all morphemes. None of these items can be further analysed. For instance, *rabbit* refers to a small furry long-eared animal that hops, but no part of *rabbit* is associated with one of these meanings. Morphemes may or may not be words: Whereas *rabbit* is a word, *-s* in *dogs* signifies plural but does not occur as a word.

Words may be simple (e.g. *rabbit/dog*), compound (*toothbrush*) or complex (*fatality/unhappy*). What differentiates a word from a morpheme is simply the fact that we have a word for those morphemes or compound/complex combinations of morphemes which can occur independently. In each case, the unit signifies one or more meanings with which it is conventionally associated.

WORD CATEGORIES

The major categories are NOUN, VERB, ADJECTIVE and ADVERB.

NOUNS

Nouns are Proper (e.g. *John, Canada*), or Common (cat, human, kindness). If common they can be countable (i.e. be singular or plural as in *boy/boys, goose/geese* etc.), or non-countable (*butter, milk, happiness* etc.). Included in this category are PRONOUNS which can substitute for noun phrases (e.g. Personal Pronouns as in *I/me/mine, we/us/ours, you/you/yours, he/him/his, she/her/hers, it/it/its, one/one/ones, they/them/theirs*). There are also Reflexive Pronouns (*myself, yourself, ourselves* etc.), Relative Pronouns (*who, whom, whose, which, which, what, that*), Indefinite Pronouns (compounds formed with *some-, any-, every-* or *no-* and *-one, -body* or *-thing* as in *somebody, anything, everyone* etc.) and two 'special' pronouns: existential *there* occuring as Subject in existential clauses (as in *There is a woman at the door*). Notice that existential *there* must be unstressed), and Ambient or 'expletive' *it* which doesn't refer to anything (as in the *it* in *it's sunny*).

Characteristic modifiers of nouns:

- DETERMINERS (e.g. the/a/an; this/that/these/those; some/any/every/no etc. as in *the dog, a man, some milk, these puppies* and so on).
- ADJECTIVAL PHRASES (e.g. *very tall women, totally unacceptable behaviour* where *very tall* and *totally unacceptable* are adjective phrases modifying the nouns *women* and *behaviour* respectively).
- PREPOSITIONAL PHRASES (e.g. *a book about physics, a manual of style, a teacher of linguistics* where *about physics, of style* and *of linguistics* are prepositional phrases modifying the nouns *book, manual* and *teacher* respectively).
- RELATIVE CLAUSES (e.g. *the man who answered the letter, the dog that bit me* where *who answered the letter* and *that bit me* are relative clauses operating as modifiers of the nouns *man* and *dog*).

It is normal for determiner and adjectival phrase modifiers to occur before the noun that they modify and for prepositional phrases and relative clauses to follow the noun they modify.

Nouns operate as the **head** element of noun phrases. Noun Phrases can occur as Subject, Complement, or Adjunct in a clause. Noun Phrases can also appear case marked by prepositions as in the above examples. That is Prepositional Phrases are Noun Phrases to which a preposition has been added. Most modern grammars describe prepositional phrases as consisting of a Preposition and a Noun Phrase complement. In English it is normal for the head noun of a noun phrase occurring as Subject of a clause to agree with the verb in person and number if the clause is indicative declarative or indicative interrogative. The bracketed phrases in the following examples are Noun Phrases operating as elements of clauses. The underlined words are nouns or pronouns.

(i) [The <u>dog</u>] eats [<u>rabbits</u>].
(ii) [A very serious <u>discussion</u> about <u>ethics</u>] was going on in [the <u>pub</u>].
(iii) [<u>John</u>] is [a <u>person</u> of considerable <u>integrity</u>].
(iv) [<u>They</u>] say [<u>he</u>] will phone again [<u>tomorrow</u>].
(v) [<u>I</u>] told [<u>them</u>] [<u>you</u>] would be [<u>home</u>].

VERBS

Verbs can be inflected for **tense** (past or present as in *walk/walked, eat/ate, go/went*), **number** (singular or plural *am/are, was/were*, though the singular/plural distinction in past tense is only relevant for the verb BE), and for present tense verbs **person** (third person, present tense singular; *he eats, she walks, it talks*; and general present *I/we/you/they eat/walk/talk*).

The 'modal' verbs are an exception. They are *can/could, may/might, will/would, shall/should, must, ought,* (and *dare, need,* and *BE* in special circumstances). Many linguists assume that modals are tensed pairs, others do not. In any case, whether they are treated as tensed or not, their forms have no clear relationship to semantic **time** (see for example *I would not care to see the crime go unpunished, I could leave tomorrow, Mary will have finished by now, ?John will have left yesterday*). Notably, they have no other inflected forms (i.e. there is no *canning, *mighted, *wills and so on). Linguists treat the modals as finite forms whether or not they recognize them as tensed.

Tensed verbs are often called **finite verb forms** and they contrast with non-tensed or **non-finite forms**. The non-finite inflection forms are:

1) the BASE FORM (*be/walk/have/eat/talk*)
2) the MARKED INFINITIVE FORM (*to be/to walk/to eat*)
3) the -ING FORM as in (*walking/eating/going*)
4) the -EN FORM (*eaten/walked/gone*).

Verbs are central to the formation of clauses for two reasons. One is that it is often the choice of verb that determines both the number and type of other elements of the clause. For example, *eat* requires both an NP subject and an NP complement and, if the clause is active, the subject will be Agent (the doer of the action) and the complement will be Theme: patient (the entity that undergoes a change of state). Thus *the boy ate the apple* is acceptable, but not **of the boy eats at the apple*, nor **the table eats the idea* and so on. The other reason for the centrality of verbs in clause formation is that only certain types of verb forms can occur in certain types of clauses. For instance, interrogatives and declaratives require that the first verb word be a finite form (modal or tensed verb). (*John is at home/ John will be at home/ Will John be at home/ Is John at home* are all acceptable but **John been at home/ *Being John at home* and so on are not.) Similarly, imperative clauses require that the first verb word is either the modal *let* or a base form (*Be quiet/ Eat your dinner/ Do study for you exam/ Let's go*).

ADJECTIVES

Adjectives are uninflected forms, although many can form comparatives and superlatives with the suffixes *-er* and *-est* repectively as in *clever, cleverer, cleverest, kind, kinder, kindest, nice, nicer, nicest*. Adjectives which cannot form a comparative or superlative with *-er* or *-est* can usually have *more* or *most* as a modifier with the same effect (e.g. **astuter, astutest* are bad, but *more astute, most astute* are acceptable). Comparatives and superlatives of adjectives (whether derived through suffixation of *-er/-est* or modification with *more/most*) function as determiners; they select or identify individuals in terms of a base attribute. These forms are consequently treated as derived rather than inflected. Adjectives realize 'attributes' and they occur either as modifiers of nouns (*clever student, kinder era, nicest dog*) or as the predicate in attributive relational clauses with a form of BE as the main verb (*This student is clever/ That era was kinder/ Susan's dog is nicest*).

ADVERBS

Adverbs are also uninflected forms. Many are derived from adjectives with the addition of an *-ly* suffix (as in *cleverly, nicely, kindly, astutely* and so on). Like adjectives, comparatives and superlatives of adverbs are formed by the addition of *more* or *most* as a modifier (as in *more cleverly, most astutely*), and they can be intensified by DEGREE ADVERBS such as *very, so, too, almost, quite* and so on. Otherwise adverbs accept neither modification nor complementation. They occur as ADJUNCTS only, modifying adjectives (e.g. *cautiously clever, totally silly*), other adverbs in the case of the degree subclass (*very cleverly, somewhat slowly, quite suddenly*), verbs (*completely exhausted, entirely gone, utterly destroyed*), verb phrases (*left the room quietly/carefully/silently*), or whole sentences (*frankly, I don't believe it/ Mary left for Montreal quite suddenly/ unfortunately, John is sick*). This description of adverbs excludes from the category comparatives and superlatives formed with *-er* and *-est*. Forms such as *quicker* and *fastest* in *Sam ran quicker (than Sue), Sam runs fastest (of all)* are regarded here as determiners derived from adjectives, not as adverbs. Note that prototypical adverbs (*suddenly, happily, quickly, botanically* etc.) do not allow suffixation of *-er/-est*.

In addition to the major categories of words above, there are also three impor-tant minor categories; PREPOSITIONS, DEICTICS and CONJUNCTIONS.

PREPOSITIONS

Prepositions are also uninflected forms. They form a closed class (as opposed to open set categories like nouns and verbs) insofar as the number of them is finite (i.e. new prepositions are very infrequently added to English). The class consists of items such as *to, by, with, for, at, in, out, on, over, up, down, under, beneath, beside, above, below* and so on. Prepositions occur as modifiers of Noun Phrases (*to John, on the table, at home, in the afternoon*) in which case the phrases are often called Prepositional Phrases. They can also occur alone as, for instance, the sole realization of a Goal: location (*John went out*) or a locative predicate (*Mary is in*).

DEICTICS

Deictics include the definite and indefinite articles *(the/a)*, the demonstratives *(this/that/these/those)*, the possessive articles (*my, our, your, our, his, her, their, its, one's*) and lexical possessives (*John's, the president's, Canada's*), quantifi-ers (*one, two, three…, first, second …*) and a few other elements. (The compar-atives and superlatives of adjectives are sometimes included among the deictic class.) All of these occur as specifiers of Noun Phrases and will precede any adjectival modifiers of the nouns as in *the dog/ the clever dog / the first clever dog* and so on, but not, for example, **clever first the dog*. Some of them, such as the demonstratives, can substitute for a whole noun phrase as in *give me the book / give me that*.

CONJUNCTIONS

Conjunctions are of three general types:

1) co-ordinating conjunctions such as *and/or/but* which can be used to co-ordinate words, phrases, and clauses,
2) subordinating conjunctions such as *because/if/although/in order/so that* which are used to subordinate one phrase or clause in relation to another,
3) sentence conjunctions such as *however, moreover, nevertheless* and so on which indicate logical relationships between independent sentences.

SOME BASIC TYPES OF GRAMMATICAL RELATION AND TERMINOLOGY

CONSTITUENCY AND DEPENDENCY

There are two fundamental types of grammatical relation, **constituency** and **dependency**.

Constituency characterizes the structure of phrases (including clauses and sentences) in terms of a vertical dimension such that, for instance, sentences consist of clauses, clauses consist of phrases, phrases consist of words and/or other phrases, and words consist of morphemes.

Dependency characterizes phrases on a horizontal dimension in terms of relationships of 'companionship'. In dependency terms, a noun phrase must have a 'head' element (a noun) and may optionally have a specifier (such as an article) as well as other pre-head and post-head modifiers. Modifiers that occur before a head noun are typically called modifiers, those after it may be called complements or adjuncts, depending on their relationship to the head noun. (Some linguists call post-head noun modifiers 'qualifiers'.) Similarly, a Verb Phrase must have a verb and may have complements and so on.

Head as a technical term refers to the element of any construction that must be present in order for the construction to occur (Noun in Noun phrases, Verb in Verb Phrases, Adjective in Adjective Phrases, Adverb in Adverb Phrases and Preposition in Prepositional Phrases).

SUBJECT

A subject is an element of clause structure. It is typically a Noun Phrase (NP) (*He/John/The tall man frightened them*), but may also be a clause (*What they saw frightened them*). If it is a Noun Phrase and the sentence is finite (has a verb that is inflected for tense, number and person) the noun will 'agree' with the verb in person and number, and will be nominative case (*He is sick/ They are sick*, but not *He are sick, Them is sick*). In Declaratives, the subject will precede all verbs (*Mary is answering the question/ Mary might have been being watched*). In Interrogatives, the subject will follow the first verb, usually an auxiliary in Modern English (*Is Mary answering the question?/ What did Mary hear?*). (Interrogatives such as *Who is sick?* are exceptions to this order.) In Imperatives (of the jussive type) the subject will be absent or it will be *you/ somebody* (*Go home!/ you go home/ somebody call an ambulance*). A vocative element may be present (*John, go home*). Some linguists treat such elements as subjects.

COMPLEMENT

A complement is an element of phrase (including clause) structure. Complements are realized by all categories of phrases except adverb phrases. They follow the main verb in clauses (unless they have been moved). There can be more than one complement in a clause. For example, verbs like *put* and *give* require two complements as well as a subject (*Sam put [the milk] [in the fridge] / Sam gave [Sue] [a ring]*), and a verb like *sell* can have three complements (*Sam sold [Fred] [the ring] [for two dollars]*). Complements are arguments of a predicate: if an element following a main verb (or other predicate) is either required or at least expected given the meaning of the verb it is a complement. (Note: in traditional grammars only NP complements are recognized. Sometimes they are referred to as indirect and direct objects as in *John gave Mary the book.*)

PREDICATE

Predicate refers to any element that enters into an argument structure that is not itself an argument. (From the point of view of the syntax of the clause, this means that anything that is not a subject or a complement must be a predicate.) Typically, the elements that count as predicates are the lexical head of any construction. Verbs are prototypical predicates insofar as they take both complements and subjects and, as we have seen, the particular verb determines the number and types of arguments that are required to make acceptable clauses (e.g. *put* requires an Agent, a Theme: transferent, and a Goal: location which, all other things being equal, are realized as Subject, Objective complement and Locative complement respectively). However, nouns and adjectives also function regularly as predicates as in *the Iraqi invasion of Kuwait* where *invasion* (a noun) has a complement (*of Kuwait*), and *John is sick* where the adjective *sick* is the predicate.

ADJUNCT

An adjunct is an element of phrase (including sentence) structure. Adjuncts are circumstantial elements usually having to do with the time, place, or manner of an event. They usually follow all complements (but they can be moved around). They are often realized by prepositional phrases (*on Wednesday, at the movies, with alacrity* etc.). Adverbs are always adjuncts. We also recognize 'logical' adjuncts (phrases beginning with *because, in order to, if, although* etc.). Adjuncts are 'optional' elements in the sense that phrases and sentences may be grammatically acceptable without adjuncts. Adjuncts predicate something about the consitutuent they are adjoined to. For example, the sentence *Mary is astute* is perfectly acceptable. When the adjunct *fortunately* is added to it we have another predication about the sentence viz. *It is fortunate that Mary is astute* or [[*Mary is astute*] *fortunately*].

Appendix B: Inventory of codes

Speech functions

Exclamations
E   after clause
Statement
S   after clause
Statement tagged
S-TAG   after clause
Question polar
QP   after clause
Question wh
QWH   after clause
Command jussive
CJ   after clause
Command optative
CO   after clause
Command fiat
CF   after clause

Checks and intonation

Checks
S-CHECK   after clause
Rising Pitch
S-RP   after clause

Address terms

Vocative + social distance
V+SD   after vocative
Politeness marker
PMR   after politeness marker

Attitudes and evaluation

Modality
M   after modal
Modality feature
MF   after modality feature
Attitude
ATT-N or ATT-P   after attitude

Appendix B (*cont.*)

Argument roles

Agent	
AGENT	after agent
Instrument	
INSTRUMENT	after instrument
Cause	
CAUSE	after cause
Experiencer	
EXPERIENCER	after experiencer
Stimulus	
STIMULUS	after stimulus
Source	
SOURCE	after source
Goal: Location	
GOAL-LOC	after Goal: Location
Goal: Recipient	
GOAL-REC	after Goal: Recipient
Goal: Beneficiary	
GOAL-BEN	after Goal: Beneficiary
Theme: Patient	
THEME-PAT	after Theme: Patient
Theme: Resultant	
THEME-RES	after Theme: Resultant
Theme: Percept	
THEME-PERC	after Theme: Percept
Theme: Message	
THEME-MESS	after Theme: Message
Theme: Range	
THEME-RAN	after Theme: Range
Theme: Identified	
THEME-IDEN'D	after Theme: Identified
Theme: Classified	
THEME-CLASS'D	after Theme: Classified
Theme: Attribuand	
THEME-ATTR	after Theme: Attribuand
Theme: Possessed	
THEME-POSS'D	after Theme: Possessed
Theme: Existent	
THEME-EX	after Theme: Existent
Theme: Ambient	
THEME-AMB	after Theme: Ambient

Circumstantial roles

Time	
TIME	after time
Place	

Appendix B (*cont.*)

PLACE	after place
Manner	
MANNER	after manner
Reason	
REASON	after reason
Purpose	
PURPOSE	after purpose
Condition	
CONDITION	after condition
Concession	
CONCESSION	after concession

Message organization

Reference	
R	after reference, co-indexed with first instance
Substitution	
SUB	after substitution, co-indexed with substituted item
Ellipsis	
Ellip	after ellipsis, co-indexed with ellipted item
Conjunction	
CONJ	after conjunction
Lexical Cohesion	
LC	after lexical item, co-indexed with presupposed item
Lexical Cohesion – Repetition	
LC-REP	after lexical item, co-indexed with first instance
Lexical Cohesion – Collocation	
LC-COL	after lexical item, co-indexed with collocate

Focus and Prominence:
Focus = <u>Underline</u>; Prominence = **Bold**.

References

Alagiakrishnan, K., McCracken, P. and Feldman, H. 2006. Treating vascular risk factors and maintaining vascular health: is this the way towards successful cognitive ageing and preventing cognitive decline? *Postgraduate Medical Journal*, **82** (964), 101–5.

Allain, P., Le Gall, D., Foucher, C. *et al.* 2008. Script representation in patients with Alzheimer's disease. *Cortex*, **44** (3), 294–304.

Almkvist, O. 1994. Neuropsychological deficits in vascular dementia in relation to Alzheimer's disease: reviewing evidence for functional similarity or divergence. *Dementia*, **55**, 203–9.

Almor, A., Kempler, D., MacDonald, M.C., Andersen, E.S. and Tyler, L.K. 1999. Why do Alzheimer patients have difficulty with pronouns? Working memory, semantics, and reference in comprehension and production in Alzheimer's disease. *Brain and Language*, **67**(3), 202–27.

Alvarez, J.A. and Emory, E. 2006. Executive function and the frontal lobes: a meta-analytic review. *Neuropsychology Review*, **16**(1), 17–42.

Alzheimer, A. 1907. On a peculiar disease of the cerebral cortex. *Allgemeine Zeitschrift fur Psychiatrie und Psychish-Gerichtlich. Medicin*, **64**, 146–8.

Alzheimer's Association 2007. *Alzheimer's Disease Facts and figures*. Report. New York: Alzheimer's Association New York City Chapter.

American Psychiatric Association 1994. *Diagnostic and Statistical Manual of Mental Disorders*, fourth edition. Washington, DC: American Psychiatric Publishing.

2000. *Diagnostic and Statistical Manual of Mental Disorders*, fourth edition. Text Revision. Washington, DC: American Psychiatric Publishing.

Anderson, R.C., Spiro, R.J., and Montague, W.E. 1977. *Schooling and the Acquisition of Knowledge*. Hillsdale, NJ: Lawrence Erlbaum.

Asp, E. 2001. How to do different things with words: some observations on speech acts in relation to a socio-cognitive grammar for English. In de Villiers, J. and Stainton, R. (eds.), *Communication in Linguistics: Vol. 1*. Toronto: Editions du Gref, pp. 1–13.

Asp, E., Song, X. and Rockwood, K. 2006a. Self-referential tags in the discourse of people with Alzheimer's disease. *Brain and Language*, **97**, 41–52.

Asp, E., Cloutier, F., Fay, S., Cook, C., Robertson, M.L., Fisk, J., Dei, D.W. and Rockwood, K. 2006b. Verbal repetition in patients with Alzheimer's disease who receive donepezil. *International Journal of Geriatric Psychiatry*, **21**, 426–31.

Asperger, H. 1944. Autistic psychopathology in childhood. In Frith, U. (ed.), *Autism and Asperger Syndrome*. Cambridge: Cambridge University Press, pp. 37–92.

Atkinson, J.M. and Heritage, J. (eds.) 1984. *Structures of Social Action: Studies in Conversation Analysis*. Cambridge: Cambridge University Press.

Austin, J.L. 1962. *How to Do Things with Words: the William James Lectures delivered at Harvard University in 1955*, (ed. Urmson, J.O.). Oxford: Clarendon.

Baba, M., Nakajo, S., Tu. P.H., Tomita, T., Nakaya, K., Lee, V.M., Trojanowski, J.Q. and Iwatsubo, T. 1998. Aggregation of alpha-synuclein in Lewy bodies of sporadic Parkinson's disease and dementia with Lewy bodies. *American Journal of Pathology*, **152**, 879–84.

Baddeley, A.D. 1998. Working memory. *Comptes rendus de l'académie des sciences*, **321**(2–3), 167–73.

  2003. Working memory and language: an overview. *Journal of Communication Disorders*, **36**, 189–208.

Baddeley, A.D. 2000. The episodic buffer: a new component of working memory? *Trends in Cognitive Sciences*, **4**(11), 417–22.

Baddeley, A.D. and Della Sala, S. 1996. Working memory and executive control. *Philosophical Transactions of the Royal Society of London B: Biological Sciences*, **351**, 1397–404.

Baddeley A.D., Baddeley, H.A., Bucks, R.S. and Wilcock, G.K. 2001. Attentional control in Alzheimer's disease. *Brain*, **124**, 1492–508.

Baltaxe, C. 1977. Pragmatic deficits in the language of autistic adolescents. *Journal of Pediatric Psychology*, **2**, 176–180.

Baron-Cohen, S. 1995. *Mindblindness: An Essay on Autism and Theory of Mind*. Massachusetts: MIT Press.

Baron-Cohen, S., Leslie, A. and Frith, U. 1985. Does the autistic child have a 'theory of mind'? *Cognition*, **21**, 37–46.

Barthes, R. 1968. *Elements of Semiology*. New York: Hill and Wang.

  1994. *The Semiotic Challenge*. Berkeley and Los Angeles: University of California Press.

Baudie, S., Dalla Barba, G., Thibaudet, M.C., Sagghe, A., Remy, P. and Traykov, L. 2006. Executive function deficits in early Alzheimer's disease and their relations with episodic memory. *Archives of Clinical Neuropsychology*, **21**, 15–21.

Bayles, K.A., Kaszniak, A.W. and Tomoeda, C. 1987. *Communication and Cognition in Normal Aging and Dementia*. Boston: Little, Brown and Company.

Bayles, K.A., Tomoeda, C.K. and Trosset, M.W. 1992. Relation of linguistic communication abilities of Alzheimer's patients to stage of disease. *Brain and Language*, **42**, 454–72.

Beauregard, M., Chertkow, H., Bub, D., Murtha, S., Dixon, R. and Evans, A. 1997. The neural substrate for concrete, abstract and emotional word lexica: a positron emission tomography study. *Journal of Cognitive Neuroscience*, **9**(4), 441–61.

Bechara, A., Damasio, H. and Damasio, A.R. 2000. Emotion, decision making and the orbitofrontal cortex. *Cerebral Cortex*, **10**, 295–307.

Beck, A.T. 2005. The current state of cognitive therapy: a 40-year retrospective. *Archives of General Psychiatry*, **62**(9), 953–9.

Bednarek, M.A. 2005. Frames revisited – the coherence-inducing function of frames. *Journal of Pragmatics*, **37**, 685–705.

Berg, C., Raminani, S., Greer, J., Harwood, M. and Safren, S. 2008. Participants' perspectives on cognitive-behavioural therapy for adherence and depression in HIV.

Psychotherapy Research: Journal for the Society of Psychotherapy Research, **18**(3), 271–80.

Berger, P. and Luckmann, T. 1966. *The Social Construction of Reality: A Treatise in the Sociology of Knowledge*. Garden City, NY: Anchor Books.

Berlin, B. and Kay, P. 1969. *Basic Color Terms*. Berkeley and Los Angeles: University of California Press.

Berlyne, N. 1972. Confabulation. *The British Journal of Psychiatry*, **120**, 31–9.

Bickel, C., Pantel, J., Eysenbach, K. and Schröder, J. 2000. Syntactic comprehension deficits in Alzheimer's disease. *Brain and Language*, **71**(3), 432–48.

Bird, H., Howard, D. and Franklin, S. 2000. Why is a verb like an inanimate object? Grammatical category and semantic category deficits. *Brain and Language*, **72**, 246–309.

Bird, T., Knopman, D., Van Swieten, J. *et al.* 2003. Epidemiology and genetics of frontotemporal dementia/Pick's disease. *Annals of Neurology*, **54**(S5), S29–31.

Birks, J. 2006. Cholinesterase inhibitors for Alzheimer's disease. *Cochrane Database Systematic Review*, **25**(1), CD005593.

Bishop, D.V. and Adams, C. 1989. Conversational characteristics of children with semantic-pragmatic disorder: II. What features lead to a judgement of inappropriacy? *British Journal of Disorders of Communication*, **24**(3), 241–63.

Black, S.E. 2007. Therapeutic issues in vascular dementia: studies, designs and approaches. Review. *Canadian Journal of Neurological Sciences*, **34**(1), S125–30.

Black, M. and Chiat, S. 2003. Noun–verb dissociations: a multi-faceted phenomenon. *Journal of Neurolinguistics*, **16** (2–3), 231–50.

Bleich, S., Romer, K., Wiltfang, J. and Kornhuber, J. 2003. Glutamate and the glutamate receptor system: a target for drug action. *International Journal of Geriatric Psychiatry*, **18**, S33–40.

Blennow, K. and Hampel, H. 2003. CSF markers for incipient Alzheimer's disease. *Lancet Neurology*, **2**(10), 605–13.

Blennow, K., de Leon, M.J. and Zetterberg, H. 2006. Alzheimer's disease. *The Lancet*, **368**, 387–403.

Bookheimer, S. 2002. Functional MRI of language: new approaches to understanding the cortical organization of semantic processing. *Annual Review of Neuroscience*, **25**, 151–88.

Bowler, J.V. and Hachinski, V. 2003. *Vascular Cognitive Impairment: Preventable Dementia*. Oxford: Oxford University Press.

Bradac, J.J. 1988. Language variables: conceptual and methodological problems of instantiations. In Tardy, C.H. (ed.), *A Handbook for the Study of Human Communication: Methods and Instruments for Observing, Measuring, and Assessing Communication Processes*. Westport, CT: Ablex Publishing, pp. 301–22.

Brazil, D. 1995. *A Grammar of Speech*. Oxford: Oxford University Press.

Brown, G. and Yule, G. 1983. *Discourse Analysis*. Cambridge: Cambridge University Press.

Brown, P. and Levinson, S.C. 1987. *Politeness*. Cambridge: Cambridge University Press.

Brunet, E. 1978. *Le vocabulaire de Jean Giraudoux: Structure et Evolution*. Genève: Skatline.

Bschor, T., Kuhl, K. P. and Reischies, F. M. 2001. Spontaneous speech of patients with dementia of the Alzheimer type and mild cognitive impairment. *International Psychogeriatrics*, **13**(3), 289–98.

Bucks, R., Singh, S., Cuerden, J. M., and Wilcock, G. 2000. Analysis of spontaneous, conversational speech in dementia of Alzheimer type: evaluation of an objective technique for analyzing lexical performance. *Aphasiology*, **14** (1), 71–91.

Burns, A., O'Brien, J., Bap Dementia Consensus Group, *et al.* 2006. Clinical practice with anti-dementia drugs: a consensus statement from the British Association for Psychopharmacology. *Journal of Psycholpharmacology*, **20**(6), 732–55.

Cabeza, R. and Nyberg, L. 2000. Imaging Cognition II: an empirical review of 275 PET and fMRI studies. *Journal of Cognitive Neuroscience*, **12**, 1–47.

Camille, N., Coricelli, G., Sallet, J., Pradat-Diehl, P., Duhamel, J. R. and Sirigu, A. 2004. The involvement of the orbitofrontal cortex in the experience of regret. *Science*, **304**, 1167–70.

Campione, E. and Veronis, J., 2002. A large-scale multilingual study of silent pause duration. ESCA-workshop on speech prosody. April 2002, *Aix-en-Provence*, pp. 199–202.

Caplan, D., Vijayan, S., Kuperberg, G. *et al.* 2001. Vascular responses to syntactic processing: event-related fMRI study of relative clauses. *Human Brain Mapping*, **15**, 26–38.

Caramazza, A. and Mahon, B. Z. 2003. The organization of conceptual knowledge: the evidence from category-specific semantic deficits. *Trends in Cognitive Sciences*, **7**(8), 354–61.

Caramazza, A and Shelton, J. R. 1998. Domain-specific knowledge systems in the brain: the animate–inanimate distinction. *Journal of Cognitive Neuroscience*, **10**, 1–34.

Cardebat, D., D'Monet, J. F. and Doyon, B. 1993. Narrative discourse in dementia. In Brownell, H. H. and Joanette, Y. (eds.), *Narrative Discourse in Neurologically Impaired and Normal Aging Adults*. San Diego: Singular, pp. 317–32.

Carlomangno, S., Santoro, A., Menditti, A., Pandolfi, M. and Marini, A. 2005. Referential communication in Alzheimer's type dementia. *Cortex*, **41**, 520–34.

Catani, M. and Mesulam, M. 2008. The arcuate fasciculus and the disconnection theme in language and aphasia: history and current state. *Cortex*, **44**, 953–61.

Catani, M. and Thiebaut de Schotten, M. 2008. A diffusion tensor imaging tractography atlas for virtual in vivo dissections. *Cortex*, **44**, 1105–32.

Catani, M., Jones, D. K. and Ffytche, D. H. 2005. Perisylvian language networks of the human brain. *Annals of Neurology*, **57**, 8–16.

Chafe, W. 1980. The deployment of consciousness in the production of a narrative. In W. Chafe (ed.), *The Pear Stories: Cognitive, Cultural, and Linguistic Aspects of Narrative Production*. Norwood, NJ: Ablex, pp. 9–50.

   1994. *Discourse, Consciousness, and Time: The Flow and Displacement of Conscious Experience in Speaking and Writing*. Chicago: University of Chicago Press.

   2001. The analysis of discourse flow. In Schiffrin, D., Tannen, D. and Hamilton, H. E. (eds.), *The Handbook of Discourse Analysis*. Malden, MN: Blackwell, pp. 673–88.

Chao, L. L., Haxby, J. V. and Martin, A. 1999. Attribute-based neural substrates in temporal cortex for perceiving and knowing about objects, *Nature Neuroscience*, **2**, 913–19.

Chertkow, H. and Bub, D. 1990. Semantic memory loss in dementia of Alzheimer's type: what do various measures measure? *Brain*, **113**, 397–417.

Chipere, N., Malvern, D. and Richards, B. 2004. Using a corpus of children's writing to test a solution to the sample size problem affecting type-token rations. In Aston, G., Bernardini, S. and Stewart, D. (eds.), *Corpora and Language Learners*. Amsterdam: John Benjamins, pp. 137–50.

Chomsky, N. 1957. *Syntactic Structures*. The Hague: Mouton.

     1995. *The Minimalist Program*. Cambridge, MA: MIT Press.

Chow, H. M., Kaup, B., Raabe, M. and Greenlee, M. W. 2008. Evidence of fronto-temporal interactions for strategic inference processes during language comprehension. *NeuroImage*, **40**, 940–54.

Chwilla, D. J. and Kolk, H. H. J. 2005. Accessing world knowledge: evidence from N400 and reaction time priming. *Cognitive Brain Research*, **25**, 589–606.

Clark, H. H. 1996. *Using Language*. Cambridge: Cambridge University Press.

Clark, H. H. and Fox Tree, J. E. 2002. Using uh and um in spontaneous speech. *Cognition*, **84**, 73–111.

Clark, H. H. and Wasow, T. 1998. Repeating words in spontaneous speech. *Cognitive Psychology*, **37**, 201–42.

Coates, J. 1996. *Women Talk*. Oxford: Blackwell.

Coates, J. and Cameron, D. (eds.) 1988. *Women in Their Speech Communities*. London and New York: Longman.

Collina, S., Marangolog, P. and Tabossi, P. 2001. The role of argument structure in the production of nouns and verbs. *Neuropsychologia*, **39**, 1125–37.

Cooper, J. O., Heron, T. E. and Heward, W. L. 2006. *Applied Behaviour Analysis*, 2nd edition. New Jersey: Prentice Hall.

Coricelli, G., Critchley, H., Joffily, M., O'Doherty, J., Sirigu, A. and Dolan, R. 2005. Regret and its avoidance: a neuroimaging study of choice behaviour. *Nature Neuroscience*, **8**(9), 1255–62.

Coricelli, G., Dolan, R. J. and Sirigu, A. 2007. Brain, emotion and decision making: the paradigmatic example of regret. *Trends in Cognitive Sciences*, **11**(6), 258–65.

Cosentino, S., Scarmeas, N., Albert, S. and Stern, Y. 2006. Verbal fluency predicts mortality in Alzheimer disease. *Cognitive and Behavioral Neurology*, **19**(3), 123–9.

Coupland, J., Robinson, J. and Coupland N. 1994. Frame negotiation in doctor–elderly patient consultations. *Discourse and Society*, **5**(1), 89–124.

Cullen B., Coen R. F., Lynch, *et al*. 2005. Repetitive behaviour in Alzheimer's disease: description, correlates, and functions. *International Journal of Geriatric Psychiatry*, **20**, 686–93.

Cummings, J. L. 1997. Neuropsychiatric manifestations of right hemisphere lesions. *Brain and Language*, **57**(1), 22–37.

Dalla Barba, G., Nedjam, Z. and Dubois, B. 1999. Confabulation, executive functions, and source memory in Alzheimer's disease. *Cognitive Neuropsychology*, **16** (3/4/5), 385–98.

Danes, F. 1974. Functional sentence perspective and the organization of the text. In Danes, F. (ed.), *Papers on Functional Sentence Perspective*. The Hague: Mouton, pp. 106–28.

D'Argembeau, A., Xue, G., Lu, Z.-L., Van der Linden, M. and Becharab, A. 2008. Neural correlates of envisioning emotional events in the near and far future. *NeuroImage*, **40**, 398–407.

Delgado, P.L. and Moreno, F.A. 2006. Neurochemistry of mood disorders. In Stein, D.J., Kupfer, D.J. and Schatzberg, A.F. *The American Psychiatric Publishing Textbook of Mood Disorders*. Arlington, VA: American Psychiatric Publishing, Inc., pp. 101–16.

De Martino, B., Kumaran, D., Seymour, B. and Dolan, R.J. 2006. Frames, biases, and rational decision-making in the human brain. *Science*, **313**(5787), 684–7.

Dennis, M., Lazenby, A.L. and Lockyer, L. 2001. Inferential language in high-functioning children with autism. *Journal of Autism and Developmental Disorders*, **31**(1), 47–54.

Den Ouden, H.E.M., Frith, U., Frith, C. and Blakemore, S.J. 2005. Thinking about intentions. *NeuroImage*, **28**, 787–96.

Desmond, D. 2003. Vascular dementia. *Clinical Neuroscience Research*, **3**(6), 437–48.

de Villiers, J. 2005. Discourse Analysis in Autism Spectrum Disorder, *Linguistics and the Human Sciences*, **1**(2): 245–60.

  2006. Syntactic and semantic patterns of pedantic speech in Asperger's syndrome. In Hwang, S., Sullivan, B. and Lommel, A., eds., *LACUS Forum XXXII: Networks*. Houston: LACUS.

de Villiers, J. and Stainton, R. (eds.) 2009. *Communication in Linguistics Vol. II: Michael Gregory's Proposals for a Communication Linguistics*. GREF.

de Villiers, J. and Szatmari, P. 2004. Message Organization in Autism Spectrum Disorder. In Fulton, G. D., Sullivan W.J. and Lommel, A.R. (eds.), *LACUS Forum XXX: Language, Thought and Reality*. Houston: LACUS, pp. 207–14.

de Villiers, J., Fine, J., Ginsberg, G., Vaccarella, L. and Szatmari, P. 2007. A scale for rating conversational impairment in autism spectrum disorder. *Journal of Autism and Developmental Disorders*, **37**(7), 1375–80.

Devlin, J.T., Moore, C.J. and Mummery, C.J. 2002. Anatomic constraints on cognitive theories of category specificity. *NeuroImage*, **15**(3), 675–85.

Dijkstra, K., Bourgeois, M.S., Allen, R.S. and Burgio, L.D. 2004. Conversational coherence: discourse analysis of older adults with and without dementia. *Journal of Neurolinguistics*, **17**(4), 263–83.

Dolcos, F., Rice, H.J. and Cabeza, R. 2002. Hemispheric asymmetry and aging: right hemisphere decline or asymmetry reduction. *Neuroscience and Biobehavioral Reviews*, **26**, 819–25.

Dolcos, F., LaBar, K. S. and Cabeza, R. 2004. Dissociable effects of arousal and valence on prefrontal activity indexing emotional evaluation and subsequent memory: an event-related fMRI study. *NeuroImage*, **23**, 64–74.

Downes, W. 2000. The language of felt experience: emotion, evaluative and intuitive. *Language and Literature*, **9**(2), 99–121.

Drai, D. and Grodzinsky, Y. 2006a. A new empirical angle on the variability debate: quantitative neurosyntactic analysis of a large data set from Broca's aphasia. *Brain and Language*, **96**, 117–28.

  2006b. The variability debate: more statistics, more linguistics. *Brain and Language*, **96** (2), 157–70.

Druks, J. 2002. Verbs and nouns – a review of the literature. *Journal of Neurolinguistics*, **15**, 289–315.

Dubois, B., Feldman, H.H., Jacova, C. *et al.* 2007. Research criteria for the diagnosis of Alzheimer's disease: revising the NINCDS-ADRDA criteria. *The Lancet: Neurology*, **6**(8), 734–46.

Duff Canning, S. J., Leach, L., Stuss, D. T. Ngo, L. and Black, S. E. 2004. Diagnostic utility of abbreviated fluency measures in Alzheimer's disease and vascular dementia. *Neurology*, **62**, 556–62.

Duncan J, and Owen A. M. 2000. Common regions of the human frontal lobe recruited by diverse cognitive demands. *Trends in Neurosciences*, **23**(10), 475–83.

Duong, A., Tardif, A. and Ska, B. 2003. Discourse about discourse: what is it and how does it progress in Alzheimer's disease? *Brain and Cognition*, **53**, 177–80.

Duong, A., Giroux, F., Tardif, A. and Ska, B. 2005. The heterogeneity of picture-supported narratives in Alzheimer's disease. *Brain and Language*, **93**, 173–84.

Ehrenreich, B., Hilden, J. and Malterud, K. 2007. Patients' written life stories: a gateway for understanding. *Scandinavian Journal of Primary Health Care*, **25**(1), 33–7.

Ellis, M. P. and Astell, A. J. 2004. The urge to communicate in severe dementia. *Brain and Language*, **91**, 51–2.

El-Manoufy, A. 1988. Intonation and meaning in spontaneous discourse. In Benson, J., Cummings, M. and Greaves, W. (eds.), *Linguistics in a Systemic Perspective*. Philadephia: John Benjamins, pp. 301–29.

Erlich, J. S., Obler, L. K. and Clark, L. 1997. Ideational and semantic contributions to narrative production in adults with dementia of the Alzheimers type. *Journal of Communication Disorders*, **30**, 79–99.

Everingham, C. R., Heading, G. and Connor, L. 2006. Couples' experiences of postnatal depression: a framing analysis of cultural identity, gender and communication. *Social Science and Medicine*, **62**(7), 1745–56.

Fangmeier, T., Knauff, M., Ruff, C. C. and Sloutsky, V. 2006. fMRI evidence for a three-stage model of deductive reasoning. *Journal of Cognitive Neuroscience*, **18**, 320–34.

Ferstl, E. C. and von Cramon, D. Y. 2001. The role of coherence and cohesion in text comprehension: an event-related fMRI study. *Cognitive Brain Research*, **11**(3), 325–40.

2002. What does the fronto-median cortex contribute to language processing: coherence or theory of mind? *NeuroImage*, **17**, 1599–612.

2007. Time, space and emotion: fMRI reveals content specific activation during text comprehension. *Neuroscience Letters*, **427**, 159–64.

Ferri, C. P., Prince, M., Brayne, C. *et al.* for Alzheimer's Disease International. 2005. Global prevalence of dementia: a Delphi consensus study. *Lancet*, **366**, 2112–17.

Ferstl, E. C., Rinck, M. and von Cramon, D. Y. 2005. Emotional and temporal aspects of situation model processing during text comprehension: an event-related fMRI study. *Journal of Cognitive Neuroscience*, **17**, 724–39.

Ferstl, E. C., Neumann, J., Bogler, C. and von Cramon, D. Y. 2008. The extended language network: a meta-analysis of neuroimaging studies on text comprehension. *Human Brain Mapping*, **29**, 581–93.

Fiebach, C. J., Schlesewsky, M., Lohmann, G., von Cramon, D. Y. and Friederici, A. D. 2005. Revisiting the localization of syntax: syntactic integration vs. syntactic working memory. *Human Brain Mapping*, **24**, 79–91.

Fillmore, C. J. 1968. The case for case. In Bach, E. and Harms, E. (eds.), *Universals in Linguistic Theory*, New York: Holt, Rinehart, and Winston, pp. 1–88.

1976. Frame semantics and the nature of language. In Harnad, S. R., Steklis, H. D. and Lancaster, J. (eds.), *Origins and Evolution of Language and Speech*. New York: Annals of the New York Academy of Sciences, Vol. 280, pp. 20–32.

1982. Frame semantics. In The Linguistic Society of Korea (ed.), *Linguistics in the Morning Calm*. Seoul: Hanshin Publishing Co, pp. 111–37.

Fine, J. 1991. The static and dynamic choices of responding: toward the process of building social reality by the developmentally disordered. In Ventola, E. (ed.) *Functional and Systemic Linguistics*. The Hague: Mouton DeGruyter. pp. 213–34.

2006. *Language in Psychiatry: A Handbook of Clinical Practice*. London: Equinox Publishing.

Fine, J., Bartolucci, G., Ginsberg, G. and Szatmari, P. 1991. The use of intonation to communicate in pervasive developmental disorders. *Journal of Child Psychiatry*, **32**(5), 771–82.

Firbas, J. 1992. *Functional Sentence Perspective in Written and Spoken Communication*. Cambridge: Cambridge University Press.

Firth, J. R. 1957. *Papers in Linguistics 1934–1951*. London: Oxford University Press.

Fletcher, P. C., Happé, F., Frith, U. *et al.* 1995. Other minds in the brain: a functional imaging study of 'theory of mind' in story comprehension. *Cognition*, **57**, 109–28.

Fletcher, P. C., Shallice, T. and Dolan, R. J. 2000. 'Sculpting the response space' – An account of left prefrontal activation at encoding. *NeuroImage*, **12**, 404–41.

Fombonne, E, Zakarian, R., Bennett, A. Meng, L. and McLean-Heywood, D. 2006. Pervasive developmental disorders in Montreal, Quebec, Canada: prevalence and links with immunizations. *Pediatrics*, **118**(1), 139–50.

Fox, N. C., Scahill, R. I., Crum, W. R. and Rossor, M. N. 1999. Correlation between rates of brain atrophy and cognitive decline in AD. *Neurology*, **52**(8), 1687–9.

Frijda, N. H. 1986. *The Emotions*. Cambridge: Cambridge University Press.

Friston, K. J., Harrison, L. and Penny, W. 2003. Dynamic causal modeling. *NeuroImage*, **19**, 1273–302.

Frith, U. 2003. *Autism: Explaining the Enigma*, 2nd edition. Oxford: Blackwell.

Frith, U., and Frith, C. D. 2003. Development and neurophysiology of mentalising. *Philosophical Transactions of the Royal Society of London (Series B)*, **358**, 459–73.

Frith, U. and Happé, F. 1994. Autism: beyond 'theory of mind'. *Cognition*, **50**, 115–32.

Galambos, J. A. 1986. Knowledge structures for common activities. In Galambos, J. A., Abelson, R. P. and Black, J. B. (eds.), *Knowledge Structures*. Hillsdale, NJ: Erlbaum, pp. 21–46.

Gallagher, H. L. and Frith, C. D. 2003. Functional imaging of theory of mind. *Trends in Cognitive Sciences*, **7**(2), 77–83.

Galvin, J. E., Lee, V. M. and Trojanowski, J. Q. 2001. Synucleinopathies: clinical and pathological implications. *Archives of Neurology*, **58**,186–90.

Garcia, L. and Joanette, Y. 1997a. Conversational topic-shifting analysis in dementia. In Bloom, L., Obler, L. K., De Santi, S. and Erlich, J. (eds.), *Discourse Analysis and Application: Studies in Adult Clinical Populations*. Hillsdale, NJ: Earlbaum, pp. 169–92.

Gensler, O. 1977. Non-syntactic anaphora and frame semantics. *Proceedings of the Third Annual Meeting of the Berkeley Linguistics Society*. Institute of Human Learning, University of California, Berkeley, pp. 321–34.

Ghaziuddin, M. and Gerstein, L. 1996. Pedantic speaking style differentiates Asperger syndrome from high-functioning autism. *Journal of Autism and Developmental Disorders*, **26**(5), 585–96.

Gilbert, S.J., Bird, G., Brindley, R. Frith, C.D. and Burgess, P.W. 2008. Atypical recruitment of medial prefrontal cortex in autism spectrum disorders: an fMRI study of two executive function tasks. *Neuropsychologia*, **46**(9), 2281–91.

Godbout, L. and Doyon, J. 1995. Mental representation of knowledge following frontal-lobe or postrolandic lesions. *Neuropsychologia*, **33**, 1671–96.

Godbout, L., Cloutier, P., Bouchard, C., Braun, C.M.J. and Gagnon, S. 2004. Script generation following frontal and parietal lesions. *Journal of Clinical and Experimental Neuropsychology*, **26**(7), 857–73.

Goel, V., Grafman, J., Tajik, D., Gana, S. and Danto, D. (1997). A study of the performance of patients with frontal lobe lesions in a financial planning task. *Brain*, **120**, 1805–22.

Goffman, E. 1959. *The Presentation of Self in Everyday Life*. New York: Doubleday.

1961. *Asylums: Essays on the Social Situation of Mental Patients and other Inmates*. New York: Doubleday Anchor.

1974. *Frame Analysis: An Essay on the Organization of Experience*. New York: Harper and Row.

1986. *Stigma: Notes on the Management of Spoiled Identity*. New York: Touchstone.

Goldin, P.R., Hutcherson, C.A.C., Ochsner, K.N., Glover, G.H., Gabrieli, J.D.E. and Gross, J.J. 2005. The neural bases of amusement and sadness: a comparison of block contrast and subject-specific emotion intensity regression approaches. *NeuroImage*, **27**, 26–36.

Goldman-Eisler, F. 1968. *Psycholinguistics: Experiments in Spontaneous Speech*. New York: Academic Press.

Grady, C., MacIntosh, A.R., Beig, S., Keightley, M., Burian, H. and Black, S. 2003. Evidence from functional imaging of a compensatory prefrontal network in Alzheimers disease. *The Journal of Neuroscience*, **23**(3), 986–93.

Graff-Radford, N.R. and Woodruff, B.K. 2007. Frontotemporal dementia. *Seminars in Neurology*, **27**(1), 48–57.

Grafman, J. 1989. Plans, actions, and mental sets: managerial knowledge units in the frontal lobes. In Perecman, E. (ed.), *Integrating Theory and Practice in Clinical Neuropsychology*. Hillsdale, NJ: Erlbaum, pp. 93–138.

2002. The structured event complex and the human prefrontal cortex. In Stuss, D.T. and Knight, R.T. (eds.), *The Frontal Lobes*. New York: Oxford University Press, pp. 292–310.

Gregory, M. 1988. Generic situation and register: a functional view of communication. In Benson, J., Cummings, M. and Greaves, W. (eds.), *Linguistics in a Systemic Perspective*. Philadelphia: John Benjamins, pp. 301–29.

2002. Phasal analysis within communication linguistics: two contrastive discourses. In Fries, P., Cummings, M., Lockwood, D. and Spruiell, W.C. (eds.), *Relations and Functions within and around Language*. London: Continuum.

2009a. Remarks on a theory of grammar for a socio-cognitive linguistics. In de Villiers, J. and Stainton, R. (eds.), pp. 269–81.

2009b. Arguments, roles, relations, prepositions and case: proposals within a socio-cognitive grammar of English. In J. de Villers and R. Stainton (eds.), pp. 282–311.

2009c. Notes on communication linguistics. In de Villiers, J. and Stainton, R. (eds.), pp. 143–266.

2009d. English patterns. In de Villiers, J. and Stainton, R. (eds.), pp. 1–142.

Grice, H.P. 1975. Logic and conversation. In Cole, P. and Morgan, J.L. (eds.), *Syntax and Semantics. Vol.* III: *Speech Acts*. New York: Academic Press, pp. 41–58.

Grill-Spector, K. 2003. The neural basis of object perception. *Current Opinion in Neurobiology*, **13**(2), 159–66.

Grossman, M., Cooke, A., DeVita, C. *et al.* 2002. Age-related changes in working memory during sentence comprehension: an fMRI study. *NeuroImage*, **15**(2), 302–17.

Gumperz, J.J. and Hymes, D. (eds.) 1972. *Directions in Sociolinguistics: The Ethnography of Communication*. New York: Rinehart and Winston.

Gussenhoven, C. 2004. *The Phonology of Tone and Intonation*. Cambridge: Cambridge University Press.

Gustafson, D., Rothenberg, E., Blennow, K., Steen, B. and Skoog, I. 2003. An 18-year follow-up of overweight and risk of Alzheimer disease. *Archives of Internal Medicine*, **163**, 1524–8.

Guye, M., Bartolomei, F. and Ranjeva, J.P. 2008. Imaging structural and functional connectivity: towards a unified description of brain organization? *Current Opinion in Neurology*, **21**(4), 393–403.

Halliday, M.A.K. 1967. *Intonation and Grammar in British English*. The Hague: Mouton.

1970. *A Course in Spoken English: Intonation*. Oxford: Oxford University Press.

1976. *Halliday: System and Function in Language: Selected Papers*, (ed. by G. Kress). London: Oxford University Press.

1977. Text as Semantic Choice in Social Contexts. In van Dijk, T., Janos, A. and Petofi, S. (eds.), *Grammars and Descriptions*. New York: Walter de Gruyter, pp. 176–225.

1978. *Language as Social Semiotic: The Social Interpretation of Language and Meaning*. London: Edward Arnold.

1984. *The Semiotics of Culture and Language*. London: Pinter.

1985. Dimensions of discourse analysis: grammar. In van Dijk, T.A. (ed.), *Handbook of Discourse Analysis, Vol.* II: *Dimensions of Discourse*. London: Academic Press, pp. 29–56.

1987. Spoken and written modes of meaning. In Horowitz, R. and Samuels, S.J. (eds.), *Comprehending Oral and Written Language*. New York: Academic Press, pp. 55–82.

1989. *Spoken and Written Language*. Oxford: Oxford University Press.

1994. *Introduction to Functional Grammar (2nd edition)*. London: Arnold.

Halliday, M.A.K. and Greaves, W.S. 2008. *Intonation and the Grammar of English*. London: Equinox.

Halliday, M.A.K. and Hasan, R. 1976. *Cohesion in English*. London: Longman.

1989. *Language, Text and Context*, 2nd edition. London: Longman.

Happé, F. 1993. Communicative competence and theory of mind in autism: a test of relevance theory, *Cognition*, **48**, 101–19.

1994. An advanced test of theory of mind: understanding of story characters' thoughts and feelings by able autistic, mentally handicapped, and normal children and adults, *Journal of Autism and Developmental Disorders*, **24**(2), 129–54.

Happé, F. 1997. Central coherence and theory of mind in autism: reading homographs in context, *British Journal of Developmental Psychology*, **15**, 1–12.

Happé, F. and Frith, U. 2006. The weak coherence account: detail-focused cognitive style in autism spectrum disorders, *Journal of Autism and Developmental Disorders*, **36**(1), 5–25.

Hasan, R. 1985. *Linguistics, Language, and Verbal Art*. Oxford: Oxford University Press.

Hébert, R., Lindsay, J., Verreault, R., Rockwood, K., Hill, G. and Dubois, M. F. 2000. Vascular dementia: incidence and risk factors in the Canadian Study of Health and Aging. *Stroke*, **31**(7), 1487–93.

Henson, R. N. A., Shallice, T, and Dolan, R. J. 1999. Right prefrontal cortex and episodic memory retrieval: a functional MRI test of the monitoring hypothesis. *Brain*, **122**, 1367–81.

Herholz, K., Salmon, E., Perani, D. *et al.* 2002. Discrimination between Alzheimer dementia and controls by automated analysis of multicenter FDG PET. *NeuroImage*, **17**, 302–16.

Heritage, J. and Maynard, D. W. (eds.) 2006. *Communication in Medical Care: Interaction Between Primary Care Physicians and Patients*. Cambridge: Cambridge University Press.

Hess, C. W., Sefton, K. M. and Landry, R. G. 1986. Sample size and type-token ratios for oral language of preschool children. *Journal of Speech and Hearing Research*, **29**(1), 129–34.

Hier, D. B., Hagenlocker, K. and Shindler, A. 1985. Language disintegration in dementia: effects of etiology and severity, *Brain and Language*, **25**(1), 117–33.

Hier, D. B., Stein, R. and Caplan, L. R. 1985. Cognitive and behavioral deficits after right hemisphere stroke. *Current Concepts in Cerebrovascular Disease*, **20**, 1–5.

Hill, E. L. 2004. Executive dysfunction in autism. *Trends in Cognitive Sciences*, **8**, 26–32.

Hill, G., Forbes, W., Berthelot, J.-M., Lindsay, J. and McDowell, I. 1996. Dementia among seniors. *Health Reports*, **8**(2), 7–10.

Hirono, N., Mori, E., Ishii, K. *et al.* 1998a. Hypofunction in the posterior cingulate gyrus correlates with disorientation for time and place in Alzheimers disease. *Journal of Neurology, Neurosugery and Psychiatry*, **64**, 552–4.

1998b. Regional metabolism: associations with dyscalculia in Alzheimer's disease. *Journal of Neurology, Neurosurgery and Psychiatry*, **65**, 913–6.

Holmes, D. I. 1992. A stylometric analysis of Mormon scripture and related texts. *Journal of the Royal Statistical Society (A)*, **155**, 91–120.

1994. Authorship attribution. *Computers and the Humanities*, **28**, 87–106.

Holmes, D. I. and Singh, S. 1996. A stylometric analysis of conversational speech of aphasic patients. *Literary and Linguistic Computing*, **11**, 45–60.

Honoré, A. 1979. Some simple measures of richness of vocabulary. *Association of Literary and Linguistic Computing Bulletin*, **7**, 172–7.

Huddleston, R. D. and Pullum, G. K. 2002. *The Cambridge Grammar of the English Language*. Cambridge: Cambridge University Press.

Hudson, R. 1984. *Word Grammar*. Oxford: Blackwell.

2007. *Language Networks. The New Word Grammar*. Oxford: Oxford University Press.

Hymes, D. 1962. The ethnography of speaking. In Gladwin, T. and Strutevant, W. C. (eds.), *Anthropology and Human Behaviour*. Washington, DC: Anthropological Society of Washington, pp. 15–53.

1971. *On Communicative Competence*. Philadelphia: University of Pennsylvania Press.

1974. *Foundations in Sociolinguistics: An Ethnographic Approach*. Philadelphia: University of Pennsylvania Press.

Hynd, M.R., Scott, H.L. and Dodd, P.R. 2004. Glutamate-mediated excitotoxicity and neurodegeneration in Alzheimer's disease. *Neurochemistry International*, **45**, 583–95.

Ilmberger, J., Rau, S., Noachtar, S., Arnold, S. and Winkler, P. 2002. Naming tools and animals: asymmetries observed during direct electrical cortical stimulation. *Neuropsychologia*, **40**(7), 695–700.

Inzitari, D., Lamassa, M., Pantoni, L. and Basile, A.M. 2004. Therapy of vascular dementias, *Archives of Gerontology and Geriatrics Supplement*, **9**, 229–34.

Jackendoff, R. 1990. *Semantic Structures*. Cambridge: MIT Press.

    2002. *Foundations of Language*. Oxford: Oxford University Press.

    (In preparation). Conceptual Semantics. To appear in *Semantics: An International Handbook of Natural Language Meaning*, de Gruyter.

Jacob, C.P., Koutsilieri, E., Bartl, J. *et al.* 2007. Alterations in expression of glutamatergic transporters and receptors in sporadic Alzheimers disease. *Journal of Alzheimer's Disease*, **11**(1), 97–116.

Jefferson, G. 1974. Error correction as an interactional resource. *Language in Society*, **2**, 181–99.

    1985. An exercise in the transcription and analysis of laughter. In van Dijk, T.A. *Handbook of Discourse Analysis, Vol. III*. London: Academic Press, pp. 25–34.

    2004. Glossary of transcript symbols with an introduction. In Lerner, G.H. (ed.), *Conversation Analysis: Studies from the First Generation*. Amsterdam: John Benjamins, pp. 13–31.

Jellinger, K.A. 2002. Vascular-ischemic dementia: an update. *Journal of Neural Transmission Supplementum*, **62**, 1–23.

    2007. The enigma of mixed dementia. *Alzheimers and Dementia*, **3**(1), 40–53.

Jellinger, K.A. and Attems, J. 2007. Neuropathological evaluation of mixed dementia. *Journal of the Neurological Sciences*, **257**(1–2), 80–7.

Jolliffe, T. and Baron-Cohen, S. 1999a. A test of central coherence theory: linguistic processing in high-functioning adults with autism or Asperger syndrome: is local coherence impaired? *Cognition*, **71**, 149–85.

    1999b. The strange stories test: a replication with high-functioning adults with autism or Asperger syndrome. *Journal of Autism and Developmental Disorders*, **29**(5), 395–419.

Jones, S., Jonsson, E. and Bäckman, L. 2006. Differential verbal fluency deficits in the preclinical stages of Alzheimer's disease and vascular dementia. *Cortex*, **42**(3), 347–55.

Just, M.A., Cherkassky V.L., Keller, T.A. and Minshew, N.J. 2004. Cortical activation and synchronization during sentence comprehension in high-functioning autism: evidence of underconnectivity. *Brain*, **127**, 1811–21.

Kahneman, D. and Frederick, S. 2007. Frames and brains: elicitation and control of response tendencies. *Trends in Cognitive Sciences*, **11**(2), 45–6.

Kanner, Leo. 1943. Autistic disturbances of affective contact. *Nervous Child*, **2**, 217–50.

Kantarci, K., Weigand, S.D., Petersen, R.C. *et al.* 2007. Longitudinal 1H MRS changes in mild cognitive impairment and Alzheimer's disease. *Neurobiology of Aging*, **28**, 1330–9.

Kashani A., Lepicard, E., Poirel, O. *et al.* 2008. Loss of VGLUT1 and VGLUT2 in the prefrontal cortex is correlated with cognitive decline in Alzheimer disease. *Neurobiology of Aging*, **29** (11), 1619–30.

Kemper, S., Herman, R. E. 2006. Age differences in memory-load interference effects in syntactic processing. *Journal of Gerontology Series B: Psychological Sciences and Social Sciences Online*, **61**, 327–32.

Kemper, S. and Sumner, A. 2001. The structure of verbal abilities in young and older adults. *Psychology and Aging*, **16**, 312–22.

Kemper, S., Greiner, L. H., Marquis, J., Prenovost, K. and Mitzner, T. L. 2001a. Language decline across the life span: findings from the Nun Study. *Psychology and Aging*, **16**(2), 227–39.

Kemper, S., Marquis, J. and Thompson, M. 2001b. Longitudinal change in language production: effects of aging and dementia on grammatical complexity and propositional content. *Psychology and Aging*, **16**, 600–14.

Kern, R. S, Van Gorp, W. G., Cummings, J. L., Brown, W. S. and Osato, S. S. 1992. Confabulation in Alzheimer's disease. *Brain and Cognition*, **19**, 172–82.

Kertesz, A. 2006. Progress in clinical neurosciences: frontotemporal dementia-Pick's disease. *Canadian Journal of Neurological Science*, **33**(2), 141–8.

Kintsch, W. 1974. *The Representation of Meaning in Memory*. Hillsdale, NJ: Lawrence Erlbaum Associates.

    1988. The role of knowledge in discourse comprehension: a construction–integration model. *Psychological Review*, **95**, 163–82.

Kintsch, W., and Keenan, J. M. 1973. Reading rate and retention as a function of the number of the propositions in the base structure of sentences. *Cognitive Psychology*, **5**, 257–74.

Klafki, H.-W., Staufenbiel, M., Kornhuber, J. and Wiltfang, J. 2006. Therapeutic approaches to Alzheimer's disease. *Brain*, **129**, 2840–55.

Klages, Jennifer. 2006. Magnetic resonance spectroscopy, magnetic resonance imaging and neuropsychology in persons with vascular cognitive impairment and mild Alzheimer's disease: will new technology help with old problems? PhD Dissertation, Department of Psychology, Dalhousie University.

Knapp, M., Prince, M., Albanese, E. *et al.* 2007. *Dementia UK*. A report to the Alzheimer's Society on the prevalence and economic cost of dementia in the UK produced by King's College London and London School of Economics. London: Alzheimer's Society.

Knopman, D. S., Parisi, J. E., Boeve, B. F. *et al.* 2003. Vascular dementia in a population-based autopsy study. *Archives of Neurology*, **60**(4), 569–75.

Kontiola, P., Laaksonen, R., Sulkava, R. and Erkinjuntti, T. 1990. Pattern of language impairment is different in Alzheimer's disease and multi-infarct dementia. *Brain and Language*, **38**, 364–83.

Kopelman, M. D. 1987. Amnesia: organic and psychogenic. *The British Journal of Psychiatry*, **150**, 428–42.

Koshino, H., Carpenter, P. A., Minshew, N. J., Cherkassky, V. L., Keller, T. A. and Just, M. A. 2005. Functional connectivity in an fMRI working memory task in high-functioning autism. *NeuroImage*, **24**, 810–21.

Koshino, H., Kana, R. K., Keller, T. A., Cherkassky, V. L., Minshew, N. J. and Just, M. A. 2008. FMRI investigation of working memory for faces in autism: visual coding and underconnectivity with frontal areas. *Cerebral Cortex*, **18**(3), 289–300.

Krawczyk, D. C. 2002. Contributions of the prefrontal cortex to the neural basis of human decision making. *Neuroscience and Biobehavioral Reviews*, **26**, 631–64.

Krishnan, K.R.R., Charles, H.C., Murali Doraiswamy, P. *et al.* 2003. Randomized, placebo-controlled trial of the effects of donepezil on neuronal markers and hippocampal volumes in Alzheimer's disease. *American Journal of Psychiatry*, **160**, 2003–11.

Kuperberg G. R., Kreher D. A., Sitnikova T., Caplan, D.N. and Holcomb, P.J. 2007. The role of animacy and thematic relationships in processing active English sentences: evidence from event-related potentials. *Brain and Language*, **100**, 223–37.

Kuperberg, G.R., Lakshmanan, B.M., Caplan, D.N. and Holcomba, P.J. 2006. Making sense of discourse: an fMRI study of causal inferencing across sentences. *NeuroImage*, **33**, 343–61.

Labov, W. and Waletzky, J. 1967. Narrative analysis. In Helm, J. (ed.), *Essays on Verbal and Visual Arts*. Seattle: University of Washington Press, pp. 12–44.

Lafosse, J.M., Reed, B.R., Mungas, D., Sterling, S.B., Wahbeh, H. and Jagust, W.J. 1997. Fluency and memory differences between ischemic vascular dementia and Alzheimer's disease. *Neuropsychology*, **11**, 514–22.

Lakoff, G. 1973. Hedges: a study in meaning criteria and the logic of fuzzy concepts. *Journal of Philosophical Logic*, **2**(4), 458–508.

    1987. *Women, Fire, and Dangerous Things: What Categories Reveal About the Mind*. Chicago: University of Chicago Press.

Lakoff, R. 1975. *Language and Woman's Place*. New York: Harper and Row.

Lamb, S.M. 1966. *Outline of Stratificational Grammar*. Washington: Georgetown University Press.

    1998. *Pathways of the Brain: The Neurocognitive Basis of Language*. Amsterdam: John Benjamins.

Lane, R.D., Fink, G.R., Chau, P.M. and Dolan, R.J. 1997. Neural activation during selective attention to selective emotional responses. *Neuroreport*, **8**(18), 3969–72.

Langa, K.M., Foster, N. L. and Larson, E.B. 2004. Mixed dementia: Emerging concepts and therapeutic implications. Review. *Journal of the American Medical Association*, **292**(23), 2901–8.

Lee, M. and Thompson, C.K. 2004. Agrammatic aphasic production and comprehension of unaccusative verbs in sentence contexts. *Journal of Neurolinguistics*, **17**(4), 315–30.

Levinson, S.C. 1983. *Pragmatics*. Cambridge: Cambridge University Press.

Li, L., Sengupta, A., Haque, N., Grundke-Iqbal, I. and Iqbal, K. 2004. Memantine inhibits and reverses the Alzheimer type abnormal hyperphosphorylation of tau and associated neurodegeneration. *FEBS Letters*, **566**, 261–9.

Looi, J.C.L. and Sachdev, P.S. 1999. Differentiation of vascular dementia from AD on neuropsychological tests. *Neurology*, **53**, 670–8.

Loukusa, S., Leinonen, E., Jussila, K. *et al.* 2007. Answering contextually demanding questions: Pragmatic errors produced by children with Asperger syndrome or high-functioning autism. *Journal of Communication Disorders*, **40**(5), 357–81.

Luan, P.K., Wager, T., Taylor, S.F. and Liberzon, I. 2002. Functional neuroanatomy of emotion: a meta-analysis of emotion activation studies in PET and fMRI. *Neuroimage*, **16**, 331–48.

Luchsinger, J.A. and Mayeux, R. 2004. Dietary factors and Alzheimer's disease. *Lancet Neurology*, **3**, 579–87.

Luria, A. R. 1965. Two kinds of motor perseveration in massive injuries of the frontal lobes. *Brain*, **88**, 1–10.

Lyons, K., Kemper, S., LaBarge, E., Ferraro, F. R., Balota, D. and Storandt, M. 1994. Oral language and Alzheimer's disease: a reduction in syntactic complexity. *Aging and Cognition*, **2**, 271–94.

McAlonan, G. M., Cheung, V., Cheung, C. *et al.* 2005. Mapping the brain in autism: a voxel-based MRI study of volumetric differences and intercorrelations in autism. *Brain*, **128**(2), 268–76.

McCawley, J. D. 1988. *The Syntactic Phenomena of English, Vol. I–II*. Chicago: University of Chicago Press.

McKeith, I. G., Galasko, D., Kosaka, K. *et al.* 1996. Consensus guidelines for the clinical and pathologic diagnosis of dementia with Lewy bodies (DLB): report of the consortium on DLB international workshop. *Neurology*, **47**, 1113–24.

McKenna, P. and Oh, T. 2005. *Schizophrenic Speech: Making Sense of Bathroots and Ponds that Fall in Doorways*. Cambridge: Cambridge University Press.

Mackenzie, C. 2000. Adult spoken discourse: the influences of age and education. *International Journal of Language and Communication Disorders*, **35**(2), 269–85.

McKhann, G., Drachman, D. A., Folstein, M., Katzman, R., Price, D. L. and Stadlan, E. M. 1984. Clinical diagnosis of Alzheimer's disease – report of the NINCDS –ADRDA work group under the auspices of Department of Health and Human Services Task Force on Alzheimer's disease. *Neurology*, **34**, 939–44.

McPherson, S. and Cummings, J. 1996. Neuropsychological aspects of vascular dementia. *Brain and Cognition*, **31**, 269–82.

McShane, R., Areosa, S. A. and Minakaran, N. 2006. Memantine for dementia. *Cochrane Database Systematic Reviews*, **19**(2), CD003154.

MacWhinney, B. 2000. *The CHILDES Project: Tools for Analyzing Talk*. 3rd edition. Mahwah, NJ: Lawrence Erlbaum Associates.

MacWhinney, B. and Osler, H. 1977. Verbal planning functions in children's speech. *Child Development*, **48**, 978–85.

Malinowski, B. 1923. The problem of meaning in primitive languages. In Ogden, C. K. and Richards, I. A. (eds.), *The Meaning of Meaning*. New York: Harcourt Brace, pp. 296–336.

  1935. An ethnographic theory of language. In *Coral Gardens and their Magic, Vol. II*. London: Allen and Unwin, pp. 4–78.

Mamelak, M. 2007. Alzheimer's disease, oxidative stress and gammahydroxybutyrate. *Neurobiology of Aging*, **28**(9),1340–60.

Marczinski, C. A. and Kertesz, A. 2006. Category and letter fluency in semantic dementia, primary progressive aphasia, and Alzheimer's disease. *Brain and Language*, **97**, 258–65.

Marini, A., Carlomagno, S., Caltagirone, C. and Nocentini, U. 2005. The role played by the right hemisphere in the organization of complex textual structures. *Brain and Language*, **93**(1), 46–54.

Martin, A. 2007. The representation of object concepts in the brain. *Annual Review of Psychology*, **58**, 25–45.

Martin, I. and McDonald, S. 2004. An exploration of causes of non-literal language problems in individuals with Asperger syndrome. *Journal of Autism and Developmental Disorders*, **34**, 311–28.

Martin, J. R. 2000. Beyond exchange: appraisal systems in English. In Hunston, S. and Thompson, G. (eds.), *Evaluation in Text: Authorial Stance and the Construction of Discourse*. Oxford: Oxford University Press, pp. 142–75.

Martin, J. R. and White, P. R. R. 2005. *Appraisal: The Language of Attitude and Intersubjective Stance*. London and New York: Palgrave.

Mason, R., and Just, M. A. 2007. Lexical ambiguity in sentence comprehension. *Brain Research*, **1146**, 115–27.

Mason, R. A., Williams, D. L., Kana, R. K., Minshew, N. and Just, M. A. 2008. Theory of mind disruption and recruitment of the right hemisphere during narrative comprehension in autism. *Neuropsychologia*, **46**(1), 269–80.

Massoud, F., Devi, G., Stern, Y. *et al.* 1999. A clinicopathological comparison of community-based and clinic-based cohorts of patients with dementia. *Archives of Neurology*, **56**, 1368–73.

Matsuda, H. 2007. Role of neuroimaging in Alzheimer's disease, with emphasis on brain perfusion SPECT. *Journal of Nuclear Medicine*, **48**(8), 1289–1300.

Mayeux, R. 2003. Epidemiology of neurodegeneration. *Annual Review of Neuroscience*, **26**, 81–104.

Mendez, M. F., Cherrier, M. M. and Perryman, K. M. 1997. Differences between Alzheimer's disease and vascular dementia on information processing measures. *Brain and Cognition*, **34**, 301–10.

Mesulam, M. M. 1998. From sensation to cognition. *Brain*, **121**(6), 1013–52.

  2000. Aging, Alzheimer's disease, and dementia: clinical and neurobiological perspectives. In *Principles of Behavioural and Cognitive Neurology*, 2nd edition. Oxford: Oxford University Press, pp. 439–522.

Michael, E. B., Keller, T. A., Carpenter, P. A. and Just, M. A. 2001. FMRI investigation of sentence comprehension by eye and by ear: modality fingerprints on cognitive processes. *Human Brain Mapping*, **13**, 239–52.

Minsky, M. 1975. A framework for representing knowledge. In Winston, P. (ed.), *The Psychology of Computer Vision*. New York: McGraw-Hill, pp. 211–77.

  1977. Frame-system theory. In Johnson-Laird, P. N. and Wason, P. C. (eds.), *Thinking: Readings in Cognitive Science*. Cambridge: Cambridge University Press, pp. 355–76.

Monti, M. M., Osherson, D. N., Martinez, M. J. and Parson, L. M. 2007. Functional neuroanatomy of deductive inference: a language-independent distributed network. *NeuroImage*, **37**, 1005–16.

Moorhouse, P. and Rockwood, K. 2008. Vascular cognitive impairment: current concepts and clinical developments. *The Lancet: Neurology*, **7**(3), 246–55.

Moss, H. E., Tyler, L. K. and Taylor, K. I. 2007. Conceptual structure. In Gaskell, G. (ed.), *Oxford Handbook of Psycholinguistics*, New York: Oxford University Press, pp. 217–33.

Nankano, H., and Blumstein, S. E. 2004. Deficits in thematic integration processes in Broca's and Wernicke's aphasia. *Brain and Language*, **88**, 96–107.

Nespoulous, J-L., Code, C., Virbel, J. and Lecours, A. R. 1998. Hypothesis on the dissociation between referential and modalizing verbal behavior in aphasia. *Applied Psycholinguistics*, **19**, 311–31.

Neuropathology Group. 2001. Medical research council cognitive function and aging study. Pathological correlates of late-onset dementia in a multicentre, community-based population in England and Wales. *Lancet*, **357**, 169–75.

Nicholas, M., Obler, L.K., Albert, M.L. and Helm-Estabrooks, N. 1985. Empty speech in Alzheimer's disease and fluent aphasia. *Journal of Speech and Hearing Research*, **28**(3), 405–10.

Nicholson, R. and P. Szatmari 2003. Genetic and neurodevelopmental influences in autistic disorder. *Canadian Journal of Psychiatry*, **48**(8), 27–38.

Nobre, A.C., Coull, J.T., Frith, C.D. and Mesulam, M.M. 1999. Orbitofrontal cortex is activated during breaches of expectation in tasks of visual attention. *Nature Neuroscience*, **2**, 11–12.

Norbury, C.F. and Bishop, D. 2002. Inferential processing and story recall in children with communication problems: a comparison of specific language impairment, pragmatic language impairment and high-functioning autism. *International Journal of Language and Communication Disorders*, **37**(3), 227–51.

Norman, D.A. and Shallice, T. 1986. Attention to action: willed and automatic control of behaviour. *Centre for Human Information Processing (Technical Report #99)*. Reprinted in revised form in Davidson, R.J., Schwartz, G.E. and Shapiro, D. (eds.) 1986, *Consciousness and Self-Regulation: Vol. IV*, New York: Plenum, pp. 1–18.

Noveck, I.A., Goel, V. and Smith, K.W. 2004. The neural basis of conditional reasoning with arbitrary content. *Cortex*, **40**, 613–22.

Nussbaum, R.L. and Ellis, C.E. 2003. Alzheimer's disease and Parkinson's disease. *New England Journal of Medicine*, **348**, 1356–64.

O'Brien, J.T. 2006. Vascular cognitive impairment. Review. *American Journal of Geriatric Psychiatry*, **14**(9), 724–33.

O'Brien, J.T., Erkinjuntti, T. and Reisberg, B. *et al.* 2003. Vascular cognitive impairment. Review. *The Lancet: Neurology*, **2**, 89–98.

Ochsner, K.N., Bunge, S.A., Gross, J.J. and Gabrieli, J.D. 2002. Rethinking feelings: an FMRI study of the cognitive regulation of emotion. *Journal of Cognitive Neuroscience*, **14**, 1215–29.

Orange, J.B. and Kertesz, A. 2000. Discourse Analyses and Dementia, *Brain and Language*, **71**, 172–4.

Owen, A.J. and Leonard, L.B. 2002. Lexical diversity in the spontaneous speech of children with specific language impairment: application of D. *Journal of Speech, Language, and Hearing Research*, **45**(5), 927–37.

Ozonoff, S. and Miller, J. 1996. An exploration of right-hemisphere contributions to the pragmatic impairments of autism. *Brain and Language*, **52**, 411–34.

Pantoni, L. and Simoni, M. 2003. Pathophysiology of cerebral small vessels in vascular cognitive impairment. *International Journal of Psychogeriatrics*, Supplement 1, 59–65.

Patry, R. and Nespoulous, J.-L. 1990. Discourse analysis in linguistics. In Joanette, Y. and Brownell, H.H. (eds.), *Discourse Ability and Brain Damage: Theoretical and Empirical Perspectives*. New York: Springer-Verlag, pp. 3–29.

Paxton, J.L., Barch, D.M., Racine, C.A. and Braver, T.S. 2008. Cognitive control, goal maintenance and prefrontal function in healthy aging. *Cerebral Cortex*, **18**(5), 1010–28.

Perry, R.J. and Hodges, J.R. 1996. Spectrum of memory dysfunction in degenerative disease. *Current Opinion in Neurology*, **9**(4), 281–5.

Petrides, M., Alivisatos, B. and Evans, A.C. 1995. Functional activation of the human ventrolateral prefrontal cortex during mnemonic retrieval of verbal information. *Proceedings of the National Academy of Science USA*, **92**, 5803–7.

Petrides, M., Alivisatos, B. and Frey, S. 2002. Differential activation of the human orbital, mid-vetrolateral, and mid-dorsolateral prefrontal cortex during the processing of visual stimuli. *Proceedings of the National Academy of Sciences, USA*, **99**, 5649–54.

Phan, K. L., Wager, T., Taylor, S. F. and Liberzon, I. 2002. Functional neuroanatomy of emotion: a meta-analysis of activation studies in PET and fMRI. *NeuroImage*, **16**, 331–48.

Pike, K. L. and Pike, E. G. 1982. *Grammatical Analysis*. Dallas: Summer Institute of Linguistics.

Poore, Q. E., Rapport, L. J., Fuerst, D. R. and Keenan, P. 2006. Word list generation performance in Alzheimer's disease and vascular dementia. *Neuropsychology, Development and Cognition. Section B, Aging, Neuropsychology and Cognition*, **13**(1), 86–94.

Powell, A. L., Cummings, J. L., Hill, M. A. and Benson, D. F. 1988. Speech and language alterations in multi-infarct dementia. *Neurology*, **38**(5), 717–9.

Prizant, B. and Duchan, J. 1981. The functions of immediate echolalia in autistic children. *Journal of Speech and Hearing Disorders*, **46**, 241–9.

Propp, V. 1928 [trans. 1958]. *The Morphology of the Folktale*. Philadelphia: American Folktale Society.

Public Health Agency of Canada. 1999. Surveillance for Creutzfeldt-Jacob disease in Canada. *Canada Communicable Disease Report – Vol. XXV*.

Creutzfeldt-Jakob Disease Surveillance System (CJD-SS) www.phac-aspc.gc.ca/hcai-iamss/cjd-mcj/cjdss-ssmcj/stats_E.html, accessed 2007.

Quirk, R., Greenbaum, S., Leech, G. and Svartik, J. 1985. *A Comprehensive Grammar of the English Language*. London: Longman.

Ramanathan-Abbott, V. 1994. Interactional differences in Alzheimer's discourse: an examination of Alzheimer's speech across two audiences. *Language and society*, **23**, 31–58.

Razvi, S. S., Davidson, R., Bone, I. and Muir, K. W. 2005. The prevalence of cerebral autosomal dominant arteriopathy with subcortical infarcts and leucoencephalopathy (CADASIL) in the west of Scotland. *Journal of Neurology, Neurosurgery and Psychiatry*, **76**(5), 739–41.

Ready, R. E., Ott, B. R. and Grace, J. 2003. Amnestic behaviour in dementia: symptoms to assist in early detection and diagnosis. *Journal of the American Geriatrics Society*, **51**, 32–7.

Riverberi, C., Cherubini, P., Rapisarda, A. *et al.* 2007. Neural basis of generation of conclusions in elementary deduction. *Journal of NeuroImage*, **38**(4), 752–62.

Rocca, W. A. and Knopman, D. S. 2003. Prevalence and incidence patterns of vascular dementia. In Bowler, J. V. and Hatchinski, V. (eds.), *Vascular Cognitive Impairment: Preventable Dementia*. New York: Oxford University Press, pp. 21–32.

Rochester, S. R. and Martin, J. R. 1979. *Crazy talk: A Study of the Discourse of Schizophrenic Speakers*. New York: Plenum.

Rockwood, K., Graham, J. E. and Fay, S. 2002. Goal setting and attainment in Alzheimer's disease patients treated with donepezil. *Journal of Neurology, Neurosurgery and Psychiatry*, **73**, 500–7.

Rockwood, K., Moorhouse, P. K., Song, X. *et al.* 2007. Disease progression in vascular cognitive impairment: cognitive, functional and behavioural outcomes in the Consortium to Investigate Vascular Impairment of Cognition (CIVIC) cohort study. *Journal of the Neurological Sciences*, **252**(2), 106–12.

Roman, G.C. 2005. Vascular dementia prevention: a risk factor analysis. Review. *Cerebrovascular Diseases*, **20** Supplement 2, 91–100. Epub 2 Dec 2005. Review.

Roman, G.C., Tatemichi, T.K., Erkinjuntti, T. *et al.* 1993. Vascular dementia – diagnostic criteria for research studies. Report of the NINDS-AIREN International Workshop. *Neurology*, **43**, 250–60.

Rosch, E. 1983. Prototype classification and logical classification: the two systems. In Scholnick, E. (ed.), *New Trends in Cognitive Representation: Challenges to Piaget's Theory*. Hillsdale, NJ: Lawrence Erlbaum Associates pp. 73–86.

Royall, D.R., Palmer, R., Chiodo, L.K. and Polk, M.J. 2005. Executive control mediates memory's association with change in instrumental activities of daily living: the Freedom House Study. *Journal of the American Geriatric Society*, **53**(1), 11–17.

Royall, D.R., Lauterbach, E.C., Cummings, J.L. *et al.* 2002. Executive control function: a review of its promise and challenges for clinical research. A report from the Committee on Research of the American Neuropsychiatric Association. Review. *Journal of Neuropsychiatry and Clinical Neurosciences*, **14**(4), 377–405.

Ruchoux, M.M. and Maurage, C.A. 1997. CADASIL: cerebral autosomal dominant arteriopathy with subcortical infarcts and leukoencephalopathy. *Journal of Neuropathology and Experimental Neurology*, **56**(9), 947–64.

Rugg, M.D., Fletcher, P.C., Frith, C.D., Frackowiak, R.S.J. and Dolan, R.J. 1996. Differential activation of the prefrontal cortex in successful and unsuccessful memory retrieval. *Brain*, **119**(6), 2073–83.

Rushworth, M.F., Behrens, T.E., Rudebeck, P.H. and Walton, M.E. 2007. Contrasting roles for cingulate and orbitofrontal cortex in decisions and social behaviour. *Trends in Cognitive Sciences*, **11**(4),168–76.

Russell, J. (ed.) 1998. *Autism as an Executive Disorder*. Oxford: Oxford University Press.

Rusted, J. and Shepherd, L. 2002. Action-based memory in Alzheimer's disease: a longitudinal look at tea-making. *Case Studies in Neuropsychology, Neuropsychiatry and Behavioural Neurology*, **8**(1–2),111–26.

Sachdev, P.S. and Looi, J.C.L. 2003. Neuropsychological separation of vascular dementia and Alzheimer's dementia. In Bowler, J.V. and Hachinski, V. (eds.), *The Vascular Dementias: A Review and Re-appraisal*. Oxford: Oxford University Press, pp. 153–75.

Sacks, H. 1992a. *Lectures on Conversation: Vol. I*. Cambridge, MA: Blackwell.
    1992b. *Lectures on Conversation: Vol. II*. Cambridge, MA: Blackwell.

Sacks, H., Schegloff, E.A. and Jefferson, G. 1974. A simplest systematics for the organization of turn-taking for conversation. *Language*, **50**, 696–735.

Saldaña, D. and Frith, U. 2007. Do readers with autism make bridging inferences from world knowledge? *Journal of Experimental Child Psychology*, **96**(4), 310–19.

Sampson, G. 2001. *Empirical Linguistics*. London: Continuum.
    2003. The structure of children's writing: moving from spoken to adult written norms. In Granger, S. and Petch-Tyson, S. (eds.), *Extending the Scope of Corpus-based Research: New Applications, New Challenges*. Amsterdam: Rodopi, pp. 177–93.

Sanford, A.J.S., Sanford, A.J., Filik, R. and Molle, J. 2005. Depth of lexical–semantic processing and sentential load. *Journal of Memory and Language*, **53**(3), 378–96.

Sanford, A.J. and Garrod, S.C. 1981. *Understanding Written Language: Explorations of Comprehension Beyond the Sentence*. Chichester: John Wiley & Sons.

Saxton, J.A., Ratcliff, G., Dodge, H., Pandav. R., Baddeley, A. and Ganguli, M. 2001. Speed and capacity of language processing test: normative data from an older American community-dwelling sample. *Applied Neuropsychology*, **8**, 193–203.

Schacter, D.L., Alpert, N.M., Savage, C.R., Rauch, S.L. and Albert, M.S. 1996. Conscious recollection and the human hippocampal formation: evidence from positron emission tomography. *Proceedings of the National Academy of Sciences, USA*, **93**, 321–25.

Schank, R.C. and Abelson, R.P. 1977. Scripts, plans, and knowledge. In Johnson-Laird, P.N. and Wason, P.C. (eds.), *Thinking: Readings in Cognitive Science*. Cambridge: Cambridge University Press, pp. 421–32.

Schegloff, E.A. 1968. Sequencing in conversational openings. *American Anthropologist*, **70**,1075–95.

2007. *Sequence Organization in Interaction: A Primer in Conversation Analysis: Vol. I*. Cambridge: Cambridge University Press.

Schegloff, E.A., Jefferson, G. and Sachs, H. 1977. The preference for self-correction in the organization of repair in conversation. *Language*, **53**, 361–82.

Schiffrin, D. 1987. *Discourse Markers. Studies in Interactional Sociolinguistics* 5. Cambridge: Cambridge University Press.

Searle, J. 1969. *Speech Acts: An Essay in the Philosophy of Language*. Cambridge: Cambridge University Press.

1979. *Expression and Meaning*. Cambridge: Cambridge University Press.

Seiborger, F.T., Ferstl, E.C. and von Cramon, D.Y. 2007. Making sense of nonsense: an fMRI stude of task induced inference processes during discourse comprehension. *Brain Research*, **1166**, 77–91.

Seitz, R.J., Nickel, J. and Azari, N.P. 2006. Functional modularity of the medial pre-frontal cortex: involvement in human empathy. *Neuropsychology*, **20**(6), 743–51.

Shallice, T. 1982. Specific impairments of planning. *Philosophical Transactions of the Royal Society of London (Series B)*, **B298**, 199–209.

Shallice, T. and Burgess, P.W. 1996. The domain of supervisory processes and temporal organisation of behaviour. *Philosophical Transactions of the Royal Society of London (Series B)*, **351**,1405–12.

Shallice, T., Fletcher, P., Frith, C.D., Grasby, P., Frackowiak, R.S.J. and Dolan, R.J. 1994. Brain regions associated with acquisition and retrieval of verbal episodic memory. *Nature*, **368**(6472), 633–5.

Shallice, T., Venable, N. and Rumiati, R.I. 1988. *From Neuropsychology to Mental Structure*. Cambridge: Cambridge University Press.

Sergerie, K., Chochol, C. and Armony, J.L. 2008. The role of the amygdala in emotional processing: a quantitative meta-analysis of functional neuroimaging studies. *Neuroscience and Biobehavioural Reviews*, **32**(4), 811–30.

Shapiro, K. and Caramazza, A. 2000. Sometimes a noun is just a noun: comments on Bird, Howard, and Franklin. *Brain and Language*, **76**, 202–12.

Shapiro, L.P., Gordon, B., Hack, N. and Killacky, J. 1993. Verb-argument structure processing in complex sentences in Broca's and Wernicke's aphasia. *Brain and Language*, **45**(3), 423–47.

Shindler, A.G., Caplan, L.R. and Hier, D.B. 1984. Intrusions and perseverations. *Brain and Language*, **23**, 148–58.

Silverman, D.H., Small, G.W., Chang, C.Y. *et al.* 2001. Positron emission tomography in evaluation of dementia: regional brain metabolism and long-term outcome. *Journal of the American Medical Association*, **286**(17), 2120–7.

Sinclair, J. (ed.) 1990. *Collins Cobuild English Grammar*. London: Harper Collins.

Singh, S. and Bookless, T. 1997. Analyzing spontaneous speech in dysphasic adults. *International Journal of Applied Linguistics*, **7**, 165–82.

Sirigu, A., Zalla, T., Pillon, B., Grafman, J., Agid, Y. and Dubois, B. 1995. Selective impairments in managerial knowledge following pre-frontal cortex damage. *Cortex*, **31**, 301–16.

Sirigu, A., Zalla, T., Pillon, B., Grafman, J., Agid, Y. and Dubois, B. 1996. Encoding of sequence and boundaries of scripts following prefrontal lesions. *Cortex*, **32**, 297–310.

Skoog, I. and Gustafson, D. 2003. Hypertension, hypertension-clustering factors and Alzheimer's disease. *Neurological Research*, **25**, 675–80.

Small, J.A., Kemper, S. and Lyons, K. 2000. Sentence repetition and processing resources in Alzheimer's disease. *Brain and Language*, **75**(2), 232–58.

Smith, E. Rhee, J., Dennis, K. and Grossman, M. 2001. Inductive reasoning in Alzheimer's disease. *Brain and Cognition*, **47**, 494–503.

Snowdon, D.A., Kemper, S.J., Mortimer, J.A., Greiner, L.H., Wekstein, D.R. and Markesbery, W.R. 1996. Linguistic ability in early life and cognitive function and Alzheimer's disease in late life: findings from the Nun Study. *Journal of the American Medical Association*, **275**, 528–32.

Sperber, D. and Wilson, D. 1986. *Relevance: Communication and Cognition*. Oxford: Blackwell.

  1995. *Relevance: Communication and Cognition*. 2nd edition. Oxford: Blackwell.

St. George, M., Mannes, S. and Hoffman, J.E. 1994. Global semantic expectancy and language comprehension. *Journal of Cognitive Neuroscience*, **6**, 70–83.

St. George, M., Kutas, M., Martinez, A. and Sereno, M.I. 1999. Semantic integration in reading: engagement of the right hemisphere during discourse processing. *Brain*, **122**, 1317–25.

Stowe, L.A., Wijers, A.A., Willemsen, A.T.M. *et al.* 1995. Effects of sentence complexity on rCBF: A PET study. Poster presented at the *Meeting of the Cognitive Neuroscience Society*, San Francisco.

Stowe, L.A., Haverkort, M. and Zwarts, F. 2005. Rethinking the neurological basis of language. *Lingua*, **115**(7), 997–1042.

Stowe, L.A., Broere, C.A.J., Paans, A.M. *et al.* 1998. Localizing components of a complex task: sentence processing and working memory. *Neuroreport*, **9**, 2995–9.

Stowe, L.A., Broere, C.A., Paans, A.M. *et al.* 1998. Localizing components of a complex task: sentence processing and working memory. *Neuroreport*, **9**(13), 2995–9.

Sturt, P., Sanford, A.J., Stewart, A.J. and Dawydiak, E. 2004. Linguistic focus and good-enough representations: an application of the change-detection paradigm. *Psychonomic Bulletin & Review*, **11**, 882–8.

Stuss, D.T. and Benson, D.F. 1986. *The Frontal Lobes*. New York: Raven.

Surian, L., Baron-Cohen, S. and van der Lely, H. 1996. Are children with autism deaf to Gricean maxims? *Cognitive Neuropsychiatry*, **1**, 55–71.

Szatmari, P. 2003. The causes of autism spectrum disorders (ASD). *British Journal of Psychiatry*, **326**, 173–74.

Tager-Flusberg, H. 1996. Brief report: Current theory and research on language and communication in autism. *Journal of Autism and Developmental Disorders*, **26**(2), 169–72.

Tannen, D. (ed.) 1993a. *Framing in discourse*. New York: Oxford University Press.
  (ed) 1993b. *Gender and Conversational Interaction*. London: Oxford University Press.

Tannen, D. and C. Wallat. 1993. Interactive frames and knowledge schemas in interaction: Examples from a medical examination/interview. In Tannen, D. (ed.), *Framing in Discourse*. New York: Oxford University Press, pp. 56–76.

Temple, V., Sabat, S. and Kroger, R. 1999. Intact use of politeness in the discourse of Alzheimer's sufferers. *Language and Communication*, **19**(2), 163–80.

Thakkar, K. N., Polli, F. E., Joseph, R. M. *et al.* 2008. Response monitoring, repetitive behaviour and anterior cingulate abnormalities in autism spectrum disorders. *Brain*, **131**, 2464–78.

Thompson, C. K. 2003. Unaccusative verb production in agrammatic aphasia: the argument structure complexity hypothesis. *Journal of Neurolinguistics*, **16**(2,3), 151–67.

Thompson-Schill, S. L. 2003. Neuroimaging studies of semantic memory: Inferring 'how' from 'where'. *Neuropsychologia Special Issue: Functional Neuroimaging of Memory*, **41**, 280–92.

Thordardottir, E. T. and Ellis Weismer, S. 1998. Mean length of utterance and other language sample measures in early Icelandic. *First Language*, **18**, 1–32.

Tierney, M. C., Black, S. E., Szalai, J. P. *et al.* 2001. Recognition memory and verbal fluency differentiate probable Alzheimer disease from subcortical vascular dementia. *Archives of Neurology* **58**, 1654–9.

Tinaz, S., Schendan, H. E., Schon, K. and Stern C. E. 2006. Evidence for the importance of basal ganglia output nuclei in semantic event sequencing: an fMRI study. *Brain Research*, **1067**, 239–49.

Tinaz, S., Schendan, H. E. and Stern, C. E. 2008. Fronto-striatal deficit in Parkinson's disease during semantic event sequencing. *Neurobiology of Aging*, **29**(3), 397–407.

Toga, A. W. and Mazziotta, J. C. 2002. *Brain Mapping: The Methods*. London: Academic Press.

Tulving, E. 1972. Episodic and semantic memory. In Tulving, E. and Donaldson, W. (eds.), *Organization of memory*. New York: Academic Press, pp. 381–403.
  1983. *Elements of Episodic Memory*. New York: Oxford University Press.
  2002. Episodic memory: from mind to brain. *Annual Review of Psychology*, **53**, 1–25.

Tune, L., Tiseo, P. J., Ieni, J. *et al.* 2003. Donepezil HCl (E2020) maintains functional brain activity in patients with Alzheimer disease. *American Journal of Geriatric Psychiatry*, **11**, 169–77.

Tyler, L. K. and Moss, H. E. 2001. Towards a distributed account of conceptual knowledge. *Trends in Cognitive Sciences*, **5**(6), 244–52.

Ulatowska, H. and Bond-Chapman, S. 1991. Discourse changes in dementia. In Lubinski, R. (ed.), *Dementia and Communication*. Philidelphia: Mosby Publishing, pp. 115–32.

Ulatowska, H., Cannito, M. P., Hayashi, M. M. and Fleming, S. G. 1985. Language abilities in the elderly. In Ulatowska, H. K. (ed.), *The Aging Brain: Communication in the Elderly*. Austin, TX: PRO-ED, pp. 125–39.

van Dijk, T. A. 1977. *Text and Context. Explorations in the Semantics and Pragmatics of Discourse*. London: Longman.

1977. Knowledge frames and speech act comprehension. *Journal of Pragmatics*, **1**, 211–32.

1981. *Studies in the Pragmatics of Discourse*. The Hague/Berlin: Mouton.

2006. Discourse, context and cognition. *Discourse Studies*, **8**(1), 159–77.

van Dijk, T. A. and Kintsch, W. 1983. *Strategies of Discourse Comprehension*. New York: Academic Press.

van Dijk, M, and van Geert, P. 2005. Disentangling behavior in early child development: interpretability of early child language and the problem of filler syllables and growing utterance length. *Infant Behavior and Development*, **28** (2), 99–117.

van Dijk, E. J., Prins, N. D., Vrooman, H. A., Hofman, A., Koudstaal, P. J. and Breteler, M. M. 2008. Progression of cerebral small vessel disease in relation to risk factors and cognitive consequences: Rotterdam Scan study. *Stroke*, **39**(10), 2712–9.

van Leeuwen, T. J. 1996. The representation of social actors. In Caldas-Coulthard, C. R. and Coulthard, M. (eds.), *Texts and Practices – Readings in Critical Discourse Analysis*. Routledge: London, pp. 32–70.

van Valin, R. 2001. *An Introduction to Syntax*. Cambridge: Cambridge University Press.

van Valin R. and LaPolla, R. J. 1997. *Syntax: Structure, Meaning and Function*. Cambridge: Cambridge University Press.

Vigneau, M., Beaucousin, V., Herve, P. Y. *et al.* 2006. Meta-analyzing left hemisphere language areas: Phonology, semantics, and sentence processing. *NeuroImage*, **30**(4), 1414–32.

Volden, J. and Johnston, J. 1999. Cognitive scripts in autistic children and adolescents. *Journal of Autism and Developmental Disorders*, **29**(3), 203–11.

Wager, T. D., Phan, K. L., Liberzon, I. and Taylor, S. F. 2003. Valence, gender, and lateralization of functional brain anatomy in emotion: a meta-analysis of findings from neuroimaging. *NeuroImage*, **19**, 513–31.

Wagner, A. D., Pare-Blagoev, E. J., Clark, J. and Poldrack, R. A., 2001. Recovering meaning: left prefrontal cortex guides controlled semantic retrieval. *Neuron*, **31**, 329–38.

Warrington, E. K. and McCarthy, R. A. 1987. Categories of knowledge: further fractionations and an attempted integration. *Brain*, **110**,1273–96.

Warrington E. K. and Shallice T. 1984. Category specific semantic impairments. *Brain*, **107**, 829–54.

Wartenburger, I., Heekeren, H. R., Burchert, F., Heinemann, S., De Bleser, R. and Villringer, A. 2004. Neural correlates of syntactic transformations. *Human Brain Mapping*, **22**, 72–81.

Watkins, R. V., Kelly, D. J., Harbers, H. M. and Hollis, W. 1995. Measuring children's lexical diversity: differentiating typical and impaired language learners. *Journal of Speech and Hearing Research*, **38**(6),1349–55.

Watt, D. L. E. 1990b. *The Phonology and Semology of Intonation in English*. PhD dissertation, York University, Toronto.

Webster, J., Franklin, S., and Howard, D. 2001. An investigation of the interaction between thematic and phrasal structure in nonfluent agrammatic subjects. *Brain and Language*, **78**, 197–211.

Wechsler, D. (1997). *Wechsler Adult Intelligence Scale*, 3rd edition. San Antonio, TX: The Psychological Corporation.

White, P.R.R. 1998. *Telling Media Tales: the News Story As Rhetoric*. Unpublished PhD dissertation, University of Sydney, Sydney.

    2000. The sixth modal: dialogism and the language of intersubjective Positioning. *First Workshop of the Systemic Functional Research Community on Interpersonal and Ideational Grammar, Leuven*, 16–18 Number 2000.

Zacccai, J., McCracken, C. and Brayne, C. 2005. A systematic review of prevalence and incidence studies of dementia with Lewy bodies. *Age and Ageing*, **34**(6), 561–6.

Zalla, T., Pradat-Diehl, P. and Sirigu, A. 2003. Perception of action boundaries in patients with frontal lobe damage. *Neuropsychologia*, **41**, 1619–27.

Zalla, T., Sirigu, A., Pillon, B., Dubois, B., Agid, Y. and Grafman, J. 2000. How patients with Parkinson's disease retrieve and manage cognitive event knowledge. *Cortex*, **36**, 163–79.

Zanini, S. 2008. Generalised script sequencing deficits following frontal lobe lesions. *Cortex*, **44**(2), 140–9.

Zanini, S., Rumiati, R.I. and Shallice, T. 2002. Action sequencing deficit following frontal lobe lesions. *Neurocase*, **8**, 88–99.

Author index

Subject index

affect
  affective processing style 139
  appraisal framework 156
  cognitive models 162
  definition 156
  iconic signalling of affect 162
  lesions studies 140
  model analyses
    AD 159–61
    autism 156–9
  modulate discourse processes 23, 136
  neural networks 146, 147, 163–5, 201
  prosody 162, 163, 167
  semantic and lexical resources 21, 161–2
Agent 59–60
Alzheimer's disease
  cause of 16
  dementia phase 5
  diagnostic criteria 15
  discourse characteristics 5, 17–18, 126–32,
    199
    confabulation 105–7, 200
  discourse monitoring 191, 200
  episodic (self-referential) checking tags
    127–8
  episodic recall 196–8, 200
  fluency 191, 200
  hesitations 191
    coherence 17, 183, 185–91, 194–8, 200
  ideational perseveration 17, 200
  incomplete utterances 183, 191
  lexicalizalization 17, 183, 185–91, 198, 200
    discourse examples 4–5, 105–7, 106,
      126–32, 182–92, 194–8
  modalization 17, 126–7, 183, 191, 200
  morphosyntax 13
    reference 183, 185–91
    repetition 17, 191, 196–7
    topic development 17, 183, 196–8
    turn-taking 199
  neurophysiology 15, 192
  prevalence 14, 15
  risk factors for 16

  treatment 17, 209
  treatment effects in 5, 126–32
  treatment monitoring 127, 192
ambient 66
argument roles (see also circumstantial roles)
  definitions 59–67
  summary 68
argument structure
  aphasia 94–5
  information processing load 95
  problems with 94–5
Asperger's syndrome
  casual conversation 12
  contextual relevance 12
  discourse examples 169–82, 192–4
  language development 12
  pedantic speech 12, 115
  topic management 12, 169–82, 193
attitude (see also affect)
  ASDs 6, 167
  lexical selection 55, 196
  linguistic resources 55–6
Attribuand 66
autism
  contextual relevance 13
  discourse examples 5–6, 7–9, 12–13,
    156–9, 165–7
  expression of attitude, examples 6, 167
  expression of evaluation, examples 8, 159
  fMRI study of inferencing 25
  morphosyntactic difficulties, examples 13
  speech characteristics 11
  topic management examples 13
autism spectrum disorders (ASDs)
  causes 11
  communication difficulties 11–12
  defined 10–11
  diagnostic criteria 10–11
  discourse characteristics 6, 200
  dysfluency 8, 9, 98–100, 181
  evaluation 104
  humour 151
  inferencing in discourse 149–54, 181